Colorado
Hut to Hut

VOLUME 2:
Southern Region

TEXT AND
PHOTOGRAPHY BY Brian Litz

WESTCLIFFE PUBLISHERS
www.westcliffepublishers.com

*No portion of this book,
either text or photography,
may be reproduced
in any form, including
electronically, without the
express written permission
of the publisher.*

INTERNATIONAL STANDARD BOOK NUMBER:
1-56579-385-4

TEXT, PHOTOGRAPHY, AND SCHEMATIC MAPS COPYRIGHT:
Brian Litz, 2000. All rights reserved.

EDITOR:
Steve Grinstead
DESIGN AND PRODUCTION:
Rebecca Finkel, F + P Graphic Design, Inc.; Boulder, CO
PRODUCTION MANAGER:
Craig Keyzer

PUBLISHED BY:
Westcliffe Publishers, Inc.
P.O. Box 1261
Englewood, Colorado 80150
www.westcliffepublishers.com

Printed in China through World Print, Ltd.

*For more information about other fine books and calendars from Westcliffe
Publishers, please contact your local bookstore, call us at 1-800-523-3692, write
for our free color catalog, or visit us on the Web at www.westcliffepublishers.com.*

LIBRARY OF CONGRESS CATALOGING-IN-PUBLICATION DATA:
Litz, Brian, 1961–.
    Colorado hut to hut / text and photography by Brian Litz.
    p. cm.
    Includes bibliographical references and index
    Contents: v.1. Northern and central regions —
    v.2. Southern regions
    ISBN: 1-56579-384-6 (vol. 1) — ISBN: 1-56579-385-4
    (vol. 2)
    1. Cross-country skiing — Colorado — Guidebooks.
    2. All terrain cycling — Colorado — Guidebooks. 3. Tourist
    camps, hostels, etc. — Colorado — Guidebooks. 4. Colorado
    — Guidebooks. I. Title

    GV854.5.C6 L575 2000
    796.93´2´09788 — DC21   00-040428

PLEASE NOTE:
Risk is always a factor
in backcountry and high-
mountain travel. Many of
the activities described in
this book can be dangerous,
especially when weather is
adverse or unpredictable,
and when unforeseen events
or conditions create a hazardous situation. The author
has done his best to provide
the reader with accurate
information about back-
country travel, as well as
to point out some of its
potential hazards. It is the
responsibility of the users
of this guide to learn the
necessary skills for safe
backcountry travel, and
to exercise caution in
potentially hazardous areas,
especially on snowfields and
avalanche-prone terrain.
The author and publisher
disclaim any liability for
injury or other damage
caused by backcountry
traveling or performing
any other activity described
in this book.

COVER PHOTO:
*Joe Ryan, Mike Miracle,
Jordan Campbell, and Rick
Leonidas head out from the
North Pole Hut for a day of
skiing on Hayden Peak.*

N96.932
L78 2c
v. 2

Acknowledgments

Through five printings and three editions of *Colorado Hut to Hut,*
many, many super people have contributed ideas, information, time,
words of encouragement, words of wisdom ("He who skis last skis
tracks!"), technical expertise—even their precious bodies (as skiing
companions and as models)—not only to help bring this project
to fruition but also to keep it going. Without their help, this book
would have been truly impossible—and it wouldn't have been nearly
as much fun to do. Whether your help was by phone, in my office,
or on the trail, it has been deeply appreciated! I would like to thank
(in no particular order) the following people, who have added their
special something to this book:

Bill Litz, Mary Kay Litz, Jon Alegranti, Bevin Wallace,
Steve Grinstead, Clint Buckner, Kurt Lankford, Greg Doubek, Craig
Gaskill, Jeff Cobb, Ken Morr, Pat Fortino, Beth Smith, Kirk Watson,
Gordon Banks, David Hiser, Doug Johnson, Bruce Ward, Bernice
Notenboom, Dan Schaefer, Lisa Paesani, Melissa Bronson, Judy
Hampton, David "Cully" Culbreth, Rick and Kiki Sayre, Jordan
"Du Telemark" Campbell, Bob Moore, Philippe Dunoyer, Paul
Parker, Jeff Parker and Nancy Coulter-Parker, Mike Miracle, Rick
Leonidas, Bruce Hayden, Dave Boardman, Steve Sterner, the
Geriatric Tele Society, Chris Quinn, Pete Stouffer, Doug Seyb, Mike
O'Brien, David and Betsy Harrower, Ace Kvale, David Eye, John
Scahill, Liz Klinga, Mark Collen, Joe Chervenak, Roland Pitts, Sally
Moser, Dianne Howie, Suzanne Venino, and Amy Duenkel. Special
thanks go to Lou Dawson for unwittingly helping me start down the
path of guidebook writing.

The following members of organizations have been
indispensable: John Fielder, Linda Doyle, Craig Keyzer, Carol Pando,
Jenna Samelson, and Carolyn Acheson (Westcliffe Publishers); Rebecca
Finkel (F + P Graphic Design, Inc.); Kim Reed (Reed Photo Imaging);
Yvonne "Bootsie" Brodzinski and Linda Thompson (Never Summer
Nordic); Steve Prim (Guinn Mountain Hut); Andy Miller (High
Lonesome Hut); Bob Allison (Squaw Mountain Fire Lookout,
Arapaho National Forest, Clear Creek Ranger District); Craig Steele
(Outward Bound School); Ralph Thomas (Hidden Treasure Yurt);

Cindy and Curt Carpenter, David Schweppe, Peter Looram, Mary Sanders, Debbie Krohn, May Eynon, and Jenifer Blomquist (10th Mountain Division); Leigh Girvin and Dr. John Warner (Summit Huts Association); Scott Messina, Hawk Greenway, and Craig Ward (Alfred Braun Memorial Hut System); Jed Frame (Elkton Cabins); Tabor Allison (Gothic Cabin); Jean and Mary Pavillard (Cement Creek Yurt); "Stormy" Coleman (Lost Wonder Hut); Doug MacLennan (Southwest Nordic System); Mary Ann DeBoer (Cumbres Nordic Adventures); Mark Mueller and Sandy Kobrock (Wolf Creek Backcountry); Ken Kutac and Curtis Larson (San Juan Snowtreks); Mark Richter and Robert Sullivan (Phoenix Ridge Yurts); Jerry Gray and Colin Gray (Hinsdale Haute Route); Christopher George (Saint Paul Lodge); Mike Turrin, Joe Ryan, Josh Weinstein, and Mark Kelley (San Juan Hut System); and Dale Atkins, Knox Williams, and Scott Toepfer (Colorado Avalanche Information Center).

In this edition of *Colorado Hut to Hut*, we have teamed up with several sponsors. Not only do these people and companies produce some of the best products to take into the backcountry, but they are also friends. Thanks go to Tom Fritz, John Cooley, and Neil Munro (Marmot); Steve Hardesty (Cima/Tua Ski); Bruce Edgerly and Bruce McGowen (Backcountry Access); Mike Hattrup (K2 Skis); Mark Peterson (Ortovox USA); John Sweitzer and Gary Richter (Garmont USA); Casey Sheahan and Ann Obenchain (Kelty Backpacks); Maile Buker, Jordy Margid, and Craig Hatton (Black Diamond Equipment Ltd.); and Mike Harrelson, Hal Thomson, and Vickie Achee (Patagonia).

Finally, I would like to thank the gang at Neptune Mountaineering, who kept my screws glued, edges sharp, and bindings (and attitude) adjusted—Gary Neptune, Chris Clark, Roland Fortin, Luke Gosselin, Scott Sutton, Mike Smith, Ryan Phinney, and Pete Mason.

This book is dedicated to my homies—Bill, Karen, and Mary Kay.
— BRIAN LITZ

Photography: John Norris

TUA = TELEMARK.

" ...to many, Tua=telemark. I've lost count of the number of times, in the dead of mountain wilderness, miles from the nearest outpost civilized enough to stock cold beer, that I've heard someone defend Tua's supremacy over all other brands, while staunchly refusing to try anything else 'because there is no point.' "

~ Leslie Anthony
Powder Magazine

Tua Ski ~ 1945 33rd Street
Boulder, CO 80301
ph 303.417.0301 ~ fax 303.417.0145
www.tuaski.com

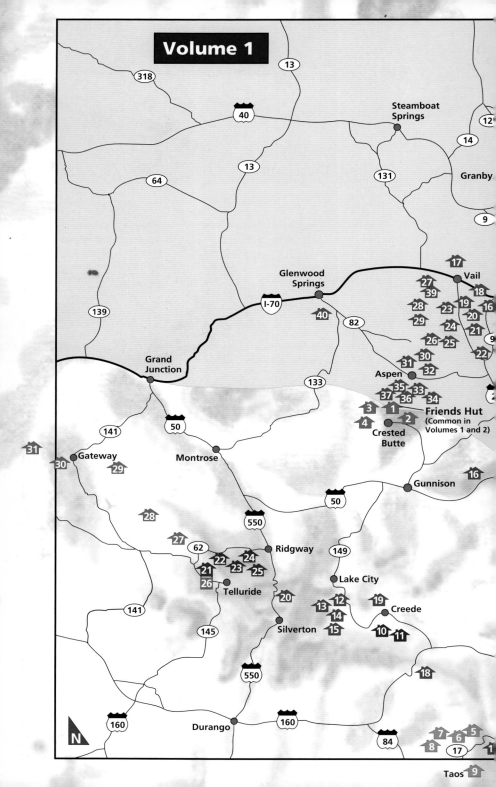

Volume 1

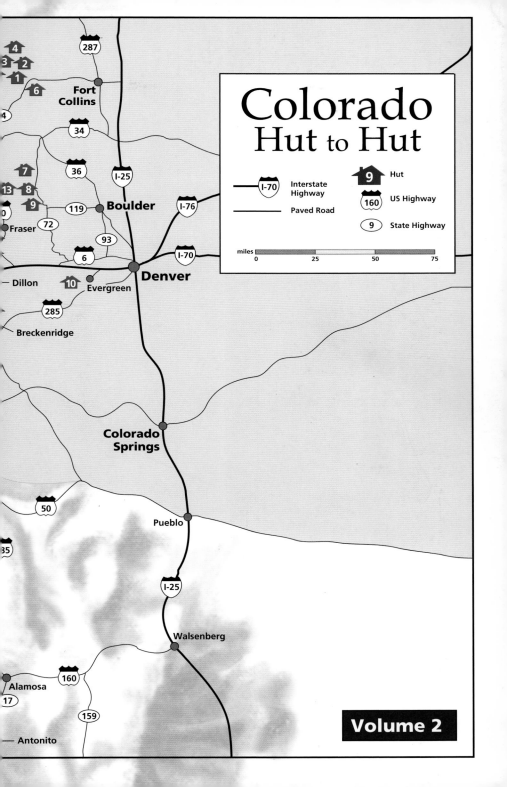

Colorado
Hut to Hut

Symbol	Meaning
I-70	Interstate Highway
	Paved Road
9	Hut
160	US Highway
9	State Highway

miles
0   25   50   75

Volume 2

Table of Contents

Foreword

The well-established and growing hut-to-hut system in Colorado provides a special recreational experience that is fast dwindling in this state and throughout the West. With increases in population and tourism, many people are seeking out more remote, secluded experiences. These huts—with their warm hearths, convenient facilities, and cozy beds—allow people to delve deeper and deeper into the forest environment. In so doing, the hustle and bustle of modern urban living falls away and the splendor of raw, wild nature takes over.

Having been to a number of these huts with my family, I've been overcome by the soothing stillness and profound silence. The winter landscape presents itself in full glory as you traverse along well-marked trails leading to each hut. Before you unfolds a brilliant expanse of sparkling, snowcapped peaks and crisp, fresh, winter mountain air. But what I treasure most is the vast openness of the crystalline, deep blue skies. It's exhilarating and rejuvenating.

Not only have I had an opportunity to experience nature in its full sense—with the added hope of spying winter wildlife—but these huts also provide physical challenges that are equally rewarding. For more than twenty years, I worked for the Colorado Outward Bound School. This school provides participants with opportunities to test themselves both physically and mentally by confronting obstacles and surviving the elements in natural surroundings. Skiing the Colorado hut-to-hut network presents similar challenges. As in the Outward Bound program, each member of your hut-to-hut group must take care of his or her own needs—warm clothing, adequate conditioning, enough food and water—while also contributing to the group by pulling together, preparing meals in the hut, and making sure each member is enjoying the trip.

The huts provide a chance for exploration, an escape, a respite. They also offer an opportunity for communal interaction with other backcountry enthusiasts. The *Colorado Hut to Hut* guidebooks are a valuable source of information on the ski hut network in Colorado, intended to enhance your own outdoor adventure and to ensure that your excursion into the winter woods is safe and enjoyable. Have fun!

—MARK UDALL
U.S. Congressman

Jordan Campbell atop Hayden Peak above the North Pole Yurt in the San Juan Hut System.

Preface

The sentinel of Hayden Peak towers over the San Juan Hut System's North Pole Hut. Though not as well known to backcountry ski mountaineers as the mountain of the same name near Aspen, this southerly Hayden is no less alluring or classic. Hayden Peak anchors the northwest corner of the Sneffels Range, slicing the westerly winds like the prow of a great ship. Few people have tread upon its summit or disturbed its snowy flanks.

Whenever I have driven across Dallas Divide between Ridgway and Telluride, I cannot help but admire the peak. I know the route by heart. Although I have summited Hayden Peak in the past, sans skis, I have always wanted to lay tracks down the beautiful hanging snowfield on its northwest flank.

In early March of 1998, I was given an opportunity to reach my goal. Two old friends, Jordan Campbell and Joe Ryan (owner of the San Juan Hut System), as well as two new friends, Rick Leonidas and Mike Miracle (an editor at *Skiing Magazine*), accompanied me. Both Jordan and Joe had considerable backcountry skiing experience, but Mike, who is an excellent alpine skier, was a novice to serious off-piste skiing.

We spent the night at the hut, and the next day headed for the summit. The route was a natural: Climb the north ridge on skins through the superb, forested powder glades to tree line. Above, the route steepened. Over unconsolidated slopes composed of talus, frozen scree, and snow, we kicked steps up to the rocky, northern summit ridge. From there, moderate high-altitude walking along the ridge-crest led to the diminutive summit cone and some tricky climbing.

For several tense minutes, we scratched our way up the exposed summit slopes on snow that ranged from bulletproof to sugar. The finale came in the form of hand-and-foot scrambling atop a teeter-totter pile of dark, ancient sedimentary blocks.

On top the weather was clear, cold, and windy—but high, thin clouds softened the sun. Mount Sneffels was to the east; to the south Telluride and the Wilson Peaks; to the west the high desert of Utah; and north was Grand Mesa. We headed back to the hut, and under the guidance of Joe Ryan we all skied the superb, low-angled powder of the hanging snowfield as well as the tricky, treacherous stair step of ramps, cliff bands, gullies, and tree clusters. It was the perfect day for the perfect sport.

Even after 23 years of backcountry hut skiing, I still find every hut trip full of nourishing adventure, unskied terrain, and exhilarating challenges. What could be better than having this adventure with friends both old and new? The summit was great, but Mike's assessment was better: "Strangely invigorating and the best skiing experience of my life."

—BRIAN LITZ

Chris George (proprietor of the Saint Paul Lodge), Brad Smith, Bob Moore, and Bill Harris ski into U.S. Basin above the lodge and Red Mountain Pass.

Introduction

Welcome to *Colorado Hut to Hut: Volume II, Southern Region.* There is much new in this third edition (and fifth printing) of this guidebook. In the introduction to the previous editions, I mentioned how popular hut-to-hut travel was becoming—illustrating with raw statistics the exaggerated growth curve that had defined the sport for 10 to 15 years. If anything, at the dawn of the new millennium, this trend is accelerating. In fact, demand for 10th Mountain Division huts has become so vigorous that in 1999 the hut system instituted a lottery system to apportion their space.

Naturally, the hut supply tries to keep pace with hut demand, and since the last edition of this book, printed in 1995, Colorado's high country has sprouted roughly 20 new huts—a 40 percent increase in five years. So one of the first things you will notice is the presence of many new faces. All 20 of Colorado's new huts are covered, including six entirely new hut systems, as well as additions to existing hut systems.

Concerns about the growing number of hut entries in the book, along with the associated growth in the number of pages, led to another major change: the metamorphosis of *Colorado Hut to Hut* from one book into a two-volume set. Volume I covers the huts detailed in the Northern and Central chapters of the old tome, and Volume II covers the Southern huts.

The line of demarcation runs east-west across the crest of the Elk Range and over to the southern end of the Sawatch Range near Monarch Pass. Although this splits the very centrally located Elk Mountains in two, it reflects the added distance and time required for most hut users (based on the Front Range) to reach Monarch Pass and the Gunnison River Valley. It is also an attempt to balance the editorial coverage in each book. This division means that the Alfred Braun Memorial Huts, which reside on the northern side of the Elk Range, will be found in Volume I, and the Crested Butte area huts and the Lost Wonder Hut are found in Volume II.

Volume I covers huts in the northern and central areas. In the north, these include the five huts of the Never Summer Nordic Yurts and the Nokhu Cabin. Central huts include those of the Summit Huts Association, the 10th Mountain Division Hut Association, the Alfred A. Braun Memorial Hut System, and two independent huts (Hidden Treasure Yurt and Sunlight Backcountry Cabin). Volume II covers the Crested Butte area huts, the Bull of the Woods Yurt in Taos, New Mexico, and the entire San Juan Mountains, including the Cumbres Pass area in the South San Juans on the New Mexico border. The last section is a guide to the San Juan Huts mountain biking route going from Telluride to Moab, Utah.

Several new huts are featured in this edition. In the Crested Butte area, the Elkton Cabins now boast the **Silver Jewel** and the **Miner's Delight** in addition to the existing Elkton Hut. The Southwest Nordic Center has added the **Grouse Creek Yurt** and **Bull of the Woods Yurt** (near Taos, New Mexico). Other new systems and huts are: San Juan Snowtreks, operating the **Fisher Mountain Hut** and the **Lime**

'Nuff said.

Creek Yurt; Cumbres Nordic Adventures and its **Spruce Hole Yurt;** Wolf Creek Backcountry's **Pass Creek Yurt;** and the Phoenix Ridge Yurts (consisting of the **Phoenix Ridge Yurt** and the **Meadow Yurt**).

Taking on this book project certainly has proven to be a double-edged sword. When I first hatched the idea back around 1990, I did not envision the never-ending construction of huts that has forced me to continually update the guide. I figured that I would need to revisit it every five to eight years or so. This obviously was not to be, as every year sees a new hut welcoming weary, chilled skiers in the winter and rain-soaked, lightning-harassed mountain bikers and hikers in the summer.

Why is hut-to-hut travel becoming more and more popular? One reason, I believe, is that many alpine skiers have become bored with an increasingly packaged, groomed, and manufactured "product" at downhill ski areas. Also, many more people are moving to the Rocky Mountain region. Another factor is that outdoor-recreation gear has greatly improved in recent years; today's equipment is lighter and performs extremely well, allowing outdoor enthusiasts of all abilities to enjoy the backcountry. And finally, hut-to-hut travel is just plain fun! The backcountry beckons a wide variety of people, with panoramic vistas, colorful sunsets, the challenge of unknown terrain, the thrill of virgin snow, and, finally, the chance to relax in a cozy cabin overlooking the heart of the Colorado Rockies.

Which all means lots of work for me. But, hey, it also keeps me out in the backcountry...doing field work! I still love this sport as much as I did the first time I strapped on a pair of old wooden Trysl-Knut skis and headed to the Markley and Tagert huts with my Colorado Mountain Club Denver Junior Group buddies for our winter outing in January 1977. Here's to Colorado remaining the hut capital of the United States!

Mark Kelley and Josh Weinstein tour to Ridgway Hut.

How to Use This Guide

Writing a guidebook presents the author with a quandary: provide directions as detailed as "go 100 feet and turn left at the 15th aspen tree" or provide only the basic data? Some guidebooks give so much information and conversation that the user becomes frustrated merely trying to assemble the relevant facts; other guidebooks are so tersely fact oriented that they leave the user cold and uninspired.

My vision for *Colorado Hut to Hut* was to create a field guide as well as a backcountry "wish book." It is intended to provide information and advice for aspiring hut-to-hut travelers and to inspire the seasoned ski mountaineer looking for new and unknown challenges. The beginner can read through the "On the Trail" section of this introduction and follow the detailed trail descriptions, while the expert might simply scan the trail summaries to get a quick overall feel for a tour or an untried hut system.

In addition to routes and hut-system information, *Colorado Hut to Hut* includes sections on equipment recommendations and hut etiquette, as well as avalanche information and help with some of the more common problems encountered on hut-to-hut expeditions. It also contains several appendixes with important phone numbers, including emergency and hut-reservation numbers. The Bibliography and Recommended Reading List (Appendix G) contains suggestions for further reading on a range of topics important to hut-to-hut skiers and bikers.

This book is certainly not the only source of information that should accompany adventurers into the wilderness, nor is it a substitute for experience. Every person heading into the backcountry needs to be proactive in obtaining the experience and knowledge necessary to ensure a safe, enjoyable adventure in the Colorado Rockies. Skiers, hikers, and bikers are strongly encouraged to carry a selection of maps, including United States Geological Survey's 7.5-minute topographic maps (topos), Trails Illustrated maps, and maps produced by the various hut systems. Books such as *The ABCs of Avalanche Safety & Snow Sense,* and *Backcountry Medical Guide* are also invaluable resources for mountain expeditions. These books fit easily into a pack and cover important topics too complex to be detailed fully in this guidebook.

To get the most out of this book, please take the time to read the following brief summary of its overall organization.

Colorado Hut to Hut: Volume I, Northern and Central Regions and *Volume II, Southern Region* contain regional headings, which each begin with a brief overview of the hut systems located in those areas, including a bit of local history, the type of skiing found nearby, and general descriptions of hut amenities.

Individual hut systems, huts, and tours are then described in detail, once again highlighting each hut's history and special features. Each tour description has two parts: The first is a capsule summary of the most important tour information, including level of difficulty, estimated travel time, mileage, elevation gain and loss, and pertinent map sources; the second portion is a detailed narrative of the route.

A route is described in detail only once. That is, if a tour that runs from Uncle Bud's Hut to Skinner Hut is described under the Uncle Bud's Hut section, it will not be described again in reverse under the Skinner Hut entry.

Hut tours are separated into two categories: trails that travel from a trailhead to a hut and tours that travel between huts—"hut to hut." As a general rule, the hut systems and trails that link huts within a system are described from north to south and/or from east to west. Many hut entries also include recommended day tours.

Jim "Massage Therapist to the Stars" Bowen takes a load off in the San Juan backcountry.

Annotated USGS 7.5-minute topo maps show routes to and surrounding each hut. These maps are for general reference only; you should purchase your own topo maps for route-finding.

Difficulty

Each tour is assigned a rating of overall difficulty. These ratings are subjective, but they do follow generally accepted criteria.

Novice routes present few difficulties, require less complex navigation, and feature minimal elevation gain. A novice rating does not mean a route is suitable for people who have never cross-country skied; a novice-level skier ideally should have completed at least five to 10 backcountry day trips and have a basic mastery of double poling and snowplowing. Because novice skiers are generally still gaining wilderness savvy in areas such as navigation and avalanche awareness, it is recommended that these skiers participate in guided trips or in group outings accompanied by more experienced skiers.

Intermediate routes are the most common type of tour in this book and most closely define the term "classic tour." Intermediate-level skiers usually have been skiing for at least several seasons and have participated in five or more hut trips. Their wilderness experience and fitness levels are solid, and they are able to ski to and from huts with ease. They also enjoy off-trail skiing, although they may not have completely mastered the telemark turn. Carrying heavy overnight backpacks is not new to these skiers.

Advanced skiers have generally been backcountry and hut skiing for many seasons, have skied and traveled in a wide variety of weather conditions, and can telemark down steep, timbered slopes and through diverse types of snow. They are very fit and have a full understanding of avalanches and rescue procedures. Most important, advanced skiers will never tell you where the best powder is!

Advanced/Expert designations indicate tours that go beyond the standard definition of "advanced"—tours that demand high fitness levels and mountain skills plus an extraordinary level of commitment. An example might be a tour with a passage over a pass or ridge that must be crossed to reach a hut. Once over the pass or ridge, you have to be committed to reaching the hut, as the distance and exertion required to retrace your steps may be simply too much. In addition, the high-altitude nature of this terrain might leave skiers particularly vulnerable to approaching storms—making a bail-out problematic, if not outright impossible. Other tours considered "expert" might require rock scrambling or extreme exposure to the elements, or the tour may be unusually long and physically taxing.

Most day-trip peak ascents are at least advanced in difficulty. Under good conditions, most peaks can be climbed quickly and safely, but it is amazing how quickly a storm can move in and within minutes drop the temperature and visibility to zero.

Advanced and expert tours are serious undertakings. In fact, any tour in this book can become advanced under certain conditions.

Icons

Icons indicating cross-country skiing, snowshoeing, bicycling, and/or hiking accompany each tour description. Hut routes with all four icons are open year-round for skiing, snowshoeing, biking, and hiking. Some huts are open only in winter (due to permit restrictions), so only winter icons will be shown. Because bicycles are prohibited in Wilderness Areas, routes that pass through them are closed to mountain bikers; therefore no bicycle icon will be shown.

Time

The travel times listed are general guesstimates of how long the average group of skiers will take to complete a route. They include time for a lunch break and several shorter breaks. While stronger parties can easily make quick work of most trails, slower groups—those new to backcountry skiing or those breaking trail in powder snow—might consider using a figure of one mile per hour plus one hour per 1,000 feet of elevation gain in estimating tour lengths.

Distance

The distance listed in each section is one-way mileage as measured from trailhead to hut or from hut to hut. (Mileage to a trailhead, as detailed in the text portion of the tour, may be slightly off due to variances in car odometers.)

Elevations

Three elevations are given in the capsule information for each tour. The first elevation is for the point where the trail begins, whether it is a trailhead or a hut. The second elevation is for the destination hut. The final pair of elevations represents the gain (+) and loss (−) accumulated over the length of a trail. (These figures should be reversed if you are traveling in the opposite direction.) In trail descriptions, an elevation that corresponds to a USGS 7.5-minute topo map reference is referred to as an "Elevation Point."

Few photos illustrate the raw power of an avalanche as this image taken from the Wolf Pass area in the San Juan Mountains, where a slide cut through spruce-fir trees like a hot knife through butter.

Avalanche

In this guidebook I use the avalanche-hazard rating system created by Richard and Betsy Armstrong, which I have used in previous skiing guides. This system is extremely useful because it gives an overall feel for the terrain. This is important because daily or seasonal avalanche hazards may change but terrain does not.

Avalanche warnings in the summaries at the beginning of each trail discussion pertain only to that specific trail, not to other hut-to-hut trails in the area or to any day tours in the area. For example, a trail to a hut or in between huts might be extremely safe and carry with it a "minimal danger" avalanche rating while the recommended day tours included with a specific hut origin might have much more dangerous ratings. A rating of "minimal danger" in a tour description has no relationship to the severity of the avalanche terrain and hazards above and around the huts.

Snow conditions can change rapidly; the decision to ski or not ski a potential avalanche route is entirely yours. Remember that many people are caught in small slides that occur in unlikely or unobvious avalanche terrain, such as in a creek drainage or in the middle of a forest. To be safe, always assume that you will be traveling in avalanche conditions.

The four categories of avalanche terrain used in this guidebook are:

1. Minimal danger. This route is safe under all conditions. However, it is still recommended that you remain alert and play it safe; an avalanche, while unlikely, is never totally impossible.

2. Some avalanche terrain encountered; easily avoided. This route is still safe in all conditions when skiers remain on standard trails. There is some dangerous terrain in the general vicinity, but it should be easy to spot and avoid.

3. Route crosses avalanche runout zones; can be dangerous during high-hazard periods. This trail's normal route lies below a known avalanche path. Skiers will not likely serve as a trigger, although they could be caught in a spontaneous slide.

4. Route crosses avalanche slopes; prone to skier-triggered avalanches during high-hazard periods. This route travels directly across a known hazard, and skiers can easily set off a slide given the right combination of conditions.

Note: If the Colorado Avalanche Information Center says the avalanche hazard is high, avoid trails with ratings of three or four as listed above. (See Appendix E for avalanche information phone numbers.)

Maps

Colorado Hut to Hut lists relevant USGS 7.5-minute topographic maps, National Forest maps, Trails Illustrated maps, special maps for each tour, and references for maps included in this book.

USGS topo maps are the mainstays of mountaineers and skiers, providing the greatest detail of elevations, contours, and natural features. National Forest maps are large-scale maps that are almost useless for navigation; however, they do provide road and trailhead information, as well as an overview of the area. Trails Illustrated maps are very useful for backcountry travelers—especially mountain bikers—because they cover the equivalent of eight USGS topo maps. These maps are up-to-date and virtually indestructible. Trails Illustrated maps are listed only if they are available for the area. Specialty maps include any maps produced by a hut association, such as the 10th Mountain Division Hut Association. These maps are revised often and are very popular.

Schematic maps included in this book are referenced by page number after each tour heading. These maps are for basic orientation only; use the maps recommended in the capsule information for route navigation. Also, keep in mind that a map's degree of usefulness is directly related to its date of publication. Old maps will not have the most current information on roads, trails, etc. Remember to check the publication date of any map.

Note: A 1:160,000-scale "topo atlas" published by DeLorme Mapping is available for Colorado. This is one of the single most useful sources of information for anyone traveling the back roads of the state and is highly recommended. See Appendix H for map sources.

On the Trail

Before You Go

As someone (perhaps a backcountry skier) once said: "Education teaches us the rules. Experience teaches the exceptions." The mountains can be a very dangerous and unpredictable place for the unknowing and ill prepared—as well as for the highly skilled and seasoned backcountry traveler. Skiers, snowshoers, hikers, and mountain bikers must understand that even the "easiest" trail can be very challenging, that weather patterns can and do change quickly and dramatically, and that equipment fails. Those headed to even the most readily accessible huts must accept responsibility for their own and their companions' safety and well-being. Self-sufficiency is a must.

For individuals who are interested in learning more about hut-to-hut travel, courses are offered by major outdoor-equipment retailers, guide services, universities, and recreational clubs, as well as many city and county recreation departments. These classes range from "layering clothes for cold weather" and "basic mountain bike repair and maintenance" to weekend avalanche seminars. These evening and weekend sessions can be excellent sources of basic and more advanced backcountry information.

Successful and safe expeditions do not just happen—they are the result of organization and planning. Use the following outline to aid in organizing your hut-to-hut adventure:

1. Use *Colorado Hut to Hut* to choose trips that match your group's interests and skill level. Talk to the hut systems' personnel to help plan a trip that is appropriate for your group's experience and fitness level, and to help you decide whether your group needs a guide. (See Appendix A for hut-system addresses, phone numbers, and websites.)

2. Call the hut system to reserve the hut(s) and dates you want. Remember that weekends, holidays, and nights with full moons are usually reserved first. Be prepared to pay for the trip in full when you make your reservation.

3. Designate a leader for your group. The leader should be responsible for disseminating information and seeing that all risk waivers (if required) are returned to the proper hut system.

4. Purchase any necessary trail and road maps.

5. Plan meals and snacks. Purchase food and repackage to reduce bulk.

6. Inspect equipment (zippers, pack straps, etc.) and take it for a dry run. Purchase flashlight and avalanche transceiver batteries, ski waxes, skin glue, etc. Restock first-aid and repair kits. Make sure all binding screws are tight and that binding cables (if any) are in good repair. Organize group gear. Rent any gear necessary. Test avalanche transceivers.

7. Practice packing your pack. Make sure essential and often-used items (sunglasses, goggles, sunscreen, maps, headlamps, compass, snacks, knives) are in a handy location.

Roanne Miller gives a clinic on fluid off-piste skiing.

8. Plan car shuttles. (Call the hut system if you need assistance in planning car shuttles; its staff may be able to recommend shuttle services.)

9. Before you leave for the trailhead, be sure to call the Colorado Avalanche Information Center (CAIC), the U.S. Weather Service, and the Colorado Department of Transportation (see Appendixes B and E) to check avalanche, weather, and road conditions.

10. Provide a responsible party back home with your trip itinerary, expected time of return, where you plan to park, and hut-system phone numbers.

11. Establish an emergency plan and assess the group's first-aid knowledge.

12. Finally, DO NOT forget hut lock combinations and/or keys. Play it safe and have several individuals carry these. Keep a flashlight handy in case you arrive at the hut after dark.

Gear

Today, a staggering amount of durable, high-performance equipment is available for conveyance through the backcountry. Though the vast majority of hut visitors arrive in winter, and on skis, more people are traveling by snowshoe and in the summer.

There is little to say about what kind of equipment to use in the summer. Bikers use standard mountain bikes, though the cyclo-cross type of bike has become more popular. Appropriate footwear for hikers ranges from heavy-duty "approach" shoes and boots to heavy-duty backpacking boots. Some summer visitors drive high-clearance or four-wheel-drive vehicles to the huts and use them as base camps for day hiking and biking trips. Many huts and hut systems are not open in the summer, so please check with each system for specifics.

Although far more durable than the backcountry ski gear of yore, today's high-precision equipment requires attention for maximum performance. Here, Mick Fairchild uses a truing bar to check for an even base.

Winter is the time when things are hopping in the huts, and there is much debate regarding the best equipment for winter travel. Snowshoes are steady and reliable, easy to master, require minimal skills to operate (especially when pointed downhill), are not temperature-temperamental (like waxes and skins), can easily be rented, and are a great choice for non-skiers who would like to sample the hut experience without the anxiety that can accompany the beginning ski experience. Even though snowshoeing is a fulfilling outdoor pursuit, I believe it ranks well below skiing on the fun scale. Think about it—you walk up a hill, then you walk back down the hill. With skis, you walk up the hill (aided by skins or waxes), then slide down the hill on a gravity-propelled free-fall.

The fact of the matter is that most of the huts in Colorado were conceived of as ski huts—plain and simple. All in all, skis are the ideal mode of transportation for those willing to master their use. You can walk on them, kick and glide on them, herringbone on them, carry them on your pack, and, most importantly, be transported straight to nirvana on them when under the influence of gravity in powder snow.

For the most part, any type of non-track (Nordic center) ski can be used in Colorado's hut systems. I have acquaintances who occasionally "skate," or kick-and-glide, their way to the huts. This usually is done only under optimal conditions. Though most of the huts and trail systems were designed for and built when most people were skiing on heavy-duty, metal-edged touring skis and when moderate-duty, free-heel telemark gear reigned supreme, today an equal number of skiers are using alpine resort-grade free-heel gear. And more and more people—though the numbers are still relatively small—are using alpine touring or ski-mountaineering equipment. It all works, and the final choice really depends on the skiers' intentions, abilities, and the type of gear they own.

Virtually every novice- to intermediate-level trail on a road can be tackled using metal-edge touring gear. Even beginners can scoot to and from huts and snowplow down roads on this gear. This category includes waxable and waxless skis with partial to full metal edges with a shovel of roughly 50 to 70 millimeters in width. If you intend to travel above tree line, off-trail (cross-country), with heavier packs, or want to make some turns on day trips, then a wider, sturdier, more aggressive heavy-duty backcountry touring or moderate-duty telemark set-up would be preferable—along with a heavier all-leather or lighter-weight plastic boot.

For many modern skiers who rip at the lift-accessed resorts using telemark and parallel turns, want to spend a lot of time skiing off peaks and ridges and through steep trees, and do multiday tours with heavy packs, the choice is the latest generation of high-end performance free-heel gear. These skis are derived from alpine ski technology. They are not meant to be waxed with "touring" waxes. Rather, they are used most often with climbing skins for forward and upward mobility. In addition, they have a single-camber construction that is optimized for turning on the steeps in a variety of snow conditions—from the deepest powder to the most problematic, wind-compacted sastrugi above tree line. For the most part, skiers using this type of "heavy metal" will most likely sport the latest generations of burly plastic boots or race-grade leather telemark boots.

Alpine touring gear hails primarily from the central European alpine countries (free-heel telemark gear originated in Scandinavia), and has been available for decades in North America. Alpine touring gear's proponents—usually introduced to it in the Alps by mountaineers who climb peaks while wearing leather or plastic mountaineering boots—are growing. This increase in popularity is for good reasons, including the fact that as "tele" gear has become higher-performance and heavier, Alpine touring gear has become increasingly light and comfortable. The bindings, which can pivot at the toe for touring and lock down like a standard resort alpine binding for downhill skiing, also incorporate sophisticated release features that appeal to skiers concerned about leg injuries from falls.

The lock-down feature also allows skiers to ski exactly as they would on standard resort equipment. This feature is beneficial for competent resort skiers who would like to experience the backcountry and do not want to learn an entirely new turn. Alpine touring gear allows downhill skiers to directly transfer their skills into backcountry skiing.

In summary, don't obsess about gear. In fact, if you make many sojourns to the huts, you can and will see every type and combination of gear imaginable. If you are new to the sport, go to a good shop and talk to experienced salespeople. Talk to friends. Keep an open mind and don't get led astray by philosophical zealots. You can find many good books and how-to videos that go over the basics (see Appendix G). Most gear is rentable. Experiment before you buy. Bottomline? It is more important to go out there and have fun while cranking face plants than to worry about what kind of gear you are using.

A note about equipment care: Modern equipment is so well-made and sophisticated that many people have become complacent concerning the proper maintenance and routine inspection of their gear. Take the time to check your equipment thoroughly. Look for loose screws and loose cables on bindings, worn laces on boots, bent poles, broken zippers, loose brakes on bikes, etc. Make sure that you have all of your gear (see checklist in Appendix F). Carry a repair kit and know how to use it. The time to learn how to repair gear is before you leave home—not in the middle of a blizzard at midnight.

General Trail Considerations

When traveling in the backcountry, be sure that your group arrives at the trailhead early; traveling hut to hut requires an equally early start. Try to build extra time into your schedule just in case problems arise.

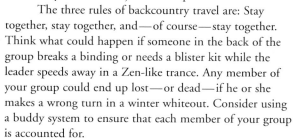

The three rules of backcountry travel are: Stay together, stay together, and—of course—stay together. Think what could happen if someone in the back of the group breaks a binding or needs a blister kit while the leader speeds away in a Zen-like trance. Any member of your group could end up lost—or dead—if he or she makes a wrong turn in a winter whiteout. Consider using a buddy system to ensure that each member of your group is accounted for.

Each group should carry emergency equipment consisting of rudimentary camping gear, such as a stove, a pot, and a tarp, in case emergency shelter is necessary. Also, each person should carry high-energy snack food and quick trailside meals (such as soups), as well as a first-aid kit, flashlight, and avalanche gear. Be sure to test your transceivers as a group each and every day and discuss emergency procedures before your group heads into the backcountry.

Above: A "hasty-pit" provides a quick, though important view of the snow crystals and deepest snowpack layers of potential ski slopes.

Finally, each member of the group should carry maps and a compass. Many skiers and mountain bikers have become too dependent on guidebooks, but map reading, navigation, and compass use are crucial skills that all backcountry travelers should acquire and practice. It is essential to keep maps and compasses handy and refer to them often, especially when confronted with a trail intersection, confusing route, and/or foul weather. Get in the habit of matching real-world landmarks to features on the map and watching out for trail markers—both the obvious and the not so obvious.

Backcountry trail markers exist in a variety of forms: blue diamonds for Nordic ski trails, orange diamonds for snowmobile routes, old tree blazes, and others. On the trails covered in this book, you may encounter any or all of these markers—or none.

GPS Coordinates

If there ever was anything that is part art and part science, it is land navigation. Though the subject is too large to cover in detail here—and there are many fine books dedicated solely to this pursuit—I find it necessary to touch on the subject, especially with regard to Global Positioning System (GPS) units and coordinates. GPS coordinates are beginning to appear in many guidebooks. This is because more people are requesting them, not necessarily because people absolutely need to have them to navigate in Colorado under normal conditions. I have been uneasy about including them and, in fact, as we went to press, I chose to leave them out entirely in this edition.

One reason is the coordinates that were available at press time, provided by the hut operators, came with caveats such as "remember that these are only as good as the person who took them," or "so-and-so did these coordinates a long time ago and we think they are reasonably accurate," and "we have two sets of numbers that differ, and we are going to do them again in the future."

This lack of confidence in the current data—much of which are many years old—is a function of several factors including the evolution of both the sophistication of commercially available GPS units over time and advancements in the general science of equipment usage in the field. In addition, the competence of the GPS operator affects the accuracy of the readings, as does the ability of the GPS unit to lock onto a maximum number of satellites—the latter being affected by local topography and forest cover. Historically, GPS units have been less effective in giving elevational readings, as opposed to latitude and longitude.

Perhaps most important, up until a few months before this book went to press, the U.S. military had purposefully hindered the accuracy of civilian units for reasons of national defense. The U.S. government's decision now allows GPS units to achieve highly accurate readings. So during the next few years, prepare for a steady stream of accurate, dependable coordinates to be available through a variety of sources, including each hut system.

And finally, bear in mind the sales hype that accompanies the arrival of GPS units that are sold today. Believe all of it, and it could lead you to swear that by carrying one (or an altimeter or a compass, for that matter), you will be immune to getting lost. What if the batteries die? Or you could come to the conclusion that GPS units' divining-rod abilities allow you to shut off your brain while you are led directly to your chosen destination. They don't and won't.

GPS units only tell you where you are—and roughly at that—not where to go. Nor will they tell you whether an avalanche path, a cliff band, or unskiable trees are in your way. Ultimately, you have to select the route.

Navigation Tips and Tools

The bottom line is that GPS units are useful for navigating in Colorado's mountains, but no more so than a map, a compass, or an altimeter. You can travel through the high country safely and efficiently by following these guidelines:

1. Give yourself time to develop a feel for the land, rates of travel, and the orientation of the mountains.

2. Learn to pay attention to landmarks.

3. Master the skills of reading a compass and USGS topo maps—7.5-minute quads still being the best tools available for navigation—and the ability to match them to the terrain around you.

4. Skillfully employ your brain (first and foremost).

In addition to good maps, everyone should have a quality compass. This, like the topo map, is an essential tool for travel. Buy a good compass that is capable of shooting real bearings, and learn how to use it. State-of-the-art compasses cost around $40 to $60 and will last forever. (Don't get hoodwinked into buying a techy, battery-operated one—the fewer the batteries, the better.) Keep your map and compass handy and break them out at every stop.

More and more people are now carrying altimeters, which are on the next tier of essential tools for navigation in the mountains. Units such as the Suunto Vector provide a steady stream of information for the user from their sophisticated altimeter/barometer, log functions, watch functions, and built-in digital compass. The compasses in these devices are actually quite nice, though still not a substitute for a quality hand-held compass. Used properly, altimeters can provide helpful information on changing weather conditions, elevation, and rate of travel; however, the key to using them is to understand what their limitations are.

Hypothermia, Frostbite, and the Sun

Hypothermia and frostbite are the two most common cold-weather injuries afflicting skiers and winter mountaineers. Both are preventable—and reversible—if caught in their earliest stages.

Hypothermia is a general cooling of the body's core temperature. It takes only a minor change in this core temperature to produce noticeable effects such as feeling chilled or cold, impairment of muscle coordination (especially of the hands), apathy, confusion, and shivering. Try to stay dry and warm, drink warm fluids, snack regularly, and check each other during the course of the day.

Frostbite is a localized freezing of soft tissue due to exposure to temperatures at or below freezing. Keep all body parts protected from the wind and cold and keep them dry! Watch for skin that turns whitish and loses sensation (frost nip and mild frostbite).

You can avoid both frostbite and hypothermia by staying dry, warm, and rested and by limiting your skin's exposure to the cold air and bitter winds. Carry and wear a variety of clothes, layering them so you can quickly regulate your body's temperature and humidity by shedding or adding garments, especially a wind-protection layer.

Your skin and eyes need "clothing," too. Pack plenty of sunblock and lip protection, at least SPF 20 to 30. Consider bringing moisturizing lotion or aloe to soothe skin. Purchase high-quality sunglasses that screen out the most dangerous ultraviolet radiation and carry an extra pair in the first-aid kit. On mountain bike trips, bring light-colored clothes, such as thin tights and long-sleeved T-shirts, that you can wear during the day to shield your skin from the sun.

Altitude

Colorado's huts are roughly between 8,500 and 12,000 feet in elevation. Unless you have been routinely exercising at higher elevations, you will probably feel the effects of altitude. Because there is less oxygen at these high elevations, your body will consequently be forced to work harder during physical exertion. It is not unlikely that you may experience the effects of altitude sickness, with symptoms such as shortness of breath, dizziness, headaches, lack of appetite, and nausea.

Slow acclimatization is the best way to minimize and eventually eliminate the effects of altitude. It takes about three weeks of continual exposure to a given altitude to become fully acclimatized. Fortunately, the human body adapts quickly, and you can easily lessen the effects of altitude by building a little time into your trip and starting out slowly. If you are visit-

A shovel—don't leave home without one.

ing the mountains from a lower elevation, say, 6,000 feet or below, plan a day or two at the beginning of your trip to stay at a mountain town before hitting the trailhead. Additionally, choose an itinerary that allows your group to gain elevation gradually; hut-system personnel can help you plan an appropriate trip. Also, stay several nights at one hut so you can further acclimatize. Remember that a hut trip is not a race—take your time and enjoy it. Be sure to consult a physician if you have any questions concerning your health and your ability to function at high altitude.

Nutrition and Hydration

Dehydration is one of the single biggest factors contributing to Acute Mountain Sickness (AMS) and High-Altitude Pulmonary Edema (HAPE), as well as leading to headaches, nausea, restless sleep, and a feeling of malaise. Colorado's dry climate and high elevations cause human bodies to work harder. It is almost impossible to drink too much water. Plan on at least three to four quarts per person per day.

Rather than waiting and watching for signs of dehydration, prevent it! Make sure you drink plenty of fluids each morning when you get up, at meals, and throughout the day. Drink tea or water after a hard day of skiing, biking, or hiking. Begin dinner with a light soup and keep a bottle of water next to your bed. Consider carrying two water bottles or one water bottle and a thermos. Fill one container with plain water and a second with soup, cider, or a fruit-flavored electrolyte-replacement beverage.

Because hut skiing allows you to travel with less camping gear, there is no excuse for not bringing enough food. Cook good, nutritious meals with plenty of carbohydrates and protein. Soups are excellent for times when your appetite is suppressed. Have healthy snacks handy on the trail and snack routinely. Taking a steady supply of fuel and liquid into the body throughout the day will work wonders at warding off exhaustion.

Weather

Colorado weather is predictable in that it is unpredictable. The weather is generally sunny and clear. Winter storms sometimes descend out of Canada, sending temperatures far below zero for extended periods, but these storms usually moderate rapidly. In winter, the midday temperatures in the high country normally remain in the +15 to +30 degree (F) range, with nighttime temperatures dropping to zero to −10 degrees. When storms move in, they seldom stay for more than a few days.

Early-season skiing (late November through early January) can range from excellent to nonexistent. During this time of year, it is often possible to travel hut to hut on packed trails, though day skiing is often limited because of shallow snow cover that leaves rocks and logs exposed. Late in the season, as snowstorms become more frequent and the snow has a higher moisture content, conditions start improving. Good off-trail skiing usually begins in January, when the snowpack starts to settle and skiers are able to float well above any obstacles beneath it, like rocks and tree stumps. The more southern huts tend to get a deeper snowpack earlier and often have great skiing as early as December.

As spring approaches, the days become longer and warmer, although winter-like storms are still very real threats in the high country. This is when storms with heavier, moisture-laden snow move through the mountains and the deepest snowpack accumulates. Many skiers—both Nordic and downhill—feel February to April is the best time to ski, especially at higher elevations.

In the summer, the high country belongs to hikers and mountain bikers. Colorado summers are beautiful, with warm to hot days and cool nights. Probably the greatest dangers to people using huts during the summer are dehydration and lightning. Summer thunderstorms build with extreme rapidity and can easily strand groups on exposed mountain peaks, high passes, or in the middle of treeless parks. These storms, which usually hit in the afternoon, often move off as quickly as they arrive. Watch the skies, including the sky behind you.

Storms should not be treated lightly. If you are caught in a storm during summer or in winter (yes, there are occasional lightning storms even in winter and spring), immediately leave high points such as ridges, passes, or peaks. Move away from lone objects such as boulders, trees, or bicycles. Sit on the ground, not in caves or gullies (because of ground currents), and wait until the storm passes.

Many Coloradans feel that autumn is the finest season in the Rockies. The weather is stable, with crisp daytime temperatures and chilly nights. Normal temperatures range from the 60s and 70s during the day and the high 30s to 40s at night. This is probably the best time of year for mountain biking and hiking. Fall can also see turbulent weather as rainstorms move across the mountains, dusting the highest peaks with snow. Keep an eye out for rainbows.

Avalanches

Perhaps the most spectacular, most widespread, and least understood threat to the winter backcountry traveler is an avalanche. By its most basic definition, an avalanche is a large mass of snow that moves downhill under the force of gravity. Avalanche activity is a very complex process that belies its apparent simplicity.

More and more people are dying in avalanches because more and more people are skiing, snowshoeing, snowboarding, and snowmobiling. People new to back-country skiing should consider a guided trip their first time out. The purpose of this discussion is to give you a rudimentary understanding of just what an avalanche is, how to avoid one, and what to do if you must cross an avalanche slope.

The best way to prepare yourself to travel safely in the Rockies is to first read *Snow Sense* and *The ABCs of Avalanche Safety*. Carry these with you. For further information, read *The Avalanche Handbook* and *Avalanche Safety for Climbers and Skiers*. Enroll in an avalanche course and spend some time really digging into the snowpack. Or check out some of the videos that have hit the market in recent years, including *Winning the Avalanche Game*. (See Appendix G for information on how to obtain these titles.)

Avalanches come in two basic varieties. The first is the loose-snow or point-release avalanche. Point-release avalanches usually begin at a specific point and flow downhill in a structureless mass, forming an inverted V. The second kind is the slab avalanche, which begins when a large, cohesive slab or sheet of snow starts sliding all at once, leaving a well-defined fracture line. Slab avalanches are the more dangerous of the two types of slides because they involve huge amounts of hard, often wind-packed snow. Slab avalanches kill the most people and cause the most property destruction.

A slab avalanche is initiated when something serves as a trigger to upset the snowpack, which may have very little internal strength. Likely triggers are the wind, weather, temperature, and, of course, people. Think of the snowpack as a cake; a cake may be made up of a single, stable layer or it may have several layers. Now think of what will happen when that cake is tilted at an angle. Often these layers are held together in a delicate equilibrium and may stay in this precarious state for days or weeks. Then, along comes a potent snowstorm, a warm spell, a wild animal, or a skier to disrupt that delicate balance.

Backcountry travelers should consider three factors when assessing a slope's potential for sliding: terrain, weather, and snowpack. When thinking about the terrain, remember that most avalanches occur on north- and east-facing slopes with angles between 25 and 55 degrees. The vast majority of avalanches occur on slopes with angles between 30 and 45 degrees. Avoid snow cornices that overhang ridges away from the prevailing winds. Keep in mind, however, that wet-snow avalanches can occur on slopes of even 10 degrees, especially on south-facing slopes during spring. Remember to check the ground cover; the more rocks and trees there are to anchor the snow, the better.

Weather factors include rapid changes in conditions such as wind, air temperature, and snowfall. Any of these factors can create a change in the structure and equilibrium of the snowpack, causing a slide. Most avalanches occur immediately after a storm as the new snow slides off the old surface. Be especially watchful during periods when there are constant winds over 15 miles per hour. Also watch for storms that dump more than one inch per hour or have a total accumulation of six inches or more. An increase in the air temperature can also strongly affect the internal integrity of the snowpack.

The third factor, snowpack, is a little more difficult to observe, as it requires digging into the snow and having some training in assessing just what you're looking at when you do. A Life-Link snow crystal card is extremely useful for assessing snow type.

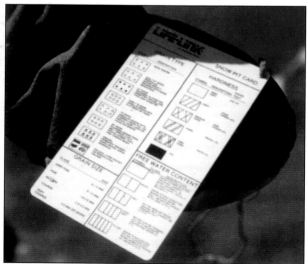

Snow crystal cards are indispensable for interpreting the dynamics of the snowpack.

Once in the backcountry, the most important thing that skiers can do to avoid tragedy is to make simple, informed observations. These include:

1. taking note of any slides or movements of snow

2. noticing any old slide paths

3. paying close attention to any settling of the snowpack (particularly after you ski across it)

4. listening for the "whumpfing" sounds that occur when air is being forced out from under the snowpack

5. looking for any cracks in the snow

Try to avoid avalanche slopes by staying in the forest or skiing along the crest of a ridge. If you must cross a known or suspected avalanche slope, first remove all ski leashes and pole straps and loosen or undo pack straps and waist belts. Cross the slope one skier at a time and observe the others in your group as they cross.

Every member of your group should wear a transceiver; make sure that your transceiver is turned on and set to transmit on the same frequency as everyone else's in your group. The new standard worldwide frequency is 457 kHz. The old 2.275 kHz transceivers that have been the standard in the United States are now being phased out. In recent years, several fully digital and analog-with-digital-function transceivers have hit the market. This means the units are getting easier to use. However, technology is still not a substitute for practice, practice, practice. No matter which model you own, you should know it intimately.

In addition to transceivers, backcountry skiers must carry a shovel and either ski poles that convert to an avalanche probe pole or a dedicated probe. Recently, more people have begun carrying lightweight dedicated probes because of their superior ability to penetrate hard snow, their simplicity, and their length, which allows them to probe more deeply into the snowpack. Obviously, you want reliable, durable gear that is still light enough not to be left at home.

Jeff Pratt whips up some comfort-food.

If you do get caught in a slide, attempt to "swim" in the snow, shedding any gear. When you sense the slide coming to a stop, place your hands in front of your face to create an air pocket. Remain calm and wait for rescuers to reach you. Individuals not caught in the slide should begin rescue operations immediately.

Before you leave on a hut trip, be sure to call the Colorado Avalanche Information Center to get the most recent snow conditions and avalanche activity reports (see Appendix E).

What You'll Find at the Hut

You've struggled all day breaking trail through two feet of fresh snow, arriving at the hut's front door late in the afternoon—spent but happy to be "home." Inside, you'll find the huts well-furnished for comfortable living. The huts do not have exactly the same assortment of stoves, lighting systems, beds, or kitchenware, but here is what you can generally expect to find.

First, all of the huts have some type of woodstove for heat. In huts with only one stove, it is used not only for heat but also to melt snow for water (accomplished with large pots), to dry wet clothes, and for limited cooking. The primary source of water in the huts is snowmelt, though a limited few have well water. To avoid contamination of the water, dogs are banned from the huts. Most huts also are stocked with firewood.

Larger huts, such as those in the 10th Mountain Division system and the Summit Huts Association, usually have a second wood-burning stove dedicated to cooking tasks. This second stove most often is a large, classic, old-time stove featuring an oven and warming bays set above the cooking surface near the chimney. Although few people cook with wood today, you would be surprised at the incredible meals and baked goods that can be produced on these stoves.

In addition to a wood-burning stove, nearly every hut is equipped with some type of propane cookstove. Fueled by large exterior tanks, these simple-to-operate workhorse stoves pull duty for most of the hut cooking and for heating water for drinks. Because of the high cost of propane, using propane stoves to melt snow for water is discouraged unless there is an emergency. Though firing up a woodstove is slower when you first arrive at the hut, producing water on a woodstove is the most efficient method. Finally, a few huts have older suburban-home-style propane stoves with integrated propane ovens.

Hut kitchens are fully stocked with the pots, pans, skillets, cups, glasses, knives, forks, and spoons that most people require. Huts typically end up with a basic assortment of spices, cooking oils, and a few staples—which can be helpful in emergency situations. Except in a few instances, however, the huts are not stocked with food. Leaving excess food is also strongly discouraged, as it can attract the local rodent population. You pack it in, you pack it out—eaten or uneaten.

The standard hut has a lighting system powered either by the large propane tanks used for cooking or by a contemporary photovoltaic lighting system. In addition, you should carry headlamps and candles. Headlamps are handy for late-night forays to the outhouse, for reading in bed, and for use on the trail.

Each hut visitor must bring a sleeping bag (except to the Spruce Hole Yurt, which is stocked with bedding). Don't worry about a foam pad, as all huts have some type of foam pads for comfortable sleeping. Some huts have pillows and some do not. If you can't sleep without a pillow and can't stand the thought of using a pillow that someone else has used, bring a small camp pillow of your own. Sleeping bag stuff-sacks are useful as makeshift pillows when stuffed with extra sweaters.

For evenings and while relaxing at the huts, bring an extra pair of pants, shorts, dry socks, hut booties or slippers, and a T-shirt. Most hut visitors just walk around in their fleece tights, which cuts down on the weight in your pack. An extra set of lightweight clothes for lounging does add a bit of weight but more than makes up for it when your ski clothes are damp and smelly and you want to get out of them.

Hut Etiquette

Hut life can be joyous, or it can be hellish. Huts are often large enough to hold up to 20 people, and more than one group may be booked at the same time. The quality of the hut experience depends on the groups sharing a hut treating each other with respect and courtesy. If sharing a hut with strangers does not appeal to you, be sure to reserve the hut exclusively for your own group. Here are a few rules to keep in mind—whether you are sharing a hut with another party or have it to yourselves. These courtesies extend to groups that may be arriving after your group departs.

When you arrive:
1. Leave skis and poles outside.
2. Clean snow from boots and clothes outside.
3. Read any hut instructions and post reservation confirmation lists.
4. Build a fire, shoveling out old ashes if necessary, and begin to melt water. Chop lots of wood.
5. Turn on electricity and propane.
6. Be tidy. Do not drop clothing and equipment all over the communal living area.
7. Be polite and quiet, especially in the evenings.
8. Wash dishes promptly and thoroughly.
9. Leave your dog at home with a multiday steak bone. "Just say no to yellow snow."

Before you leave:
1. Make sure fires are out.
2. Shut and lock all windows and doors.
3. Turn off propane (if required) and photovoltaic electric system.
4. Shut outhouse doors.
5. Pour out water to prevent freezing.
6. Sweep floor.
7. Pack out trash and extra food.
8. Chop some wood and kindling for the next group.

Cellular Phones

Believe it or not, cell phones have become an issue in the backcountry. They can be a very effective way to summon help in the event of an emergency. The problems arise in the hut. Many people find them to be an unnecessary intrusion of technology into the serenity of a wilderness adventure. Use them judiciously and thoughtfully.

Crested Butte Area

Crested Butte is a conical peak surrounded by meandering rivers that course through rural, agriculturally rich valleys. A number of large valleys radiate away from the peak like the spokes of a mountain-bike wheel. Across the Elk Mountains from Aspen and Ashcroft, this area maintains a delicate balance among the demands of recreation, wilderness, and country living. The pace is slower, the smell of wild summer grasses stronger, and the people more inclined to stop and chat. The town of Crested Butte has grown relatively slowly and still blends Victorian charm with Western cowtown energy.

Circled by the sweeping ridges of the Elk Mountains, the West Elks, and the Ruby and Anthracite Ranges, the town and the downhill ski area lie at the center of an outdoor enthusiast's recreational mecca. Many consider Crested Butte to be the birthplace of the modern American telemark turn.

Old mining roads stripe the valleys, connecting abandoned mining camps and deserted town sites like delicate threads. During the summer, mountain bikers from all over the country converge here, huffing and puffing up 12,000-foot passes and white-knuckling their way back down. In the winter these same roads and trails become popular Nordic routes.

Backcountry hut skiing in the southern Elks and in the Ruby and Anthracite Ranges consists of only six huts. What the area lacks in the quantity of huts, however, it more than makes up for in quality. These independent huts are Friends Hut, Cement Creek Yurt, Gothic Cabin, and Elkton Cabins (Elkton Hut, Silver Jewel, and Miner's Delight). The routes are very scenic, featuring pleasant touring to the huts, as well as excellent backcountry skiing around them.

All of these huts are equipped for overnight skiers with an assortment of wood-burning stoves, beds with sleeping pads, cookware, and outhouse facilities. The huts are open only for the winter season.

A skier battles the backcountry crowds for first tracks.

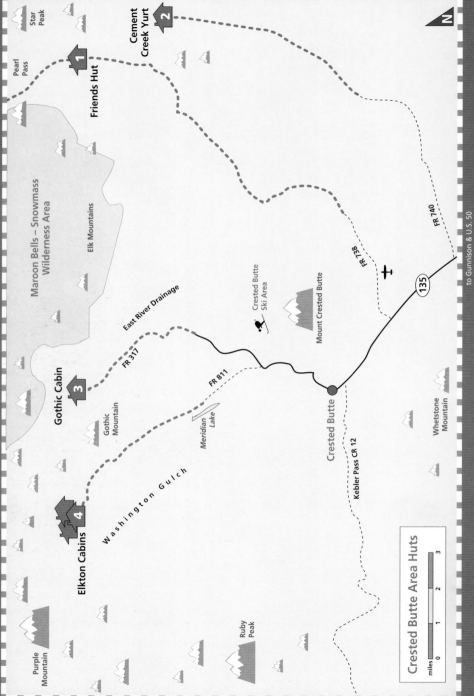

Crested Butte Area Huts

miles
0   1   2   3

1

Friends Hut

HUT ELEVATION	11,500'
DATE BUILT	1984–1985
SEASONS	Thanksgiving through end of May
CAPACITY	8
HUT LAYOUT	Log cabin with upstairs sleeping loft for 6; 2 couch-beds for 2 on main floor
HUT ESSENTIALS	Wood-burning stove for heat, propane cookstove with oven, photovoltaic lighting, all kitchenware, running water nearby (has to be treated)

The legendary Friends Hut awakens on a quiet winter morning.

A sign in Friends Hut says the hut is for serious skiers—and I agree! This hut offers expert skiers a total Rocky Mountain ski adventure. Located below the south faces of Star and Crystal Peaks, Friends Hut provides access to many acres of skiable alpine terrain, as well as long, challenging routes to the hut.

Friends Hut was constructed as a memorial to 10 residents of Aspen and Crested Butte who died in a plane crash above East Maroon Pass. Volunteers provided the labor to build the hut, which opened during the winter of 1985–1986. Today, Friends Hut stands as a backcountry link between the mountain communities of

Aspen and Crested Butte—a fitting tribute to a group of people who loved the Colorado Rockies.

This hut is recommended for advanced skiers who understand the severity of backcountry skiing and are capable of self-sufficient winter travel. Strong intermediate-level skiers can also enjoy this trip if they are accompanied by experienced partners or guides. Because of the remoteness of this cabin, it is recommended that groups book the hut for a minimum of two nights so skiers can enjoy a full day of rest or day touring. Extra time spent at the hut also provides good weather insurance if parties need to re-cross Pearl Pass.

Located to the south 1,000 feet below the summit of Pearl Pass, Friends Hut completes the hut system across the Elk Mountains. Many—if not most—skiers tour to Friends Hut via Pearl Pass; the Braun system's Tagert and Green-Wilson huts work well as a jumping-off point for crossing the pass. Because skiers depend on windows of settled mountain weather to ensure a safe crossing, this itinerary is committing. (Refer to the Tagert and Green-Wilson Huts description in the Alfred A. Braun Memorial Hut System, *Colorado Hut to Hut, Volume I: Northern and Central Regions,* page 262).

Approaching Friends Hut from Crested Butte, skiers are faced with a long trek up Brush Creek. This route is less spectacular than skiing from Ashcroft, but it is also considerably less alpine and exposed to far less avalanche danger. (For information on the approach route from Ashcroft, please see *Colorado Hut to Hut, Volume I: Northern and Central Regions,* page 272.)

The hut's rough-hewn timbers and wood paneling create a warm and restful winter oasis. The hut sleeps eight on beds in a sleeping loft and around the wood-burning stove on the main floor. Amenities include a photovoltaic lighting system, propane cookstove, cookware, a wood-chopping and ski storage room, and an outhouse with a large window (to inspire contemplative thought). Water can be drawn from the creek for most of the winter; notices in the hut direct skiers to the most reliable water sources. Creek water should be treated or boiled before using.

RESERVATION NOTE: Friends Hut is open only during the winter, and additional groups may be booked into the hut if your group does not fully occupy it. Make reservations through the 10th Mountain Division Hut Association (see Appendix A).

Seventy years young, Philippe Dunoyer mocks the nasty conditions atop Pearl Pass.

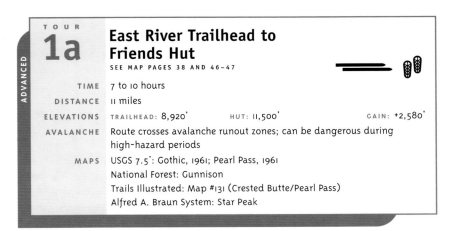

TOUR

ADVANCED

1a
East River Trailhead to Friends Hut
SEE MAP PAGES 38 AND 46–47

TIME	7 to 10 hours
DISTANCE	11 miles
ELEVATIONS	TRAILHEAD: 8,920ʼ HUT: 11,500ʼ GAIN: +2,580ʼ
AVALANCHE	Route crosses avalanche runout zones; can be dangerous during high-hazard periods
MAPS	USGS 7.5ʼ: Gothic, 1961; Pearl Pass, 1961 National Forest: Gunnison Trails Illustrated: Map #131 (Crested Butte/Pearl Pass) Alfred A. Braun System: Star Peak

TOUR OVERVIEW: The route to Friends Hut from Crested Butte is one of the longest and most arduous tours to any backcountry hut. Classic cross-country skiing follows Brush Creek Road and then East Brush Creek Road on a consistent climb from the East River near the Cold Spring Ranch to tree line below Star Peak. This route takes a lot of work, but it's worth the effort. Get an early start and be prepared for a long day if you expect to have to break trail.

Especially in upper East Brush Creek, the route passes near the runout zones of several large slide paths. Skiers should be able to assess avalanche danger and to make necessary adjustments in selecting a route. Your group should also be prepared for severe winter conditions. The trail lies within deep valleys and is well marked, so route-finding is not too difficult. The trickiest task is to locate the hut as you approach it through the woods.

DIRECTIONS TO TRAILHEAD: From the town of Crested Butte, drive for 2 miles south on CO 135 to the Skyland Country Club/Airport Road (County Road 738). This turn is immediately southeast of the bridge across the Slate River. Follow the road as it curves past the entrance to Skyland Country Club on the left. Continue along the road as it skirts the southeast flank of Mount Crested Butte. After driving 2.5 miles, you'll arrive at a small, plowed parking area on the left. Park here. Do not drive past the Lazy F Bar Outfitters sign; there is no public parking beyond this point.

THE ROUTE: Ski on the road past the Lazy F Bar Outfitters sign and contour north past the ranch on the left. Near the 1.5-mile mark, you'll reach the broad, treeless mouth of Brush Creek. Turn northeast and follow the summer four-wheel-drive road along the left side of the creek. Turn right at the marked intersection of the West Brush Creek Trail (Forest Road 738.2A) and the Brush Creek/Middle Brush Creek Trail (Forest Road 738).

Ski down and across the creek and begin a short ascent to a fork in the trail near the 4-mile mark. Take the left fork on a steep climb high above a narrow and precipitous constriction in the valley bottom. After making a traverse across the toe of lower Teocalli Ridge, drop back down into Brush Creek and ski up the drainage along the broad valley bottom.

The trail eventually crosses the creek via snow bridges in an area filled with willows. Near the end of the valley, ascend east onto East Brush Creek Road (Forest Road 738.2B). Follow the road into thicker spruce forests and continue up the valley. The road in the upper valley is on the west side of the creek and leads

directly under several avalanche runout zones. Many skiers cross to the east side of the creek and ski in the relative safety of the thicker trees on that bank. The actual point of creek crossing is left to the discretion of the group.

Friends Hut sits above the confluence of the two highest, unnamed forks of East Brush Creek. By traversing upward above the northeast fork of the creek, near the upper limit of the forest, you ski directly to the hut, which sits atop a tiny knoll protected by tall spruce trees.

Cully Culbreth tucks himself in at the Friends Hut.

2 Cement Creek Yurt

HUT ELEVATION	10,160'
DATE BUILT	1994
SEASONS	Year-round
CAPACITY	6
HUT LAYOUT	20-foot yurt with one fan-shaped bed that sleeps 6 on individual sleeping pads; all kitchenware; windows with plastic and screens; a see-through, 10-foot-high dome in the roof
HUT ESSENTIALS	Propane stoves for cooking and heating, table with benches, shelving for kitchen food and supplies, contained outhouse (waste is hauled out)
OTHER GOODIES	Custom-designed tours and avalanche courses

Cement Creek Yurt is a winter backcountry drop camp in the Elk Mountains, near Crested Butte, owned and operated by Adventures to the Edge. This commercial guiding and adventure travel business in turn is owned and operated by Jean and Mary Pavilliard of Crested Butte. Jean is a certified guide with the American Mountain Guides Examiner and European Guiding Association who leads trips not only to this yurt but also to the farthest reaches—and altitudes—on earth. Currently, because of Forest Service restrictions, the Cement Creek Yurt is open only to guided trips.

Cement Creek, which lies to the east of Crested Butte, has pleasant ski touring. Interestingly enough, it was the site of one of Colorado's first downhill ski areas, although the area consisted of only one run cut through the woods.

In addition to being a destination unto itself, this hut is used for extended multiday tours to other huts in the area, including Friends Hut and the Alfred A. Braun Huts. (See Appendix A for reservation information.)

RECOMMENDED DAY TRIPS:

For day trips, skiers can continue up Cement Creek or explore a side valley. Exercise caution, for there are potential-avalanche slopes in the higher valleys. All groups should carry avalanche safety equipment. In addition to being a destination unto itself, this hut is used in extended multiday tours to other huts in the area, including Friends Hut and the Alfred A. Braun Huts. (See Appendix A for reservation information.)

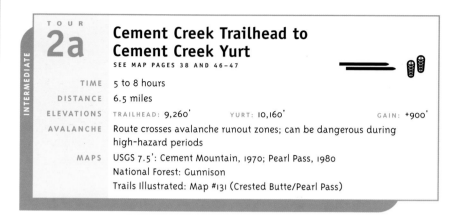

TOUR

2a

Cement Creek Trailhead to Cement Creek Yurt

SEE MAP PAGES 38 AND 46–47

INTERMEDIATE

TIME	5 to 8 hours
DISTANCE	6.5 miles
ELEVATIONS	TRAILHEAD: 9,260' YURT: 10,160' GAIN: +900'
AVALANCHE	Route crosses avalanche runout zones; can be dangerous during high-hazard periods
MAPS	USGS 7.5': Cement Mountain, 1970; Pearl Pass, 1980 National Forest: Gunnison Trails Illustrated: Map #131 (Crested Butte/Pearl Pass)

DIRECTIONS TO TRAILHEAD: Take CO 135 to the Cement Creek Road (County Road 740) turnoff, which is roughly 8 miles south of Crested Butte. Turn east onto this road, pass the Crested Butte South subdivision, and continue to the end of the plowed road. The ultimate length of this tour depends on how far up-valley the road is plowed.

THE ROUTE: Basically, this route is a straight shot along a valley floor, following a summer road (CR 740), which then becomes Forest Road 740. Leave the parking area and begin skiing along the road. The first few miles are popular with local cross-country skiers and snowmobilers and are usually snow-packed.

Near the 3-mile mark, the valley narrows considerably, exposing skiers to potential avalanche hazards on both sides for about a mile. Cross a bridge, then ski through several switchbacks on the eastern side of Cement Creek. Above the switchbacks, the valley begins to widen again. Continue due north upstream for 2.5 miles to the yurt. Cement Creek Yurt sits right in the middle of the valley, due south of the base of the southern ridge of 12,618-foot Hunter's Hill.

laser

uphill comfort.
downhill control.

Two position forward-lean heel mechanism.
Dynafit binding compatible.
Designed and tested by Backcountry skiers.

⊘ **SCARPA**

Distributed by Black Diamond Equipment, Ltd.

SEE VOLUME 1

37b*

38a*

MAROON BELLS - SNOWMASS
WILDERNESS

1.60 miles to Friends Hut
2.60 miles to Tagert & Green-Wilson Huts

Friends Hut
11,500'

Cement Creek Yurt
10,160'

GUNNISON NATIONAL FOREST

GUNNISON   NATIONAL   FOREST

NOTE: The Pearl Pass tour to the
Braun System (#37b) is covered in
*Colorado Hut to Hut, Volume 1:
Northern and Central Regions*.
(Tour 1a in volume 2 is
Tour 38a in volume 1.)

Friends Hut & Cement Creek Yurt

5.80 miles to East River Trailhead

2.00 miles to East River Trailhead
9.00 miles to Friends Hut

Friends Hut &
Cement Creek Yurt

Scale 1:24,000   Contour Interval 40 Feet

0   1/2   1

SCALE IN MILES

MN 12°

Hut

Trailhead ●

Wilderness – – – –

Trails, including US Forest Service trails, may or may
not be marked. USFS trails and roads are not maintained and their exact location may vary. This map is
not a substitute for good route-finding skills. This map
is agood to help locate routes. These are suggested
routes only. Hazards exist in the backcountry, including
avalanches. Common sense and good judgment can
reduce but not eliminate these hazards.

© 2000 Brian Litz

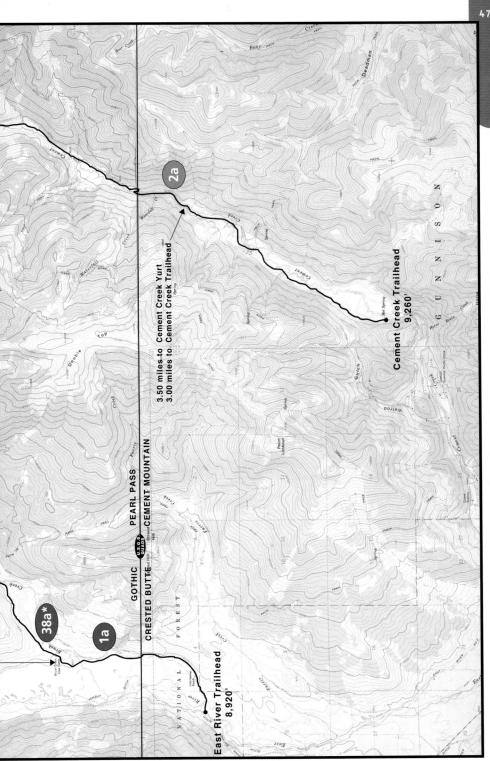

GUNNISON

NATIONAL FOREST

Cement Creek Trailhead
9,260'

3.50 miles to Cement Creek Yurt
3.00 miles to Cement Creek Trailhead

U.S.G.S. QUADS
GOTHIC
PEARL PASS
CRESTED BUTTE
CEMENT MOUNTAIN

East River Trailhead
8,920'

38a*

1a

2a

3 Gothic Cabin

HUT ELEVATION	9,480'
DATE BUILT	Mid-1960s
SEASONS	Varies; generally mid-November to mid-April
CAPACITY	6
HUT LAYOUT	Rectangular cabin with half sleeping loft and one private room on main floor; beds and mattresses can be moved around
HUT ESSENTIALS	Wood-burning stove for heat, snowmelt for water, propane cookstove and oven, electric lighting, outhouse

Tucked away in a valley below Gothic Mountain, Scofield Pass, and Copper Creek is the community of Gothic. During the late 1800s, Gothic was a highly profitable gold- and silver-mining community, as well as a supply point for the surrounding mines and mining camps. According to Perry Eberhart's *Guide to the Colorado Ghost Towns and Mining Camps,* Gothic boasted a population of around 8,000 during its heyday. In addition to being the wealthiest town in Gunnison County, Gothic had a reputation as one of the wildest towns in all of Colorado.

Today, Gothic is a haven for recreationists and budding naturalists. The Rocky Mountain Biological Labs are the center of activity, offering a multitude of summer workshops and classes for college students and others interested in the ecology of the Rockies. Winter finds Gothic deserted except for caretakers, snow-shoe hares, and the occasional Nordic skier. It's a great place to escape to in the winter and makes an excellent base camp, allowing skiers many day explorations into the beautiful valleys surrounding the town.

Cabins used by summer students are available to cross-country skiers for a fee during the winter and are booked through the Crested Butte Nordic Center (see Appendix A). The exact number of cabins available to skiers may change from year to year, so call the Center for the latest information. The cabins are well equipped with stoves, cookware, beds, and outhouse facilities.

RECOMMENDED DAY TRIPS:

Continue up-valley toward Scofield Pass via the road. Also, for the adventurous, consider a tour up Copper Creek. This magnificent valley leads up into the Maroon Bells–Snowmass Wilderness Area and skiers can eventually cross one of several remote, committing passes that lead to, among other things, Conundrum Creek. A long tour into the upper reaches of any of these valleys takes you through serious mountain terrain and the associated hazards. Be prepared.

NOVICE

TOUR 3a
Gothic Road Trailhead to Gothic Cabin
SEE MAP PAGES 38 AND 53

TIME	3 to 5 hours
DISTANCE	3.5 miles
ELEVATIONS	TRAILHEAD: 9,580' CABIN: 9,480' GAIN/LOSS: +140'/-240'
AVALANCHE	Route crosses avalanche runout zones; can be dangerous during high-hazard periods
MAPS	USGS 7.5': Gothic, 1961
	National Forest: Gunnison
	Trails Illustrated: Map #131 (Crested Butte/Pearl Pass)

TOUR OVERVIEW: The trail follows the snow-covered summer road that begins near the Crested Butte downhill ski area. Be aware of several potential slide paths that drop off the northeast aspect of Snodgrass Mountain. Stop in or call the Crested Butte Nordic Center for the latest information on avalanche activity.

DIRECTIONS TO TRAILHEAD:
From the town of Crested Butte, drive north on County Road 317 (CO 135 turns into CR 317), go past the ski resort to the winter road closure, and park. The total distance from old town Crested Butte to the public winter road closure is roughly 4.4 miles.

THE ROUTE: The road (Forest Road 317) is obvious and easy to follow. Begin skiing along the exposed trail traversing above the East River. Ski around a sharp curve that overlooks the river and begin a gradual descent for 1.8 miles, until you cross the river. From the crossing, a gentle climb takes you up to the center of Gothic.

Gothic Cabin glows warmly under a cobalt alpenglow.

Elkton Cabins:
Elkton Hut, Silver Jewel, Miner's Delight

ELKTON HUT	
HUT ELEVATION	10,680'
DATE BUILT	1859; opened early 1980s for skiers
SEASONS	Mid-November through April (winter; varies with snowpack); July through October (summer)
CAPACITY	6
HUT LAYOUT	1-story cabin with 2 rooms; 3 beds in main room (with kitchen), 3 in separate tiny bedroom; 1 bunk bed in each room
HUT ESSENTIALS	Propane lights and cookstove, wood-burning stove for heat, all kitchenware
OTHER GOODIES	Running water from a nearby spring

SILVER JEWEL	
HUT ELEVATION	10,680'
DATE BUILT	Small main cabin built in 1859; additions made late 1960s and early 1970s
SEASONS	Mid-November through April (winter; varies with snowpack); July through October (summer)
CAPACITY	4 (in summer of 2000; could increase)
HUT LAYOUT	2-story log cabin with 2 beds in "secret" sleeping loft/room; queen pullout bed in living room; caretaker's quarters upstairs
HUT ESSENTIALS	Photovoltaic lights, propane cookstove with oven, wood-burning stove for heat, all kitchenware
OTHER GOODIES	Operates like a bed-and-breakfast, fully stocked and catered; running water from a nearby spring

MINER'S DELIGHT	
HUT ELEVATION	10,400'
DATE BUILT	Mid-1970s
SEASONS	Mid-November through April (winter; varies with snowpack); July through October (summer)
CAPACITY	12
HUT LAYOUT	2-story log cabin; 12 beds upstairs in dorm-style sleeping loft (bunks and singles)
HUT ESSENTIALS	Propane lights and cookstove with oven, wood-burning stove for heat, all kitchenware
OTHER GOODIES	Large south-facing porch

The Elkton Cabins are a trio of privately owned and operated cabins near the abandoned mining camp of Elkton, which sits upstream from Crested Butte near the headwaters of Washington Gulch. The trip to the cabins is just over 5 miles. The elevation gain is moderate, averaging a little more than 200 feet per mile, making the route to these cabins appropriate for most skiers on all types of gear. If you are just heading in for a quick overnight tour, you'll find touring gear quite adequate. This is a popular day tour in the area, so expect to see some traffic.

The three cabins consist of Elkton Hut (the original cabin opened for hut skiing in the area), Silver Jewel, and Miner's Delight (the newest structure). Elkton Hut and the original core-cabin of the Silver Jewel are historic structures—dating back to the area's glory days, when Washington Gulch produced gold and Crested Butte served as a shipping and transportation hub for area mining camps.

At its peak, 1,400 people called Elkton home! Later, Crested Butte itself struck "gold" when high-grade bituminous coal was discovered in the 1870s. The coal found here was the only bituminous coal discovered in the United States west of Pennsylvania.

The route to the huts traces the easy-to-follow Washington Gulch Road. There are two relatively steep climbs: The first is near the 3-mile mark; the second is the final approach to Elkton Hut. Although the hut is a simple log cabin, it serves well as a backcountry shelter and base camp for skiers making day excursions to surrounding glades and peaks.

Sitting nearest to Elkton Hut is the Silver Jewel. This hut serves as the hutmaster's quarters and operates like a bed-and-breakfast for four guests. The Miner's Delight sits roughly 200 feet below the other two huts. The Elkton Cabins are now open year-round and provide great access to many miles of high-country mountain biking and hiking. Book reservations through Elkton Cabins (see Appendix A).

RECOMMENDED DAY TRIPS:

"The Butte" is known as a free-heel and mountain-bike mecca, and the Elkton Cabins sit atop a motherlode of great skiing, mountain biking, and hiking. Less "aggro" (aggressive) skiers can play around, touring on the rolling hills above the huts, while more industrious and advanced skiers can climb up to the summit of Mount Baldy (two hours) for the mind-blowing 360-degree vista of the Elk Mountains, the Anthracite Range, the Rubys, and the San Juans off to the south and southwest.

In addition, the forested slopes to the south and southwest—an area known as Anthracite Mesa—hold acres of great tele-skiing terrain. This skiing can be reached with a short 20-minute climb. Ask caretakers for more recommendations and local conditions.

NOVICE/INTERMEDIATE

TOUR 4a
Meridian Lake Trailhead to Elkton Cabins
SEE MAP PAGES 38 AND 53

TIME	3 to 5 hours
DISTANCE	5.2 miles
ELEVATIONS	TRAILHEAD: 9,450' CABINS: 10,680' GAIN: +1,250'
AVALANCHE	Some avalanche terrain encountered; easily avoided
MAPS	USGS 7.5': Gothic, 1961; Oh-Be-Joyful, 1961
	National Forest: Gunnison
	Trails Illustrated: Map #131 (Crested Butte/Pearl Pass);
	Map #133 (Kebler Pass/Paonia Reservoir)

DIRECTIONS TO TRAILHEAD: Not far from the town of Crested Butte, the trailhead for Elkton Hut is near the Meridian Lake development and is easy to locate at the end of a well-marked and well-traveled county road. From the stop sign at the intersection of Elk Avenue and County Road 317 in Crested Butte (CO 135 turns into CR 317), drive north 1.7 miles to the turnoff for Washington Gulch and Meridian Lake. Turn left onto Washington Gulch Road (Forest Road 811) and proceed along the main thoroughfare to the plowed parking area at the winter road closure.

THE ROUTE: From the parking area and the trailhead signs, ski up the valley over moderate terrain. After several miles of touring along the snow-covered road, you'll come to a noticeable climb near the southwest corner of Gothic Mountain. Once past this ascent, the road climbs gradually, passing below the mountain's southwest face. From here, the terrain becomes increasingly steep as you cross the mouth of a drainage (to the northeast), then contour west and south across a creek and the head of Washington Gulch.

After crossing the creek, make the final ascent to Elkton by climbing around a switchback, heading northwest. When you arrive at Elkton, which sits on top of a flat bench, look for two cabins off to the right. The first cabin, the one closest to the road, is Elkton Hut. It is roughly 100 feet south of the other, larger cabin.

John Fielder enjoys a fine April afternoon at the Elkton Cabins.

Gothic Cabin & Elkton Cabins

GUNNISON NATIONAL FOREST

Elkton Cabins
10,680'

Gothic Cabin
9,480'

4a

3a

Gothic Road Trailhead
9,580'

Meridian Lake Trailhead
9,450'

Gothic & Elkton Cabins

Scale 1:24,000 Contour Interval 40 Feet

0 — 1/2 — 1
SCALE IN MILES

Hut 🏠
Trailhead ●
Wilderness — — —   MN 12°

Trails, including US Forest Service trails, may or may not be marked. USFS trails and roads are not maintained and their exact location may vary. This map is not a substitute for good route-finding skills. This map is an aid to help locate routes. These are suggested routes only. Hazards exist in the backcountry, including avalanches. Common sense and good judgment can reduce but not eliminate these hazards.

© 2000 Brian Litz

OH-BE-JOYFUL U.S.G.S. QUADS GOTHIC

San Juan Mountains

Three distinct regions make up Colorado. Delineated geologically and ecologically, these zones divide the state longitudinally into relatively equal areas. The Great Plains extend across the eastern third of the state, the Rocky Mountains form the middle, and plateaus and high desert carve out the western third of the state.

In the southwestern corner of Colorado, a mighty mountain range juts from the central Rockies into the desert lands of the Four Corners. These are the San Juans, one of the largest mountain ranges (covering roughly 10,000 square miles) in the lower 48 states. Former home of the grizzly bear and birthplace of the San Juan and Rio Grande Rivers, the San Juans are an alpine wilderness equaled in scenic beauty by few other North American ranges.

The San Juan Mountains are curious in that they were one of the most volcanically active ranges in prehistoric Colorado. Today's San Juans are the result of a complex mountain-building process that began more than 500 million years ago. Although the basement rocks of the San Juans are Precambrian granites and quartzite, the bulk of the high peaks, especially around Red Mountain Pass and the Sneffels Range, were formed from ancient upthrust sediments and geologically young (25 to 35 million years old) volcanic lavas, tuffs, and breccias. Nature put the finishing touches on the San Juans during the last 3 to 5 million years, as Pleistocene glaciers bulldozed the alpine uplands into the deep, U-shaped valleys and cirques where we ski and ride today.

The irregular ridges, minarets, and peaks of the San Juans seem to tear at the azure Colorado skies, forming a spectacular backdrop for wilderness skiing. Because there are no metropolitan areas nearby, skiers encounter few crowds here. Those willing to strap on climbing skins will find much untracked backcountry terrain.

Near the Colorado/New Mexico border, atop Cumbres Pass, is the Southwest Nordic Center. In contrast to the severe topography of the central and western San Juans, the terrain here in the southeastern San Juans is mostly gentle and rolling, with flat plateau and ridgelike peaks that are easy to scale and relatively free of serious avalanche hazard— though avalanche hazard still does exist! And the snowpack is one of the deepest in the southern Rocky Mountains.

Powder to the people!

This is an ideal destination for those looking for quiet touring and for newcomers to the backcountry hut-to-hut skiing experience. The Southwest

Nordic Center also opens up mountains that most skiers overlook. Northeast of the center's main group of yurts is a new neighbor—the Spruce Hole Yurt—operated by Cumbres Nordic Adventures. This yurt is easy to get to, affords scenic views, and serves up classic touring terrain.

In the central San Juans is the Hinsdale Haute Route. This system offers skiers excellent Nordic and backcountry powder skiing in an environment relatively free of the dangerous avalanche slopes and gullies usually associated with skiing the San Juan backcountry. Situated between Lake City and Creede, the Hinsdale Haute Route opens up vast areas of rolling, high-altitude terrain for free-heel skiing. This area is too far from most population areas to be used with any frequency. As the system continues to grow, it ranks as one of the state's most scenic—and safe—ski tours.

The Hinsdale Haute Route sits atop the Continental Divide near Slumgullion and Spring Creek Passes, which are more like one contiguous rolling plateau than distinct passes. South of the passes is Mineral County, home of the town of Creede and its world-famous repertory theater. Creede now is sandwiched between two new hut systems. To the north, near the Wheeler Geologic Area, are the Phoenix Ridge Yurts. Immediately south of Creede is San Juan Snowtrek Tours' Fisher Mountain Hut and Lime Creek Yurt. Both of these two new systems pioneer new turf for skiing—terrain that is quite different from other areas of Colorado and familiar to few skiers other than a handful of locals.

Either of these hut systems is great for skiers using touring equipment, as well as those with heavier gear and steeper intentions. San Juan Snowtrek Tours has designs on ultimately connecting the Creede area to Wolf Creek Pass to the south with a system of at least four structures.

And speaking of Wolf Creek—someone has finally made the effort to build a hut system in the land of bottomless powder. This new system will hopefully operate yurts farther east of the pass and the ski area and likewise gives skiers a chance to ski in some old logging areas choked with powder.

Between Ouray, the "Switzerland of America," and historic Silverton is Red Mountain Pass and its "Million Dollar Highway." Just off the summit of the pass is the Saint Paul Lodge, most likely the highest-altitude bed-and-breakfast in the United States. Reached by a straightforward one-mile ski tour, it is one of the closest backcountry huts to any trailhead that offers quick access to true off-trail ski mountaineering. Saint Paul Lodge is open only to guided trips and winter mountaineering courses.

On the western side of the San Juans, near Telluride and Ridgway, is the San Juan Hut System, the largest single hut system in the region. Five winter huts are strung out along the northern escarpment of the Sneffels Range, with terrain that features everything from classic Nordic trail skiing to extreme telemark chute skiing. The 200-mile summer mountain-bike San Juan Hut System from Telluride to Moab, Utah, crosses every ecozone in Colorado and was one of the first hut-to-hut bike tours in the country.

Sadly, we mourn the passing of a yurt that was included in past editions. The Scotch Creek Yurt near Rico is no longer in operation. Keep your fingers crossed that one day someone will take over this site, as it accesses some truly fine terrain.

Southwest Nordic Center

The mountains around Cumbres Pass (CO 17) are a southern extension of Colorado's San Juans, although they are certainly less alpine than their mighty northern siblings are. A long, linear mountain range runs from Wolf Creek Pass south to the Colorado/New Mexico border. It forms the western boundary of the San Luis Valley and the extensive Rio Grande drainage.

The region's rolling topography is forested and laced with logging trails and roads, yet it offers many open vistas of the surrounding mountains. The snowpack here is legendary. What these ingredients add up to is a recipe for adventurous, yet user-friendly, touring and telemark skiing. The Southwest Nordic Center yurts are ideal for all skiers, especially novice and intermediate skiers who like cross-country touring. The Neff Mountain Yurt is easy to reach, even after a long drive. For those wishing to experience a bit more adventure, the Flat Mountain and Trujillo Meadows Yurts offer easy, yet longer, tours.

Adding to the user-friendly nature of this system is owner/operator Doug MacLennan's unique and comprehensive trail-marking system. Doug hangs wooden diamonds from strategic tree limbs along the trails. These markers are easy to see and swing in the wind, making them even more visible. Also unique is the color-coded system for the markers: Those for the routes to the Neff and Trujillo yurts are painted blue; the Continental Divide route to the Flat Mountain Yurt is marked in orange; and the markers for the small sections of trail that connect to form the hut-to-hut routes are yellow. The markers make this one of the most easily navigable hut systems included in this book. In addition, there is very little in the way of major avalanche hazard. In fact, the overall level of potential hazard along these trails is minimal at best.

With this third edition, two new offspring join the family. The first is the Grouse Creek Yurt, which lies north of the core group of three yurts. This yurt sits off by itself and is not conducive to hut-to-hut travel with the three southern huts. Also new to the system is the Bull of the Woods Yurt near Taos, New Mexico in the Sangre de Cristo Mountains. This yurt has been "in the works" for years as the system has negotiated the permitting process. Though obviously not a Colorado hut, it is included here as part of the greater Southwest Nordic System.

Keep in mind that this system is a long way from any major towns. The closest towns are the small communities of Chama to the south, and Antonito and Conejos to the east. Alamosa, a large town with gas stations and grocery stores, is roughly one hour to the northeast, and Taos is about two hours to the south. Be sure to fill up with gas and bring all of your food and other supplies.

The entire region is flavored with a strong Spanish/Mexican influence. Place names such as Chama, Antonito, Del Norte, Alamosa, Conejos, Culebra Peak, and Montezuma Peak conjure up images of explorers searching for gold and other riches in a land inhabited by American Indians. Some of the oldest churches in North America can be found in this region. This is quite a historic and magical area!

Rick Sayre makes the best of a gray backcountry day.

Southwest Nordic Center

miles
0 1 2 3 4 5 6

FR 250

to Antonito

17

Grouse Creek
Yurt

5

La Manga Pass

17

Spruce Hole Yurt

Jarosa
Peak

Rio de los piños Creek

Trujillo Meadows
Reservoir

7

Trujillo Meadows Yurt

8

Flat
Mountain Yurt

6

Neff Mountain
Yurt

Neff Mountain

Cumbres & Toltec Railroad

17

Cumbres & Toltec Railroad

Rio de los Piños Creek

COLORADO

NEW MEXICO

N

5 Grouse Creek Yurt

HUT ELEVATION	11,200'
DATE BUILT	1996
SEASONS	Thanksgiving through April (depending on snowpack)
CAPACITY	4 to 6
HUT LAYOUT	16-foot yurt with 2 bunks with single beds; mats for 2
HUT ESSENTIALS	Wood-burning stove for heat, propane for cooking, gas lanterns, all kitchenware, outhouse

The Grouse Creek Yurt opened for business in 1997. This hut sits north of the original three yurts in the system and is separated by the massive drainage of the Rio de los Piños Creek and by enough distance to discourage hut-to-hut skiing with the other three shelters. Consequently, the hut should be enjoyed as a destination unto itself.

The trail to this yurt is like the rest of the system—well-marked and characterized by rounded, low ridges and knolls mottled with evergreen trees and scattered meadows and clearings. Under the canopy of a blue southwestern sky, old logging roads snake through these woods up the gentle creek beds toward the higher ridges to the west. The challenge of skiing here is to stay on course through the maze of trees. You will be aided in this task by the thorough system of markers established by the hut system. The elevation gain is reasonable for a tour of this length, so you will encounter the greatest physical challenges when you break trail or if you have drawn the short straw, leaving you to tote the box o' wine!

RECOMMENDED DAY TRIPS:

There are literally thousands of acres of terrain for touring around the yurt. Simply point your ski tips and follow your nose. Behind the yurt to the west is a high ridge that can be ascended more easily by heading west/southwest. Some of the steeper, eastern shots can be skied in the winter when conditions are safe, though they are ideal in the spring. Once on top of the ridge, you can head up to Jarosa Peak or toward the Red Lake area for a longer tour and excellent views of the San Luis Valley and the distant Sangre de Cristo Mountains off to the northeast.

You can ski above the cliffs and get to Elk Creek to the north and loop back around south under the cliffs to the yurt. Elk Creek can also be reached by heading due north from the yurt.

As a final option, you can head to Jarosa Peak, drop off the road, and hit the first meadow.

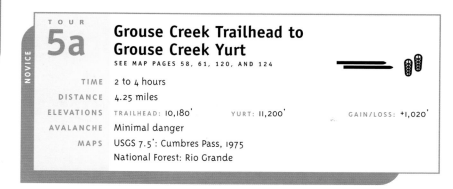

NOVICE

TOUR

5a Grouse Creek Trailhead to Grouse Creek Yurt

SEE MAP PAGES 58, 61, 120, AND 124

TIME	2 to 4 hours
DISTANCE	4.25 miles
ELEVATIONS	TRAILHEAD: 10,180' YURT: 11,200' GAIN/LOSS: +1,020'
AVALANCHE	Minimal danger
MAPS	USGS 7.5': Cumbres Pass, 1975
	National Forest: Rio Grande

DIRECTIONS TO TRAILHEAD: The trailhead for the Grouse Creek Yurt is 0.65 mile south of the sign at La Manga Pass and 6.75 miles north of the Cumbres Pass sign. Park on the eastern side on the road, just north of the creek, along the plowed parking area.

Hydrate...or headache...or worse!

THE ROUTE: Walk across the road, put on your skis, and glide out across the meadow, heading southwest, following the trail markers. Cross the creek and ski toward the woods. This is the first of three clearings you will pass through before you reach the forest logging road that you will follow for most of the second half of the journey.

After you cross the meadow, enter the woods and begin following a small drainage west. Once out of the trees, you will enter a second clearing. Ski straight across to the west side of the clearing. Enter the woods and ascend a tiny spine. This will turn into a traverse along a sidehill of a creek until you blend into the creek drainage itself.

Next, reach the third meadow, which is across in a westerly heading. At the far end, return into the forest, where you will reach a Forest Service logging road. Head to the right on this road. From now through the remainder of the trip, you will be heading roughly north/northwest. You will have to keep an eye out for other subsidiary logging roads that lace the area. The primary route is well-marked.

Eventually you will leave the road and traverse up through a meadow until you reach the final road, which heads north to the clearing. This is where the yurt sits.

Grouse Creek & Spruce Hole Yurts

Spruce Hole Yurt
10,600'

17a

Spruce Hole

MOUNTAIN

PACK TRAIL

PINOREALOSA

LA MANGA

OSIER

MOUNTAIN

PINOREALOSA

CUMBRES PASS

U.S. 6 & 84
285

La Manga Summit T.H.
10,200'

La Manga Pass

La Manga
Dos Caños

STOCK

North Fork

La Manga Dos Caños

Grouse Creek Trailhead
10,180'

Creek

LA MANGA

5a

Creek

R I O   G R A N D E

La Manga

PACK TRAIL

De Herrera Lake

Grouse Creek

N A T I O N A L   F O R E S T

1/2

Grouse Creek Yurt
11,200'

Jacobs Peak

Scale

Grouse Creek and Spruce Hole Yurts

Scale 1:24,000   Contour Interval 40 Feet

SCALE IN MILES

0   1

MN 12°

Hut
Trailhead ●
Wilderness — — — —

Trails, including US Forest Service trails, may or may
not be marked. USFS trails and roads are not maintained and their exact location may vary. This map is
not a substitute for good route-finding skills. This map
is an aid to help locate routes. These are suggested
routes only. Hazards exist in the backcountry, including
avalanches. Common sense and good judgment can
reduce but not eliminate these hazards.

© 2000 Brian Litz

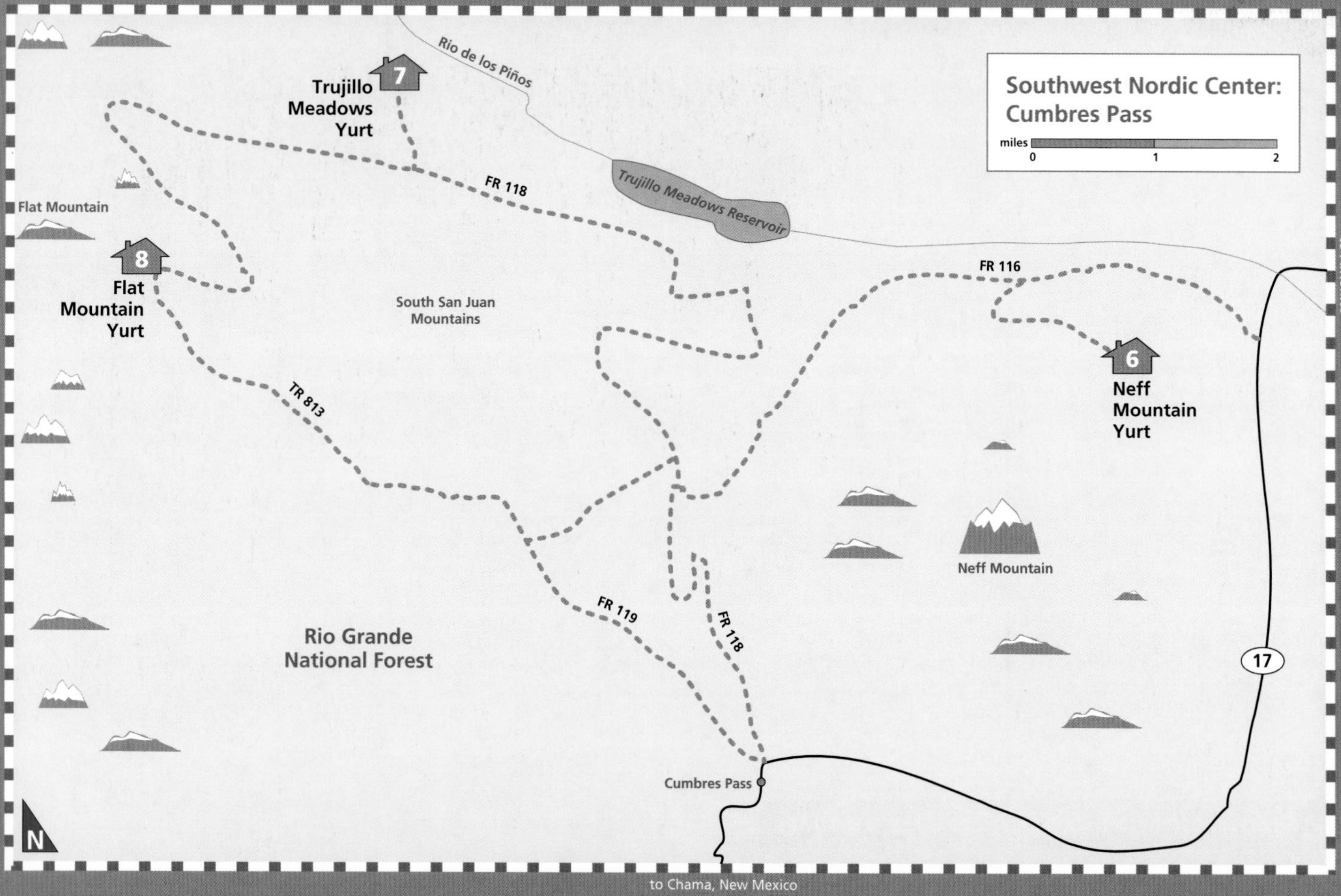

Southwest Nordic Center:
Cumbres Pass

miles
0   1   2

to Antonito

17

to Chama, New Mexico

Rio de los Piños

Trujillo Meadows Reservoir

FR 116

FR 118

7
Trujillo
Meadows
Yurt

6
Neff
Mountain
Yurt

Neff Mountain

FR 118

FR 119

Cumbres Pass

South San Juan
Mountains

TR 813

Rio Grande
National Forest

8
Flat
Mountain
Yurt

Flat Mountain

N

Neff Mountain Yurt

HUT ELEVATION	10,400'
DATE BUILT	1987
SEASONS	Thanksgiving through April (depending on snowpack)
CAPACITY	6
HUT LAYOUT	16-foot yurt with 2 bunks with single beds; mats for 2
HUT ESSENTIALS	Wood-burning stove for heat, propane for cooking, gas lanterns, all kitchenware, outhouse

Neff Mountain Yurt has the shortest approach route of any of the yurts managed by the Southwest Nordic Center. For a reasonably strong party with an early start, it is possible to drive all the way from Denver and still have enough time to reach the yurt. The most popular of the three yurts, it has one of the best views and some of the most readily available telemark skiing in the area. Immediately behind the yurt to the south is Neff Mountain.

Book reservations through the Southwest Nordic Center (see Appendix A).

Lisa Sieman takes time out on the trail for map and compass work.

RECOMMENDED DAY TRIPS:

The mountain's broad northern flank consists of a large, treeless meadow that is perfect for powder skiing. There is enough skiable acreage here for a group to last several days. The eastern side of the mountain also has some nice glades and open slopes and is a good route for skiing to the top of Neff Mountain, a recommended day trip. You can also do a counterclockwise loop around the top of the mountain.

TOUR
6a
Neff Mountain Trailhead to Neff Mountain Yurt
SEE MAP PAGES 58, 62, 72, AND 120

TIME	2 to 4 hours
DISTANCE	2.9 miles
ELEVATIONS	TRAILHEAD: 9,820' YURT: 10,400' GAIN: +580'
AVALANCHE	Minimal danger
MAPS	USGS 7.5': Cumbres Pass, 1975
	National Forest: Rio Grande

DIRECTIONS TO TRAILHEAD: The Neff Mountain Trailhead is 3.9 miles south of La Manga Summit and 3.4 miles north of Cumbres Pass. It is immediately south of where CO 17 crosses Rio de los Piños Creek (near a small cabin development and the yellow water tank for the Cumbres & Toltec Scenic Railroad line). It is marked by a large blue disk on the west side of the road. Park on the east side of the road.

The Neff Mountain Yurt is tucked into a slope below exceptional tele terrain.

THE ROUTE: Cross the road and gain Forest Road 116, an old four-wheel-drive road. Pass the yurt sign and begin skiing north, slowly gaining elevation above Rio de los Piños Creek. Follow this well-marked route 1.9 miles until you reach a fork in the trail. The right fork is marked with yellow diamonds—the connecting trail to the Flat Mountain and Trujillo Meadows Yurts—and blue diamonds lead up a steeper trail to the southwest. Climb this steeper trail for a few hundred feet, then switchback to the east.

Follow the obvious road (a closed logging road) for roughly 0.8 mile as it traverses east, passing two treeless gullies and some steep terrain below and to the north. When you reach the large, flat shoulder on the northeastern flank of Neff Mountain, you will enter a meadow.

Continue east through a stand of trees, then angle to the southeast and follow blue diamonds through small, sparse evergreens to the yurt, which sits on the southern edge of the meadow directly below the steeper slopes of Neff Mountain.

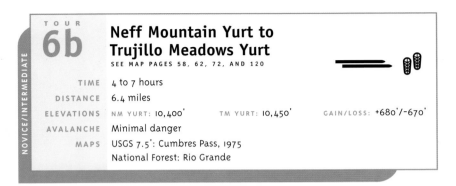

TOUR

6b Neff Mountain Yurt to Trujillo Meadows Yurt

SEE MAP PAGES 58, 62, 72, AND 120

NOVICE/INTERMEDIATE

TIME	4 to 7 hours
DISTANCE	6.4 miles
ELEVATIONS	NM YURT: 10,400' TM YURT: 10,450' GAIN/LOSS: +680'/-670'
AVALANCHE	Minimal danger
MAPS	USGS 7.5': Cumbres Pass, 1975
	National Forest: Rio Grande

TOUR OVERVIEW: Although this route is technically easy skiing, it is more than 6 miles long. If you have to break trail, it can be a strenuous outing.

THE ROUTE: From the Neff Mountain Yurt, retrace your tracks down to Forest Road 116. Turn left (west) onto FR 116 and follow the yellow diamonds. Easy to follow, the route contours up and around Elevation Point 10,445' before it hooks to the west and descends slightly to Forest Road 118, a major backcountry road that leads to Trujillo Meadows Reservoir. Snowmobilers frequent this road, so watch out! From here, follow Tour 7a (see page 68) to the Trujillo Meadows Yurt.

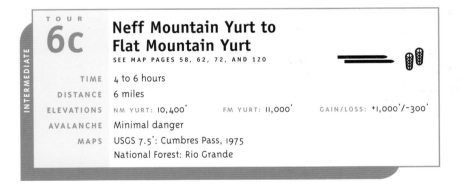

TOUR

6c Neff Mountain Yurt to Flat Mountain Yurt

SEE MAP PAGES 58, 62, 72, AND 120

INTERMEDIATE

TIME	4 to 6 hours
DISTANCE	6 miles
ELEVATIONS	NM YURT: 10,400' FM YURT: 11,000' GAIN/LOSS: +1,000'/-300'
AVALANCHE	Minimal danger
MAPS	USGS 7.5': Cumbres Pass, 1975
	National Forest: Rio Grande

THE ROUTE: This route is exactly the same as Tour 6b (see above) up to the point where you reach Forest Road 118 and ski north 0.2 mile to the yellow diamonds marking the small Forest Service trail/road that connects FR 118 to the Cumbres Pass/Flat Mountain Route. From here, turn west onto this trail and ski 0.6 mile until you reach the Cumbres Pass/Flat Mountain Trail—marked by orange diamonds. Follow Tour 8a (see page 70) to the Flat Mountain Yurt.

7 Trujillo Meadows Yurt

HUT ELEVATION	10,450'
DATE BUILT	1993
SEASONS	Thanksgiving through April (depending on snowpack)
CAPACITY	4 to 6
HUT LAYOUT	16-foot yurt with 2 bunks with single beds; mats for 2
HUT ESSENTIALS	Wood-burning stove for heat, propane for cooking, gas lanterns, all kitchenware, outhouse

The Trujillo Meadows Yurt sits in a sparsely timbered clearing overlooking Rio de los Piños Creek and Trujillo Meadows. The main route to the yurt is a moderately long, moderately difficult tour. If you can put one foot in front of the other, you can reach this hut. The standard route simply follows a wide, summer four-wheel-drive road for its entire length. This road is often used—and packed—by snowmobilers, so you rarely will have to break trail. The terrain around the yurt is also gentle—well-suited for short day tours. There are some steeper glades to the south, back across Forest Road 118, where more proficient skiers can find some telemark terrain.

Book reservations through the Southwest Nordic Center (see Appendix A).

Dave Mention breaks though superb late winter snow in the San Juans.

RECOMMENDED DAY TRIPS:

The Trujillo Meadows Yurt is surrounded by unlimited nontechnical terrain for touring. One popular tour follows the main road back upstream to the large switchback. Leave the road behind and head cross-country upstream.

Many people also enjoy skiing out to the reservoir. Leave the road at the switchback and go cross-country. Enjoy!

Cully Culbreth is footloose in the San Juans.

TOUR

7a   Cumbres Pass Trailhead to Trujillo Meadows Yurt

SEE MAP PAGES 58, 62, 72, AND 120

NOVICE

TIME	4 to 6 hours
DISTANCE	4.8 miles
ELEVATIONS	TRAILHEAD: 9,987' YURT: 10,450' GAIN/LOSS: +773'/-350'
AVALANCHE	Minimal danger
MAPS	USGS 7.5': Cumbres Pass, 1975
	National Forest: Rio Grande

DIRECTIONS TO TRAILHEAD: The trailhead for this route is immediately north of Cumbres Pass at the plowed pullout just before the well-marked turnoff to Trujillo Meadows Reservoir. The parking area is 14.2 miles north of the town of Cumbres and 7.3 miles south of La Manga Summit.

THE ROUTE: Follow Trujillo Meadows Reservoir Road (Forest Road 118) as it climbs north/northwest along a road cut on the right, or eastern, edge of a large meadow. (You'll pass the Neff Mountain Yurt Trail/Forest Road 116 turnoff to the right at mile 1.4, which is marked by yellow diamonds.) Cross a gentle pass at 1.5 miles and, after a brief 0.1 mile, descend past a left turn (marked by yellow diamonds) to the small forest road that connects to the Flat Mountain Yurt Trail.

Follow the marked road north and downhill through a large switchback and into a meadow until you reach a fork in the road. The right fork leads to Trujillo Meadows Campground. Take the left fork and, after 0.1 mile, take a sharp left turn onto another road. Climb southwest up this road for a few hundred feet until the road switchbacks north. Continue along this well-marked road for roughly 1 mile to the marked turnoff to the yurt. Turn here and follow the markers down to the Trujillo Meadows Yurt.

Flat Mountain Yurt

HUT ELEVATION	11,000´
DATE BUILT	1990
SEASONS	Thanksgiving through April (depending on snowpack)
CAPACITY	4 to 6
HUT LAYOUT	16-foot yurt with 2 bunks with single beds; mats for 2
HUT ESSENTIALS	Wood-burning stove for heat, propane for cooking, gas lanterns, all kitchenware, outhouse

Of the yurts in this system, the Flat Mountain Yurt is probably the most difficult to reach—and it is not that difficult. It sits just off the Continental Divide Trail close to a large, treeless ridge on the west—a good destination for a day trip. The reason this trip is slightly more demanding than the others is that the trail crosses a number of meadows, which are a little bit harder to navigate. In addition, the trail gains slightly more than 1,100 feet in roughly 4 miles.

The yurt is well-hidden in a little forested cove at the corner of a small, treeless clearing. There are nice views to the southeast. Book reservations through the Southwest Nordic Center (see Appendix A).

RECOMMENDED DAY TRIPS:

The ridge to the west has a variety of runs off the northern aspects, and you can ski to the summit of Flat Mountain. The eastern flank also has some shots that generally tend to be better in the spring.

Taking the time for a weekend avalanche course will pay huge dividends down the trail.

TOUR
8a
Cumbres Pass Trailhead to Flat Mountain Yurt

SEE MAP PAGES 58, 62, 72, AND 120

INTERMEDIATE

TIME	3 to 5 hours
DISTANCE	3.8 miles
ELEVATIONS	TRAILHEAD: 9,987′ YURT: 11,000′ GAIN/LOSS: + 1,153′/40′
AVALANCHE	Minimal danger
MAPS	USGS 7.5′: Cumbres Pass, 1975; Archuleta Creek, 1984 (for day trips) National Forest: Rio Grande

DIRECTIONS TO TRAILHEAD: Follow the directions to the same trailhead as Tour 7a (see page 68).

THE ROUTE: Head northwest on Forest Road 119/Trail 813, which is the Continental Divide Trail. A large orange disc on a post marks the starting point. Follow the orange diamonds as the trail climbs steadily through the woods past the turnoff to Neff Mountain Yurt and Forest Road 118 at roughly 1.6 miles. Near mile 2, the

trail enters a large, treeless meadow. Ski to the west/northwest, leaving Trail 813 at a junked car, which is usually buried in snow. Keep an eye out for the trail markers that lead to the left through the meadow.

Eventually the trail regains a more obvious road/trail that continues to the west/northwest into the upper reaches of Wolf Creek. As you begin the final ascent to the yurt, the valley becomes noticeably steeper and narrower, and a high, corniced ridge to the west also becomes visible. Finally the trail approaches a treeless clearing, which from below looks like a natural site for a yurt— and it is. Once you enter the clearing, head to the northwest corner and find the yurt tucked into the edge of a grove of evergreens.

Poles apart—be prepared to cobble broken gear with creativity (and a wad of duct tape).

TOUR

8b

Flat Mountain Yurt to Trujillo Meadows Yurt

SEE MAP PAGES 58, 62, 72, AND 120

TIME	2 to 4 hours
DISTANCE	3.8 miles
ELEVATIONS	FM YURT: 11,020' TM YURT: 10,450' GAIN/LOSS: +60'/-580'
AVALANCHE	Minimal danger
MAPS	USGS 7.5': Cumbres Pass, 1975; Archuleta Creek, 1984 National Forest: Rio Grande

TOUR OVERVIEW: This straightforward trail follows a road for its entire length. The route can be skied in either direction, although its difficulty depends on which direction you happen to be traveling. I skied it from south to north under "fast" conditions and it took only an hour. If you ski the route in reverse, from the Trujillo Meadows Yurt to the Flat Mountain Yurt, you will be climbing rather than descending for most of the trip, so it will take considerably longer.

THE ROUTE: From the front porch of Flat Mountain Yurt, head east/southeast through the clearing, remaining on the left (north) side of the meadow. Ski around a small ridge and make a slight descending traverse toward a tiny creek. On the far side of the creek, a road enters the forest. This is the marked route.

Simply follow the yellow diamonds as the road heads east, then north, and finally take a long descent to a spruce park, a large meadow that marks the end of the upper descent. Continue along the road as it switchbacks to the east/southeast and descends along a broad drainage. After roughly 1 mile, you will reach a well-marked turn (blue diamonds) on the left. Turn and follow the road until you reach another sign, where you leave the road and drop north into a clearing. There you'll find the Trujillo Meadows Yurt.

Neff Mountain Yurt, Trujillo Meadows Yurt, and Flat Mountain Yurt

Neff Mountain T.H.
9,820'

1.90 miles to Neff Mountain Trailhead
1.00 mile to Neff Mountain Yurt
2.00 miles to Forest Road 118

6a

Neff Mountain Yurt
10,400'

2.20 miles to Trujillo Meadows Yurt
2.60 miles to Cumbres Pass Trailhead

6c

6b

3.00 miles to Neff Mountain Yurt
1.40 miles to Cumbres Pass Trailhead
3.00 miles to Flat Mountain Yurt
3.40 miles to Trujillo Meadows Yurt

7a

Cumbres Pass Trailhead
9,987'

6c

8a

RIO GRANDE
NATIONAL FOREST

CUMBRES PASS

Trujillo Meadows Yurt
10,450'

8b

6b **7a**

0.40 mile to Trujillo Meadows Yurt
3.50 miles to Flat Mountain Yurt
4.40 miles to Cumbres Pass Trailhead
6.00 miles to Neff Mountain Yurt

3.20 miles to Neff Mountain Yurt
1.60 miles to Cumbres Pass Trailhead
2.80 miles to Flat Mountain Yurt
3.20 miles to Trujillo Meadows Yurt

6c

8a **6c**

Flat Mountain
Yurt
11,000'

3.80 miles to Neff Mountain Yurt
1.60 miles to Cumbres Pass Trailhead
2.20 miles to Flat Mountain Yurt

8b

Trails connect
just beyond edge
of map

8b

Neff Mountain Yurt, Trujillo Meadows Yurt, and Flat Mountain Yurt

Scale 1:24,000   Contour Interval 40 Feet

0   1/2
SCALE IN MILES

MN 12°

Hut
Trailhead ●
Wilderness – – – –

© 2000 Brian Litz

Trails, including US Forest Service trails, may or may
not be marked. USFS trails and roads are not maintained and their exact location may vary. This map is
not a substitute for good route-finding skills. This map
is an aid to help locate routes. These are suggested
routes only. Hazards exist in the backcountry, including
avalanches. Common sense and good judgment can
reduce but not eliminate these hazards.

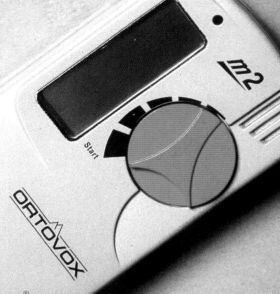

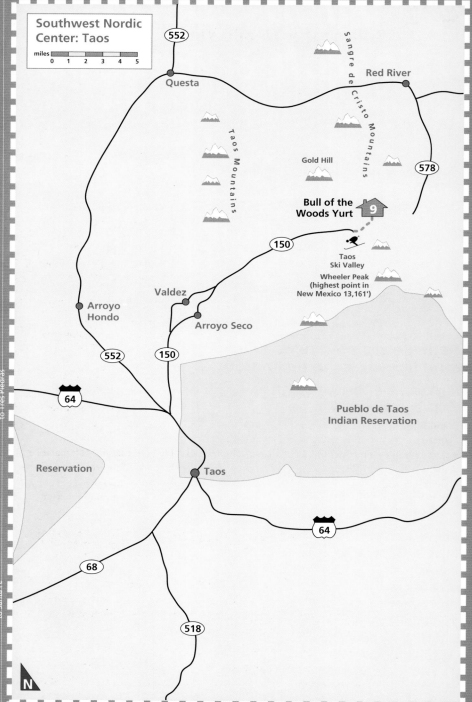

Southwest Nordic Center: Taos

miles
0 1 2 3 4 5

to Costilla

552

Questa

Sangre de Cristo Mountains

Red River

to Eagle Nest

578

Taos Mountains

Gold Hill

Bull of the Woods Yurt

9

150

Taos Ski Valley

Wheeler Peak (highest point in New Mexico 13,161')

Valdez

Arroyo Hondo

Arroyo Seco

552

150

Pueblo de Taos Indian Reservation

64

to Tres Piedras

Reservation

Taos

64

68

to Santa Fe

518

N

to Truchas

Bull of the Woods Yurt
(Sangre de Cristo Mtns./Taos)

HUT ELEVATION	10,800'
DATE BUILT	1999
SEASONS	Winter only
CAPACITY	10
HUT LAYOUT	24-foot yurt with fold-out futon bunks to sleep 6 people; 4 more mattresses that can be spread on the floor
HUT ESSENTIALS	Wood-burning stove, propane cookstove, all kitchenware, outhouse, propane lighting, games

Granted, this hut is not in Colorado, but it is part of a yurt system that exists primarily in Colorado. And there is no New Mexico hut guide to turn people on to the mystical beauty of the southern Sangre de Cristo Mountains near Taos—a storied, upthrust, fault-block mountain range that runs north to Salida, Colorado.

The hut sits atop a ridge near the Bull of the Woods Meadow between Gold Hill and 13,161-foot Wheeler Peak, which is the highest point in our southern-neighbor state. Although it is straightforward to reach in terms of route-finding, the trail to get there is steep. Once you're at the yurt, there is much to do, including glade skiing behind the yurt on the lower flanks of Gold Hill. Skiers and snowshoers can climb Gold Hill and also, with minimal technical difficulty or exposure to avalanche hazard, ascend to the highest point in New Mexico.

Although a few snowmobiles operate in the area, overall the landscape is isolated and beautiful in a southwestern-alpine kind of way. The hut sits on the edge of the meadow in the trees near the boundary of the Twining-Columbine Wilderness Study Area, which encompasses Gold Hill. Sandwiched between the yurt, the study area, and the Wheeler Peak Wilderness Area is a private in-holding where a local snowmobile outfitter runs some tours—so be aware. Overall, this is a highly commended destination.

Remember, too, that this new yurt sleeps up to 10 and is a premium structure with futon beds, and a deluxe stove that keeps everybody toasty warm all night long.

RECOMMENDED DAY TRIPS:

From the yurt, you can head in two obvious directions. The first is toward Gold Hill, and the other is toward Wheeler Peak. The tours flow along the ridgetops and are typical above–tree-line terrain. Alpine winds keep the open country free of heavy snow and there is little avalanche hazard. Generally, people will encounter a mix of touring and snowshoeing interspersed with walking—though at times it is possible to ski or snowshoe the entire distance.

Be careful in the vicinity of La Cal Basin en route to Wheeler Peak, as this is the only area that poses a real potential for avalanches. Also, people looking for vertical turns should consider skiing the 700-foot shots (20 to 35 degrees) above the yurt on the flanks of Gold Hill.

INTERMEDIATE/ADVANCED

TOUR

9a   Taos Ski Valley Trailhead to Bull of the Woods Yurt

SEE MAP PAGES 74 AND 79

TIME	2 to 4 hours
DISTANCE	2 miles
ELEVATIONS	TRAILHEAD: 9,300' YURT: 10,800' GAIN/LOSS: +1,500'
AVALANCHE	Minimal danger
MAPS	USGS: 7.5': Wheeler Peak, 1995
	National Forest: Carson National Forest

TOUR OVERVIEW: The route to the yurt is short, sweet, and steep. The well-marked summer trails and roads are easy to follow. Skiers should definitely consider tossing on skins for the ascent, and possibly to slow their return trip to the car. Some portions of the trail can be baked by the sun and have an ice crust.

DIRECTIONS TO TRAILHEAD: The trailhead is near the highest point of the parking area of Taos Ski Valley (the downhill resort). To reach the trailhead (from Taos), drive 4 miles north from the center of town to the last light in Taos proper. At this intersection, Hwy 64 heads west, Hwy 522 north, and Hwy 150 east. Turn right (east) onto Hwy 150 and follow the signed road, which deadends at the ski area.

Park near the highest reaches of the parking area, taking care to avoid the "no overnight parking" areas. Everything else is fair game.

Doug MacClennan

The high Sangre de Cristo Mountains near the Bull of the Woods Yurt.

The end of another day....

Bull of the Woods Yurt opens up new terrain in New Mexico.

THE ROUTE: Unlike the other yurts in the Southwest Nordic Center system atop Cumbres Pass, this yurt trail is not marked with "system" trail markers. It has only Forest Service trailmarkers.

After parking, and after you have prepared yourself for the rigorous ascent that lies ahead by saddling your body with your load, hop on the trail marked by Wheeler Peak and Bull of the Woods Meadow Forest Service signs and an interpretive sign about bighorn sheep. There are several numbered Forest Service trails in the general vicinity. The trail to the yurts begins on Trails #90 (Wheeler Peak) and #64 (Gold Hill), which are one and the same at this point.

Ascend along the creek for roughly 0.75 mile to the point where the Long Canyon Trail (#63) strikes off to the left. Bypass this turnoff and continue on the main Wheeler Peak Trail (#90) a bit farther until the trail veers left. Follow this trail until it reaches a Forest Road near the 1.0-mile mark. (There are trail mileage signs at the Long Canyon trail junction—visible on the way down—that do not match the measured mileage on the trail. Don't pay any attention to these.)

Travel on this road up a drainage until you near the edge of the Bull of the Woods Meadow. At this point, the Wheeler Peak Trail (signed) turns to the right and the Gold Hill Trail turns to the left. Hut-to-hut skiers should avoid both of these trails and instead ski directly into the large open meadow. Cross the meadow to the yurt, which is visible on the far edge of the meadow on the northwest corner. (*Note:* Occasional day visitors climb Wheeler Peak and the trail is often broken. Don't be led astray by their tracks as you near the yurt.)

"Four-play": relaxing at the Bull.

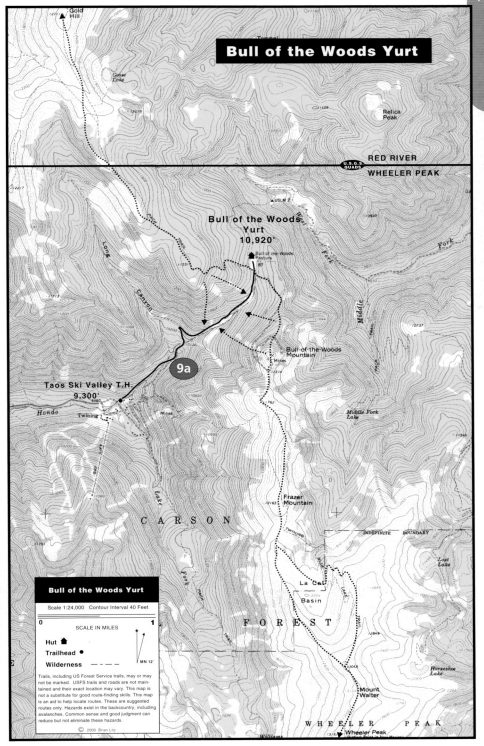

Bull of the Woods Yurt

Gold Hill

Goose Lake

Relica Peak

RED RIVER

U.S.G.S QUADS

WHEELER PEAK

USLM 2

Bull of the Woods Yurt 10,920'

Bull of the Woods Pasture

Bull-of-the-Woods Mountain

Mines

9a

Taos Ski Valley T.H. 9,300'

Hondo

Twining

Mines

Middle Fork Lake

CARSON

Frazer Mountain

INDEFINITE BOUNDARY

Lost Lake

La Cal Basin

FOREST

Horseshoe Lake

Mount Walter

WHEELER PEAK

Wheeler Peak

Bull of the Woods Yurt

Scale 1:24,000   Contour Interval 40 Feet

0 ——————————— 1
SCALE IN MILES

MN 12'

Hut

Trailhead

Wilderness – – –

Trails, including US Forest Service trails, may or may not be marked. USFS trails and roads are not maintained and their exact location may vary. This map is not a substitute for good route-finding skills. This map is an aid to help locate routes. These are suggested routes only. Hazards exist in the backcountry, including avalanches. Common sense and good judgment can reduce but not eliminate these hazards.

© 2000 Brian Litz

San Juan Snowtreks

The eastern end of the mighty San Juans is a land of deep, quiet forests, hidden valleys, and lower, less-well-known peaks. It is also the birthplace of the storied Rio Grande River. You will not find any of the highly coveted 14,000-foot peaks or nationally prominent transcontinental trails—just solitude, especially in the heart of winter—in this recreational backwater. Thankfully, what it lacks in the pure topographical ruggedness associated with the Grenadier and Needle Mountains of the western San Juans, it more than makes up for with its rarely visited, untrammeled beauty and pristine wilderness essence.

About the only things that mar this pristine picture are the scattered summer logging roads that thread through the mountains, and the occasional defunct mining camp or town. So wild and natural is this landscape that it was one of the sites chosen to reintroduce the lynx. Keep an eye out and you may catch a glimpse of these stunning feral cats.

No huts existed here until the mid- and late 1900s, and the few snowshoers and skiers who explored the area were primarily locals. In general geographic terms, this system lies west of South Fork and Del Norte and north of Wolf Creek, though it is closest to and south of the town of Creede. Indeed, there is still much unexplored terrain to venture into, and in even the more popular areas, skiers are few and far between. You will not have to fend off competition in your pursuit for powder.

Until the Lime Creek Yurt opened in 1999, only the Fisher Mountain Hut was here. Now you can ski hut to hut via the Emma Mine Road. This shelf-type road traverses the northern flank of Fisher Mountain, allowing an easy interconnection between the huts via moderate kick-and-glide skiing or snowshoeing. Either of these huts offers an ideal setting for a first hut trip, and even less experienced skiers can ski hut to hut.

The hut system is working on the permitting process for two more huts, which, if approved, eventually will allow skiers to travel from the trailheads just south of Creede to either U.S. 160 near Big Meadows Reservoir (between South Fork and Wolf Creek Pass) or directly to the summit of Wolf Creek Pass. What a magnificent wilderness excursion those "point A to point B" trips would be!

This panoramic view from near the Fisher Mountain Hut takes in the distant Uncompahgre Wilderness. Sunshine (14,001 feet) and Redcloud (14,034 feet) Peaks are on the left and Uncompahgre (14,309 feet) is on the far right.

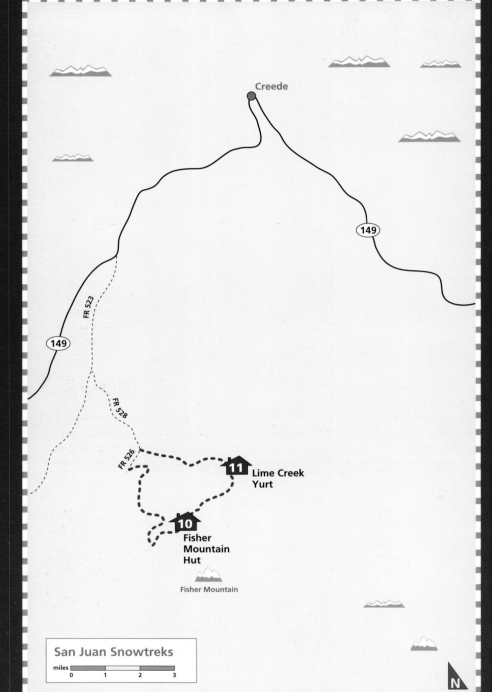

Creede

149

FR 523

149

FR 528

FR 526

11 Lime Creek
Yurt

10 Fisher
Mountain
Hut

Fisher Mountain

San Juan Snowtreks

miles
0   1   2   3

N

Fisher Mountain Hut

HUT ELEVATION	10,864'
DATE BUILT	1995
SEASONS	November 15 through April 1 (winter only)
CAPACITY	6
HUT LAYOUT	12' x 24' wooden building with 2 bunkbeds and extra mattresses
HUT ESSENTIALS	Woodstove for heat, propane cookstove, lanterns, complete kitchenware, attached indoor composting toilet

The compact, simple, one-room Fisher Mountain Hut is located near the end of a logging road at the base of a large bowl. Sparsely dotted with trees and old stumps, when this bowl is filled with powder, it is a skier's delight. You can reach the hut by pleasant and easy skiing along a road. Once you're at the hut, you'll find other logging and old mining roads that are great for longer tours, as is an ascent of unspoiled Fisher Mountain. As you ski to the hut, the vista to the north and west includes Uncompahgre (14,309') and Wetterhorn (14,015') Peaks. Few people get to see this view of the peaks.

RECOMMENDED DAY TRIPS:

You can climb up behind the hut as far as you like for turns. For a longer trip, ascend to **Fisher Peak**. If you're interested in a pleasant, scenic tour, drop down to the road and follow it out and around to the **Emma Mine**.

Cully Culbreth inspects conditions around Fisher Mountain Hut.

TOUR

10a Forest Road 526/527 Trailhead to Fisher Mountain Hut

SEE MAP PAGES 82 AND 89

TIME	3 to 6 hours
DISTANCE	5.5 miles
ELEVATIONS	TRAILHEAD: 9,300' HUT: 10,864' GAIN: +1,564'
AVALANCHE	Minimal danger
MAPS	USGS 7.5': Spar City, 1986
	National Forest: Rio Grande

TOUR OVERVIEW: This primary route to the hut is straightforward and of a moderate grade. The route follows the road for its entire length and you will find nice views across the headwaters of the Rio Grande. The main challenge here is to avoid being drawn astray by other secondary roads and trails in the area. If you pay attention, they are easy to avoid.

DIRECTIONS TO TRAILHEAD: Drive on CO 149 to an intersection that lies 7 miles southwest (toward Lake City) of Creede. Turn south onto Middle Creek Road (Forest Road 523). Drive 4.4 miles to the intersection with Ivy Creek Road (Forest Road 528). Take the left fork and drive 2.7 miles on FR 528 to the inter-

section with the Spar City Road. Take the right fork (FR 528) and drive 0.25 mile to the intersection with Forest Road 526—the road that heads straight southwest.

Occasionally the road is plowed another 0.8 mile to the turnoff to Forest Road 527. If this is the case, or if the snowpack is low, you can park at this intersection.

photo by K. Koutec

The San Juans provide an expansive vista for Spar City Trail.

THE ROUTE: From the parking area at the intersection of FR 528 and FR 526, ski south west along FR 526 for 0.8 mile to the intersection with FR 527. Turn left onto this road and follow it roughly 4.7 miles to the hut. Remember to remain on the main road and bypass the lefthand roads at 0.9 and 1.8 miles. Ski across a creek at 3.1 miles and through a large switchback at 3.9 miles. You will arrive at an orange gate at 4.7 miles. Ski past the gate and proceed uphill to the east (right) directly from the gate or along the road beyond the gate for 50 to 100 feet, then cut up to the light-gray hut.

TOUR
10b Fisher Mountain Hut to Lime Creek Yurt

SEE MAP PAGES 82 AND 89

INTERMEDIATE/ADVANCED

TIME	3 to 6 hours
DISTANCE	5.35 miles
ELEVATIONS	FM HUT: 10,864' LC YURT: 10,500' GAIN/LOSS: +596'/-1,164'
AVALANCHE	Minimal danger
MAPS	USGS 7.5': Spar City, 1986
	National Forest: Rio Grande

TOUR OVERVIEW: This tour is described as going from Fisher Mountain Hut to Lime Creek Yurt—though it certainly is possible to ski in the other direction. Overall, it is easier to travel the former, as the route loses nearly 1,000 feet throughout its duration. The trail follows an old mining road and is noticeably steep. Less adept skiers may want to keep skins on in either direction.

THE ROUTE: From the Fisher Mountain Hut, drop down off the front porch onto the obvious road (Forest Road 527), which traverses north on a gradual ascent around the ridge of Elevation Point 11,521'. This section of the tour offers stellar vistas of the upper Rio Grande Valley. Once around the ridge, the road heads east/southeast, arriving at a set of sheep corrals (used by summer sheep-herders) near the 2.5-mile mark. Continue traversing along the road, skiing past an orange gate at 3.0 miles. Eventually you will arrive at the old 1890s Emma Mine site at 3.25 miles.

Once past the mine, begin a 0.6-mile descent to a three-way intersection. This section is steep and narrow and may require skins for ascending and descending skiers alike. Turn to the right and ski past the orange gate.

Continue east, then northeast, 0.5 mile to another orange gate. Pass this gate and then take the immediate sharp turn to the left, which places you on a 1.0-mile descent to the yurt. Follow the trail downhill for 0.7 mile until you reach a blow-down logging area. Take a sharp left near a large pile of trees. Ski along the road for 0.25 mile until you reach an area with lots of flagging and signs.

Take a left turn onto a side road and go up a small slope until you reach a meadow. The yurt is located in the trees to the left at the edge of the meadow. Red and orange flagging marks this final stretch of trail.

Lime Creek Yurt

HUT ELEVATION	10,500'
DATE BUILT	1999
SEASONS	November 15 through April 1 (winter only)
CAPACITY	4
HUT LAYOUT	16-foot yurt with 2 single bunks and extra sleeping pad
HUT ESSENTIALS	Woodstove for heat, propane cookstove, lanterns, complete kitchenware, attached indoor composting toilet

The Lime Creek Yurt is the newest hut in the San Juan Snowtrek system. Like the Fisher Mountain Hut, it is positioned along old summer logging roads. The presence of the yurt opens up acres of terrain heretofore rarely skied or snowshoed by anyone other than locals. The yurt can be reached via the Fisher Mountain Hut and the Emma Mine Road or via its own dedicated approach tour. Novice skiers should access the yurt via the standard approach tour, as it is much less demanding than the Fisher Mountain Hut/ Emma Mine Road traverse. In the future, if all goes according to plan, this hut will provide a jumping-off point for an extended hut-to-hut tour that will reach Wolf Creek Pass.

photo by K. Koutec

Lime Creek Yurt offers a take-off point for easy day tours.

RECOMMENDED DAY TRIPS:

The road to the Fisher Mountain Yurt works well as an easy day tour and can be pushed as far as your group wants to go. The mountain south of the hut is skiable off several flanks.

If it's too steep, you're too old! Former state BLM director Bob Moore makes good use of his "golden years," cranking crisp tele turns.

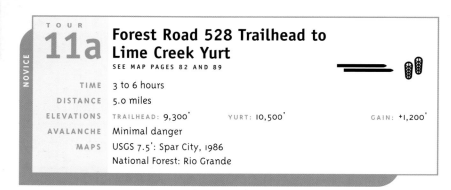

TOUR

11a

Forest Road 528 Trailhead to Lime Creek Yurt

SEE MAP PAGES 82 AND 89

NOVICE

TIME	3 to 6 hours
DISTANCE	5.0 miles
ELEVATIONS	TRAILHEAD: 9,300' YURT: 10,500' GAIN: +1,200'
AVALANCHE	Minimal danger
MAPS	USGS 7.5': Spar City, 1986
	National Forest: Rio Grande

TOUR OVERVIEW: This route—a straight shot up the Lime Creek drainage—is the primary route to the yurt. It is similar in nature to the route to the Fisher Mountain Hut (Tour 10a, see page 84), as this is a straightforward and moderately inclined tour along a Forest Service road. Keep to the main route and avoid other trails and roads in this area that head off at several intersections.

DIRECTIONS TO TRAILHEAD: Follow directions to the trailhead for Tour 10a (see page 84).

THE ROUTE: From the car, ski southeast by following Forest Road 528 up into the Lime Creek drainage. Ski up the road and go straight through an intersection, bypassing left- and righthand turns at 1.75 miles and another righthand turn at 2.0 miles. Pass a cattle guard at the 3.0-mile mark and reach a large meadow at 4.0 miles.

At 4.5 miles, you will come to a well-marked intersection with Forest Road 528A. Turn right and ski 0.5 mile to the yurt. You will ski through one major switchback, then traverse southeast until you reach a small meadow, where you will turn to the right toward the yurt. The spot where you leave the trail is also well marked, and the hut sits several hundred feet off the trail at the edge of the meadow.

Fisher Mountain Hut & Lime Creek Yurt

**Fisher Mountain Hut
& Lime Creek Yurt**

Scale 1:24,000   Contour Interval 40 Feet

SCALE IN MILES

MN 12°

Hut

Trailhead

Wilderness — — — —

© 2000 Brian Litz

Trails, including US Forest Service trails, may or may not be marked. USFS trails and roads are not maintained and their exact location may vary. This map is not a substitute for good route-finding skills. This map is an aid to help locate routes. These are suggested routes only. Hazards exist in the backcountry, including avalanches. Common sense and good judgment can reduce but not eliminate these hazards.

RIO GRANDE

NATIONAL FOREST

Lime Creek Yurt
10,500'

3.25 miles to Fisher Mountain Hut
2.10 miles to Lime Creek Yurt

Fisher Mountain Hut
10,864'

11a

10b

10a

FR 528 Trailhead
9,300'

FR 526/527
Trailhead
9,412'

0 miles to FR 526/527 T.H.
0 miles to Fisher Mtn. Hut

Hinsdale Haute Route

Colorado's Hinsdale County is a beautiful, remote area protected by the tower-ing San Juans, a region of rolling ranchlands and rich forests hemmed by some of Colorado's tallest mountains. A favorite summer vacation destination, Lake City (the county seat and only town) is nearly deserted during the winter months, the holdout of a few hundred determined year-round residents. Hinsdale County is one of the least populated counties in the nation. It also contains the highest percentage of alpine tundra of any place outside of Alaska and has the highest mean elevation of any county in the United States (10,000 feet). Federally pro-tected Wilderness Areas comprise 46 percent of this land.

Aside from the county's notoriety as a vastly profitable gold, silver, and lead mining district from 1874 until the turn of the century, perhaps its greatest claim to fame is Alferd Packer. Packer had an appetite for adventure and living on the edge of the law. During the winter of 1874–1875, Packer, an "experienced" moun-tain guide, collected a fee to lead prospectors through the rugged San Juans. The group encountered severe weather and food became scarce. Several weeks later, Packer stumbled back into civilization. Suspicious townspeople tried him for mur-der and cannibalism, and Packer served 18 years of hard labor.

Hinsdale County's hut system anchors an intriguing backcountry trail network, which, like the rest of this area, is remote and isolated. It is also ideally suited to Nordic cross-country skiing. The most unusual feature of the Hinsdale Haute Route is, in fact, its route. Beginning near Cebolla Creek between Slumgullion Pass and Spring Creek Pass on CO 149 (which connects Lake City to Creede and South Fork), the route follows the old La Garita stock trail along the Continental Divide, where cowboys once drove herds of cattle.

This route along the Continental Divide probably has the highest overall average elevation of any hut system in the state. Amazingly though, given its stratospheric elevation and the associated physiological effects of exercising in this rarified air, the touring is manageable even for less experienced, less fit skiers. This is partly because the huts, trails, and trailheads are all relatively high so there is not an inordinate amount of elevation gain skiing hut to hut.

Perhaps the greatest challenge here is in the open, unprotected nature of the terrain, which leaves travelers exposed to the elements. Poor weather can find skiers floundering about, vainly trying to navigate. An added drawback is the presence of local recreational snowmobilers, especially near the Rambouillet Yurt.

On the other hand, because the La Garita stock trail runs along a broad, gently rolling ridge, this route is almost completely free of serious avalanche danger, yet it covers a great deal of true alpine terrain. Spectacular and rarely seen winter panoramas of the Big Blue Wilderness and five 14,000-foot peaks—Handies, Redcloud, Sunshine, Wetterhorn, and Uncompahgre—are visible along the way.

The first shelter, the Jon Wilson Memorial Yurt, which opened during the winter of 1991–1992, remains one of Colorado's easiest-to-reach huts. This hut and the Rambouillet Yurt are excellent destinations for novice skiers. The more distant and committing Colorado Trail Friends Memorial Yurt and Fawn Lakes

Yurt, while still not demanding expert skiing skills, add a real alpine flavor to the system. Long-term plans call for the possible construction of enough huts to allow skiers to go all the way southwest to the old Carson townsite, where a descent into the Lake City valley and shuttle cars is feasible.

All of the yurts are large and light-filled. They are carpeted, are designed to sleep six to eight people on bunks and cots, and are well-stocked with wood-burning stoves, lanterns, propane cookstoves, pots, pans, utensils, and dishes. Of special interest are the "out-yurts"—outdoor toilets built like tiny versions of the main yurts. These out-yurts are some of the nicest backcountry commodes that I have had the pleasure to ruminate in. Call the yurt system for up-to-date trail and reservation information (see Appendix A).

Sunshine Peak lives up to its name at sunrise over Colorado Trail Friends Memorial Yurt.

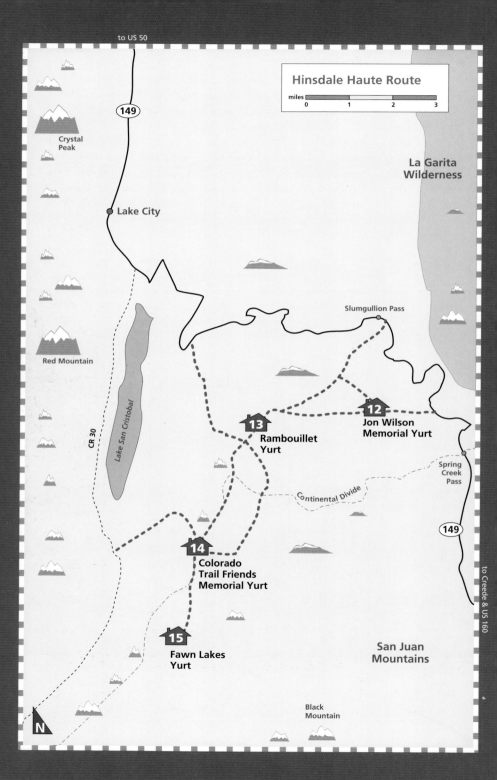

12

Jon Wilson Memorial Yurt

HUT ELEVATION	10,840'
DATE BUILT	1991
SEASONS	Late December through end of April (depending on snowpack)
CAPACITY	8
HUT LAYOUT	16-foot handmade yurt with cots and bunks
HUT ESSENTIALS	Wood-burning stove for heat, propane cookstove, propane lights, "out-yurts"

Constructed as a memorial to a young man killed in a tragic auto accident, the Jon Wilson Memorial Yurt is located near the junction of the West Fork and Middle Fork of Cebolla Creek. This yurt, the first shelter erected along the Hinsdale Haute Route, is one of the easiest huts to reach, because of the short distance and simple route-finding.

Easily handled by Nordic skiers of all abilities, the most popular trail to the yurt follows gentle Cebolla (Spanish for "onion") Creek to just slightly beyond an obvious fork in the tributary at 10,780 feet. The trail to the yurt is basically free of avalanche danger, making this an ideal introductory overnight ski trip for novices and families. From the yurt, skiers can tour up the drainages to the higher ridges or explore the surrounding forests.

Jerry Gray of the Hinsdale Haute Route tours near the Continental Divide above the yurts.

It is a large yurt filled with sunlight, thanks to clear vinyl panels built into the ceiling and around the front door. The yurt sleeps six to eight and can be reserved through the Hinsdale Haute Route (see Appendix A).

RECOMMENDED DAY TRIPS:

Day touring around this yurt is the most limited of any of the Hinsdale Haute Route yurts. You can continue up the valley following the most natural route to the Rambouillet Yurt. Pay attention through this valley, though, as it is a textbook avalanche terrain trap.

TOUR

NOVICE

12a Cebolla Creek Trailhead to Jon Wilson Memorial Yurt

SEE MAP PAGES 92 AND 112–113

TIME	1 to 3 hours
DISTANCE	1.8 miles
ELEVATIONS	TRAILHEAD: 10,440' YURT: 10,840' GAIN: +400'
AVALANCHE	Minimal danger
MAPS	USGS 7.5': Slumgullion Pass, 1986
	National Forest: Gunnison
	Trails Illustrated: Map #141 (Silverton/Ouray/Telluride/Lake City)

DIRECTIONS TO TRAILHEAD: Take CO 149 to its crossing of Cebolla Creek, approximately 15 miles southeast from Lake City or 57 miles northwest from the town of South Fork. There is a plowed parking area near mile marker 57 on the South Fork/Creede side of the creek. The trailhead is on the south side of the creek at a yurt system map.

THE ROUTE: The trail is blazed with wands that have colored circles on top. These markers, mounted on white stakes, are used on a number of trails in the Hinsdale Haute Route.

Directions are simple: Follow the marked trail along the creek. There are no side canyons to turn into until you reach Cebolla Creek's main fork at the 1.5-mile mark. Take the left fork, skiing to the southwest toward the yurt, which sits on the northwest (right) side of the creek in a small clearing. The right fork is the alternate route to the Rambouillet Yurt (Tour 13b, see page 97).

Jon Wilson Memorial Yurt was the first yurt in the Hinsdale Haute Route and remains one of the easiest to reach in the state.

13 Rambouillet Yurt

HUT ELEVATION	11,680'
DATE BUILT	1992
SEASONS	Late December through end of April (depending on snowpack)
CAPACITY	8
HUT LAYOUT	16-foot handmade yurt with cots and bunks
HUT ESSENTIALS	Wood-burning stove for heat, propane cookstove, propane lights, "out-yurts"

The Rambouillet (pronounced ram-bo-lay) Yurt, the second shelter to be built in the Hinsdale Haute Route system, provides skiers with access to safe, classic, backcountry touring terrain while also providing an intermediate stop for longer, more advanced trips to yurts farther along the Continental Divide. Tucked into the trees below Hill 71, the yurt is surrounded by acres of moderate-to-advanced ski terrain. The short tour to the summit of Hill 71—a 12,067-foot "hill"— affords an unbelievable panorama of the rugged San Juan Mountains to the west. Strong beginning skiers traveling with experienced partners should be able to reach this yurt despite its intermediate rating.

The first route begins at the Jon Wilson Memorial Yurt, although strong skiers could easily ski directly from the parking area at Cebolla Creek to the Rambouillet Yurt. Make reservations for the Rambouillet Yurt, which sleeps six to eight, through the Hinsdale Haute Route office (see Appendix A).

RECOMMENDED DAY TRIPS:

This area defines wide-open terrain for cross-country skiing. Granted, there can be snowmobiles in the area, but so it goes. From the yurt, you can ascend the high ridge to the west and south following the Continental Divide and the high trail to the Colorado Trail Friends Memorial Yurt. The return trip from the ridge and highpoint down to the yurt affords nice tele turns. At times the ridge crest can harbor wind-affected snow, but the glades to the skier's right (east) can hold better, protected snow. Be careful through here. For a safer, easier day tour, you can follow the lower Colorado Trail Friends Memorial Yurt route. Finally, the meadows to the east and the knoll to the northwest are excellent for quick kick-and-glide jaunts.

INTERMEDIATE

TOUR
13a
Jon Wilson Memorial Yurt to Rambouillet Yurt via West Fork of Cebolla Creek
SEE MAP PAGES 92 AND 112–113

TIME	3 to 4 hours
DISTANCE	3.2 miles
ELEVATIONS	JWM YURT: 10,840' R YURT: 11,680' GAIN: +840'
AVALANCHE	Route crosses avalanche slopes; prone to skier-triggered avalanches during high-hazard periods
MAPS	USGS 7.5': Lake San Cristobal, 1973; Slumgullion Pass, 1986 National Forest: Gunnison Trails Illustrated: Map #141 (Silverton/Ouray/Telluride/Lake City)

THE ROUTE: You have a choice of two routes from the Jon Wilson Memorial Yurt to the Rambouillet Yurt. The West Fork of Cebolla Creek is easier and shorter. This route, however, passes under many avalanche runout zones that are potentially dangerous. Therefore, it should be used only when conditions are entirely safe. In addition, you should use avalanche terrain travel procedures and equipment, including transceivers and shovels. If conditions are questionable, use the Middle Fork route (Tour 13b, opposite). This route is recommended during periods of avalanche hazard because the creek is better protected by trees throughout the ascent to Rambouillet Park. Both tours are straightforward, take a half day or less, and should present few problems.

Jerry Gray tours near the Rambouillet Yurt.

For the West Fork route from the Jon Wilson Memorial Yurt, follow the creek upstream for 2 miles until you pass a constriction in the valley between a knob on the south and steeper slopes on the north. Continue due west past a tributary coming in from the north to a fork in the creek, where a large meadow contours south. Begin climbing out of the drainage on a northwest heading, aiming for the east side of the south ridge of Hill 71. The Rambouillet Yurt is at 11,680 feet in a tiny meadow, just below a small, flat shoulder and rock outcrops on the south ridge of Hill 71.

INTERMEDIATE

TOUR
13b
Jon Wilson Memorial Yurt to Rambouillet Yurt via Middle Fork of Cebolla Creek

SEE MAP PAGES 92 AND 112–113

TIME	3 to 5 hours
DISTANCE	3.7 miles
ELEVATIONS	JWM YURT: 10,840' R YURT: 11,680' GAIN: +840'
AVALANCHE	Some avalanche terrain encountered; easily avoided
MAPS	USGS 7.5': Lake San Cristobal, 1973; Slumgullion Pass, 1986 National Forest: Gunnison Trails Illustrated: Map #141 (Silverton/Ouray/Telluride/Lake City)

TOUR OVERVIEW: This is a safer path to the Rambouillet Yurt from the Jon Wilson Memorial Yurt when compared to the West Fork route (Tour 13a, opposite). Use this route if avalanche conditions are questionable. If you follow the route directly along the creek in the canyon, it runs under some potentially dangerous slopes during moderate to high snowpack instability. A safer variation, the "Ridge Route," (shown as dotted line, page 113) and is recommended for those times.

THE ROUTE: From the Jon Wilson Memorial Yurt, return downstream to the junction of the West Fork and the Middle Fork of Cebolla Creek. From this point, turn and proceed upstream through the Middle Fork drainage (which is on the left). Heading due west, climb out of the drainage and enter Rambouillet Park. Intercept the Lake City Continental Divide Snowmobile Club (LCCDSC) snowmobile trail and follow it as it contours south around the small basin between Slumgullion Point and Hill 71 (see the western half of Tour 13b, shown on page 113). Rambouillet Yurt is at 11,680 feet, situated on the south ridge of Hill 71.

During periods of snowpack instability, do not follow the route up the canyon bottom. Instead, use the "Ridge Route." Leave the yurt and begin climbing directly behind it, angling upward to the right (north/northeast). There is no best route here. The goal, though, is to arrive at the top of the rock outcrop that sits on top of the ridge. Once you have climbed onto the ridge above the rock, begin climbing straight up the ridge-crest through the trees. Initially this climb is somewhat steep, but it levels off as you near the top of the climb with its flat terrain above and to the west.

Once on top, strike out roughly west/northwest and follow the path of least resistance to the well-marked snowmobile trail (the portion of the trail shared with Tour 13c, Slumgullion Pass Trailhead to Rambouillet Yurt route). Once you've reached this trail, turn southwest and follow the markers to the yurt.

TOUR
13c
Slumgullion Pass Trailhead to Rambouillet Yurt

SEE MAP PAGES 92 AND 112–113

INTERMEDIATE

TIME	4 to 6 hours
DISTANCE	4.0 miles
ELEVATIONS	TRAILHEAD: 11,540' YURT: 11,680' GAIN: +960'
AVALANCHE	Some avalanche terrain encountered; easily avoided
MAPS	USGS 7.5': Lake San Cristobal, 1973; Slumgullion Pass, 1986
	National Forest: Gunnison
	Trails Illustrated: Map #141 (Silverton/Ouray/Telluride/Lake City)

TOUR OVERVIEW: As long as the weather is stable and clear, this high-altitude traverse is quite moderate. Parts of this trail may not be marked, so skiers should be experienced in basic backcountry route-finding, navigation, and avalanche awareness.

DIRECTIONS TO TRAILHEAD: This trail begins on CO 149, on the summit of Slumgullion Pass near the snow measuring station, which is roughly 4 miles west of Cebolla Creek and 8.15 miles southeast of town on CO 149 toward Creede. This auto mileage from Lake City is measured from the spot where CO 149 crosses the Lake Fork of the Gunnison River near the Alferd Packer Memorial Site immediately south of Lake City. Park on the north side of the road in the small, plowed parking area. From the parking area, cross the road, pass the Slumgullion Snow Measuring Station stake, and follow blue diamonds southwest as they ascend into thick timber. This trail is intermittently marked with blue diamonds.

THE ROUTE: From the trailhead at the Slumgullion snow measuring station, the route ascends to the top of Elevation Point 12,047', the most difficult section of the trail.

From here, you can stay on top of the ridge and ski over Slumgullion Pass and Hill 71 for a slightly higher elevation gain and a view of the incredible scenery. Or you can take another route that descends onto an 11,800-foot shelf and follows the snowmobile trail south to the yurt. This route is more protected from the elements. During periods of severe weather and wind, skiers are advised to choose the route via Cebolla Creek and the Jon Wilson Memorial Yurt (see Tour 12a, page 94, and Tour 13b, page 97) rather than the route from Slumgullion Pass.

Rambouillet Yurt glows under a crystal-clear night sky.

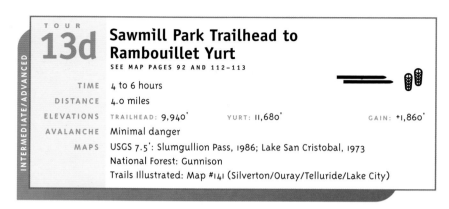

TOUR

13d Sawmill Park Trailhead to Rambouillet Yurt

SEE MAP PAGES 92 AND 112–113

TIME	4 to 6 hours
DISTANCE	4.0 miles
ELEVATIONS	TRAILHEAD: 9,940' YURT: 11,680' GAIN: +1,860'
AVALANCHE	Minimal danger
MAPS	USGS 7.5': Slumgullion Pass, 1986; Lake San Cristobal, 1973 National Forest: Gunnison Trails Illustrated: Map #141 (Silverton/Ouray/Telluride/Lake City)

TOUR OVERVIEW: This trail, although not new, was not included in previous editions of this book because it is part of the LCCDSC trail system. Despite the presence of snowmobiles, Jerry Gray, director of the Hinsdale Haute Route system, likes the trail because it is the shortest route to the Rambouillet Yurt. Route-finding is easy, as the trail is protected by trees most of the way. On the other hand, the trail does climb steeply and is more strenuous than other routes to this yurt.

DIRECTIONS TO TRAILHEAD: The trailhead is on the south side of CO 149 just past the Lake San Cristobal overlook, which is the first sharp switchback above Lake City on the way up to Slumgullion Pass. From the point where CO 149 crosses the Lake Fork of the Gunnison, go 2.85 miles to the turnoff. You'll see a steep road, marked with a sign, ascending straight uphill into the forest to the south. Park along the south side of the road on the shoulder. If you're coming from Creede, the turnoff is 5.3 miles west of Slumgullion Pass.

THE ROUTE: Climb directly up the road and follow it past a left turn, which is marked with snowmobile signs. (If you're descending, this trail bypass will appear as a right fork; it leads to another, larger snowmobile parking area farther up the pass from the trailhead.)

Follow the road for roughly 1.3 miles until you reach the meadow of Sawmill Park, which presents about the only route-finding complications on this tour. First of all, be careful not to be misdirected by the confusion of snowmobile tracks in Sawmill Park. Snowmobilers like to tour around this meadow, which can obscure the main trail. To keep on the main route, ski along the very eastern (left) edge of the park, near the trees. Keep an eye out for the spot where the trail leaves the park and re-enters the woods, along a tiny creek. This stretch of trail is normally marked with wands.

Once back in the woods, the trail climbs even more steeply up to the pass on the western edge of Rambouillet Park. This ascent doesn't let up until you gain roughly 1,000 feet. As you enter Rambouillet Park, the snowmobile trail markers lead off to the southeast, directly into the heart of this vast, open meadow. Look to the left (northeast) for the hut system wands that lead past the edge of the trees another 0.7 mile to the Rambouillet Yurt.

Good company.

Your only chance to survive an avalanche burial is to be rescued by a companion. Who are you touring with?

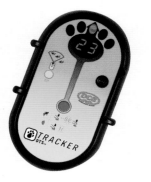

 TRACKER
DTS™

- The world's first digital, dual antenna beacon
- The top-selling beacon in North America
- Eliminates complex "grid" and "tangent" searching
- Visual displays, no volume controls
- Recommended by the Swiss, German, and Austrian alpine clubs

Companion
Shovel & Probe

- High-strength, oversized oval shaft
- Aluminum blade with reinforced cross-section
- Reversible offset grip that decreases back strain
- Optional 6-foot Companion Probe can be stored in shaft
- Light and compact

Also available: SR260 2.6-meter search-and-rescue probe

![bca backcountry access]

The leader in companion rescue technology.

Learn to recognize and avoid avalanche hazards. Practice regularly with your transceiver. For a list of avalanche education providers, see our website.

Backcountry Access, Inc. • Boulder, CO USA • www.bcaccess.com • 800-670-8735

Photo: Larry Prosor

14 Colorado Trail Friends Memorial Yurt

HUT ELEVATION	11,800'
DATE BUILT	1995
SEASONS	Late December through end of April (depending on snowpack)
CAPACITY	8
HUT LAYOUT	16-foot handmade yurt with cots and bunks
HUT ESSENTIALS	Wood-burning stove for heat, propane cookstove, propane lights, "out-yurts"

The Colorado Trail Friends Memorial Yurt was built with donations from the Colorado Trail Foundation and came on-line during the spring of 1995. It opened up adventurous terrain that truly puts the "haute" in the Hinsdale Haute Route. The yurt sits directly atop a saddle that straddles both the Continental Divide and the Colorado Trail, and it has the best views of all of the shelters in this system. All you have to do is walk out the front door to delight in a panorama of the Lake City group of the San Juan Mountains, including 14,309-foot Uncompahgre Peak to the northwest and 14,001-foot Sunshine Peak and 14,034-foot Redcloud Peak to the west/southwest. Out to the east is the peculiar, sphinx-like summit of Bristol Head.

From the Slumgullion Pass and Spring Creek side of the system, skiers must travel hut to hut from the Rambouillet Yurt or the Wilson Yurt to reach the Colorado Trail Friends Memorial Yurt. The trails are more challenging and more committing than the routes to the Rambouillet and Wilson Yurts, but the destination also may be more rewarding.

The standard route follows a high, treeless ridge separating the Rambouillet Yurt and the Colorado Trail Friends Memorial Yurt and overlooking the multi-thousand-foot escarpment above Lake San Cristobal. It is about as exposed to weather as a trail can be, and it also travels through avalanche-prone terrain. A longer, alternate route to the Colorado Trail Friends Memorial Yurt from the Rambouillet Yurt, which follows Big Buck Creek, is a better choice in foul weather.

Finally, another trail climbs directly to the yurt out of the Lake Fork Valley, gaining more than 2,500 feet en route. Called the Camp Trail, it is a newer Forest Service trail that does not appear on any maps, although it has a parking lot and official trailhead up-valley from Lake San Cristobal.

What all of this means is that a ski trip to this hut is less suitable for beginning hut skiers. Even so, strong beginners can certainly make the journey under optimal conditions.

Note: The Colorado Trail Friends Memorial Yurt has been moved slightly to the west and now sits protected on the eastern side of a small stand of evergreens. This new location is a short walk from the old one and does not affect route access information.

RECOMMENDED DAY TRIPS:

Spring is a great time to visit this hut, as the days are longer and the more stable snowpack allows better touring. Also of interest are the forested slopes high above the hut to the south, where short powder runs abound. Another option is to head east and tour into the lower valleys, where you can explore the potential for shots off the western edge of the ridge. Or follow the Colorado Trail Friends Memorial Yurt to Fawn Lakes Yurt route (Tour 15a, see page 110) as far as you like for a nice, moderate tour up to some overlooks to the south.

An old snag snags a bit of sunlight at dawn at the Colorado Trail Friends Memorial Yurt.

TOUR 14a

Rambouillet Yurt to Colorado Trail Friends Memorial Yurt via Continental Divide

SEE MAP PAGES 92 AND 112-113

INTERMEDIATE/ADVANCED

TIME	4 to 6 hours
DISTANCE	4.25 miles
ELEVATIONS	R YURT: 11,680' CTFM YURT: 11,800' GAIN/LOSS: + 800'/-1,000'
AVALANCHE	Route crosses avalanche runout zones; can be dangerous during high-hazard periods
MAPS	USGS 7.5': Slumgullion Pass, 1986; Lake San Cristobal, 1973 National Forest: Gunnison Trails Illustrated: Map #141 (Silverton/Ouray/Telluride/Lake City)

TOUR OVERVIEW: This standard route to the Colorado Trail Friends Memorial Yurt is an exciting, high-elevation tour. In clear weather it presents skiers with some of the most scenic touring in the state, navigation is easy, and, for the most part, moderately capable skiers should be able to traverse the route. If weather threatens, avoid it like the plague and take the Big Buck Creek route instead (Tour 14b, opposite).

Avalanche hazards here are minimal under normal conditions and, because of the wide-open nature of the terrain, most potential hazards are visible. Probably the most dangerous stretch is a short slope that must be negotiated to gain a narrow ridge near the 3-mile mark just before the final descent to the hut.

THE ROUTE: Leave the Rambouillet Yurt and traverse southwest to the saddle at 11,600 feet. Cross the marked snowmobile route and continue on a westerly course up and onto a ridge, where you can overlook the Lake Fork Valley below to the west.

Follow the ridge-crest south, up through a thinning stand of trees, until you reach tree line. From here the goal is to reach Elevation Point 12,305' by choosing the path of least resistance directly up the ridge. Exercise caution by trying the safest route up this slope, which is usually the windblown sastrugi that forms the transition from the windward and leeward aspects of the ridge.

Continue over the summit of Elevation Point 12,305' and past a radio tower. Descend roughly 240 feet to a saddle, then climb 160 feet toward Elevation Point 12,282'. You can ski directly over this summit or traverse around its eastern flank. Continue on this rollercoaster ride by descending to another, less obvious saddle.

From here the route continues south along a narrow ridge before descending directly to the yurt. The short climb on this ridge near Elevation Point 12,105' puts you in close proximity to some wind-loaded slopes, so once again exercise extreme caution. If this slope causes anxiety, you can avoid it by descending due south from the less obvious saddle toward Big Buck Creek for about 400 feet, then traversing around to a tributary that leads up to the saddle and the yurt.

Actually, you can abandon the route at many points for the safety of the Big Buck Creek drainage if the weather begins to deteriorate or if the level of avalanche hazard is deemed too great.

INTERMEDIATE

TOUR
14b
Rambouillet Yurt to Colorado Trail Friends Memorial Yurt via Big Buck Creek
SEE MAP PAGES 92 AND 112–113

TIME	5 to 7 hours
DISTANCE	5.4 miles
ELEVATIONS	R YURT: 11,680' CTFM YURT: 11,800' GAIN/LOSS: +800'/-880'
AVALANCHE	Route crosses avalanche runout zones; can be dangerous during high-hazard periods
MAPS	USGS 7.5': Slumgullion Pass, 1986; Lake San Cristobal, 1973 National Forest: Gunnison Trails Illustrated: Map #141 (Silverton/Ouray/Telluride/Lake City)

TOUR OVERVIEW: Big Buck Creek is the foul-weather tour to the Colorado Trail Friends Memorial Yurt. It remains well below the Continental Divide in the shelter of forests. Skiers still must cross several large, windswept meadows en route, and some small, yet potential, avalanche slopes during high-hazard periods.

THE ROUTE: From the Rambouillet Yurt, ski south to the marked snowmobile route that comes up from Sawmill Park. Turn to the southeast and follow the wands of the snowmobile route about 1 mile across Rambouillet Park to a point where the route heads south up a draw, still following the snowmobile route. Not much trail-breaking is required here under normal conditions.

From the top of the draw at the trail junction sign, cross the snowmobile trail and begin a gentle descent down the west (right) side of Big Buck Creek. After you descend about 2 miles and roughly 500 feet in elevation, a side tributary to the west (right) becomes apparent where the forest begins to thin out. Contour out of main Big Buck Creek and head directly west up a large tributary, gaining roughly 600 feet to a saddle and the Colorado Trail Friends Memorial Yurt.

Colorado Trail Friends Memorial Yurt welcomes the dawn.

TOUR

14c Camp Trail Trailhead to Colorado Trail Friends Memorial Yurt

SEE MAP PAGES 92 AND 112–113

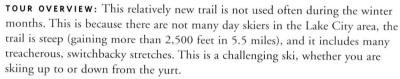

ADVANCED/EXPERT

TIME	2 to 7 hours (depending on direction)
DISTANCE	5.5 miles
ELEVATIONS	TRAILHEAD: 9,250′ YURT: 11,800′ GAIN: +2,530′
AVALANCHE	Some avalanche terrain encountered; easily avoided
MAPS	USGS 7.5′: Slumgullion Pass, 1986; Lake San Cristobal, 1973 National Forest: Gunnison Trails Illustrated: Map #141 (Silverton/Ouray/Telluride/Lake City)

TOUR OVERVIEW: This relatively new trail is not used often during the winter months. This is because there are not many day skiers in the Lake City area, the trail is steep (gaining more than 2,500 feet in 5.5 miles), and it includes many treacherous, switchbacky stretches. This is a challenging ski, whether you are skiing up to or down from the yurt.

And if that's not enough, navigation is tricky throughout, especially on the lower sections, where the trail weaves through confusing aspen forests. The trail is so new that it has not been marked, although the upper section is marked with blue spray paint on trees. The route indicated on the topo map in this book (see pages 112–113) is a close approximation, as the trail does not yet appear on the latest USGS map.

This is unfortunate for hut skiers because it is the shortest, most direct route to the Colorado Trail Friends Memorial Yurt (all other routes go via the Rambouillet and Jon Wilson Memorial Yurts). Consequently, this trail is recommended only for strong, competent skiers who are good backcountry route-finders.

Note: Although described as an ingress route, this trail works better for most people as an egress, or descent, route from the Colorado Trail Friends Memorial Yurt. Skiers can park on Slumgullion Pass, ski to either the Rambouillet or the Jon Wilson Memorial Yurt, then ski to this yurt, and finally exit via the Camp Trail to an awaiting shuttle car.

DIRECTIONS TO TRAILHEAD: Drive south of Lake City to the turnoff to Lake San Cristobal (County Road 30). Drive up this road, first on pavement, then on gravel for a total of 8 miles to the trailhead parking area on the left. The parking area is marked.

THE ROUTE: Ski or walk past the sign and begin traveling on the obvious trail. The first section is easy to follow, although it is sometimes free of snow because of its southern exposure and low elevation. From here the trail ascends on a traverse to the north/northeast and eventually enters an aspen forest. Keep an eye out for the trail, especially if no one has skied in the area lately.

The trail continues upward through the forest, both aspen and evergreen, until it begins to climb onto a distinct ridge that runs east-west and connects with the Continental Divide high above to the east. The trail continues up the sunbaked south face of this ridge through more aspen forests—an area where the trail, now more obvious, is often free of snow. Near the top of the ridge, the trail switchbacks up to the east/northeast and then gains the narrow top of the ridge. There are great views here of the surrounding mountains.

Now turn east and ski directly along the top of the ridge for a few hundred feet through more aspens. Follow the ridge until it becomes a flat shoulder, just below very steep terrain. From here, the trail veers off to the north (left) and begins to climb along a creek that parallels the upper ridge. This is where the blue spray paint markers begin to appear.

Once you are in the shaded forest on the north (left) side of the ridge, keep an eye out for blue markers and climb east toward the higher terrain above. The trail runs along a creek for a short while, then begins to ascend dramatically up a smaller, parallel ridge connected to the main one. To the north is a large, treeless talus slope that comes down from the Continental Divide. Never enter this feature; stay in the safety of the trees to the south (right).

The trail just barely enters the high, southeastern corner of the talus slopes, below a large rockface. Keep an eye out for a faint trail and markers that indicate where the trail traverses due south toward the yurt, up and away from the talus slope. The trail continues traversing until it reaches the edge of another expansive, treeless gullylike feature. Once you enter it, turn uphill to the east/southeast, past two trail markers up to a saddle and the Colorado Trail Friends Memorial Yurt.

Note: For those heading out on this route: To find the trail, leave the yurt and ski north across a meadow. Due west of the yurt is the large, treeless, gullylike feature. Head for the trees along this feature's northern edge. Go past a post, then veer more to the west and drop past another postlike trail marker. Just past this marker the terrain begins to steepen. Drop another 10 to 15 feet past two dead tree stumps and a few trees, then stop. The trail now veers due north (right) and traverses down and around to the left edge of the talus slope. Refer to the above trail descriptions from here on.

Jim Bowen skis in the fluff in the San Juans.

15

Fawn Lakes Yurt

HUT ELEVATION	12,100'
DATE BUILT	1996
SEASONS	Late December through end of April (depending on snowpack)
CAPACITY	4 to 6
HUT LAYOUT	14-foot handmade yurt with cots and bunks
HUT ESSENTIALS	Wood-burning stove for heat, propane cookstove, propane lights, "out-yurts"

Secluded and many miles from civilization, the Fawn Lakes Yurt embodies all that is special about contemporary hut life. This small, 14-foot yurt is located on a forested knoll on the snow-covered shores of the Fawn Lakes at 12,100', making it the most remote and highest of all the Hinsdale Haute Route shelters. The elevated knoll affords nice vistas to the north and east. Towering above the site to the south and west are heavily corniced cirque walls, which can pose potential avalanche threats for anyone who meanders too closely. They also reflect the morning alpenglow, bathing the entire cirque in warm light. Note that to leave Fawn Lakes Yurt, parties must retrace their ingress route back through the system as no trailheads offer direct access to it.

True backcountry telemark skiing here is probably the most unlimited of any in the Hinsdale Haute Route system. Directly north of the Fawn Lakes Yurt are many gladed slopes for powder skiing and a huge basin and gentle peaks to the north and west that offer moderate skiing above tree line.

Call the Hinsdale Haute Route system for the status of this yurt (see Appendix A).

RECOMMENDED DAY TRIPS:

You can easily access the high ridge to the south and west of the yurt by skiing east from the hut on a traverse to a spot where you can scoot up onto the lower reaches of an eastern spur of the ridge. Once on top of the broad spur, change course and head west as far as you feel inclined. The peak known as the Rio Grande Pyramid (13,821') lies far off to the south, and the rugged uplift of Bristol Head is far off to the east near Creede.

You'll also find many acres to explore on the knob immediately west of the yurt and to the north.

The remote, quaint Fawn Lakes Yurt embodies hut life.

INTERMEDIATE/ADVANCED

SEE MAP PAGES 92 AND 112–113

TOUR

15a Colorado Trail Friends Memorial Yurt to Fawn Lakes Yurt via Continental Divide

TIME	4 to 6 hours
DISTANCE	4.2 miles
ELEVATIONS	CTFM YURT: 11,800' FL YURT: 12,100' GAIN/LOSS: +980'/-680'
AVALANCHE	Route crosses avalanche runout zones; can be dangerous during high-hazard periods
MAPS	USGS 7.5': Slumgullion Pass, 1986; Lake San Cristobal, 1973 National Forest: Gunnison Trails Illustrated: Map #141 (Silverton/Ouray/Telluride/Lake City)

TOUR OVERVIEW: This route is similar in character to the route between the Rambouillet Yurt and the Colorado Trail Friends Memorial Yurt (Tour 14a, see page 104). But this tour is shorter, exposes skiers to fewer potential avalanche hazards, and, overall, seems less strenuous. Under clear skies and on a solid snowpack, you can make quick progress across the ridge. Probably the most difficult stretch is navigating the hummocky terrain on the final half-mile.

An alternate foul-weather route traverses roughly 500 feet below to the east (see dotted line, page 112). It is about as difficult and approximately the same length as this tour, and the route is obvious.

Above and south of Fawn Lakes Yurt, Jerry Gray gazes at 13,821-foot Rio Grande Pyramid.

THE ROUTE: Begin the tour by leaving the Colorado Trail Friends Memorial Yurt and descending down-valley to the east over gentle terrain. After only about 100 feet of elevation, look for a narrow finger of meadow (visible from the yurt) that cuts directly into the forest on the south. Head into this clearing and ski to the far southeastern (left) corner. From here, markers and a trail cut (the Colorado Trail) lead due south through the forest and up onto the top of a wide-open ridge. From this vantage point, the rest of the route is visible to the west and south.

Turn due west (right) and begin the slow, gradual ascent toward Elevation Point 12,490'. You do not have to climb directly to the top of this point, but on a clear day the views make it worthwhile. From here, either travel south directly along the crest of the Continental Divide or traverse lower along the eastern flank. This second option may provide more protection from the elements. *Note:* The foul-weather route descends off the point for about 200 feet, then makes a long traverse south toward Fawn Lakes.

Continue south until the ridge begins to fade into a large basin. Contour slightly to the west and descend as you cross the basin. Aim for the left (eastern) side of the highest forested knoll, which is framed against the cirque walls to the south/southeast. Navigation tools are handy here for choosing the most direct route to the yurt. Just remember to stay around 12,000 feet as you ski back into the woods and traverse east toward the southeastern boundary of the basin. Also be sure to traverse below the short, steep, forested slopes that protect the northern aspects of the knoll.

Once you're on the east side of the knoll, climb up through an indistinct creek

Morning has broken at Fawn Lakes Yurt.

drainage to the edge of the trees and a small lake just below the eastern flank of the knoll. The Fawn Lakes Yurt is located directly on top of a small, flat, bench-like knoll on the northern edge of the largest lake. The southeastern-most of the Fawn Lakes, it is marked at 12,062 feet on the USGS topo map. Bear in mind that all of these small lakes are often covered with a deep layer of snow and the area may look more like a meadow.

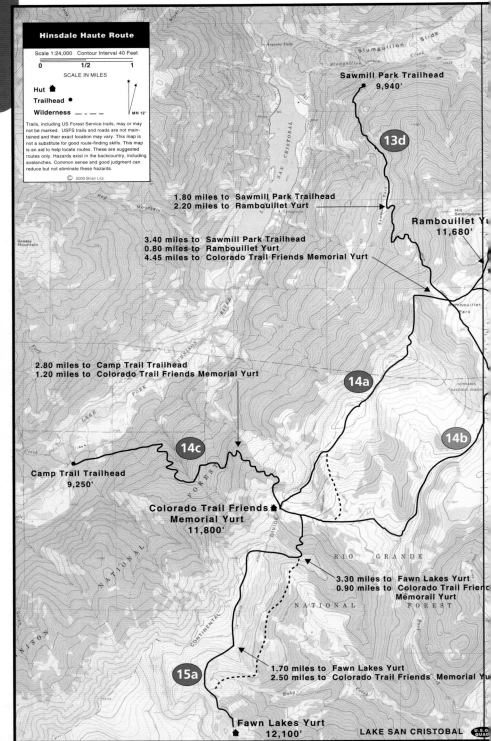

Hinsdale Haute Route

Scale 1:24,000   Contour Interval 40 Feet

0   1/2   1

SCALE IN MILES

Hut 🏠

Trailhead ●

Wilderness — – – — / MN 12°

Trails, including US Forest Service trails, may or may not be marked. USFS trails and roads are not maintained and their exact location may vary. This map is not a substitute for good route-finding skills. This map is an aid to help locate routes. These are suggested routes only. Hazards exist in the backcountry, including avalanches. Common sense and good judgment can reduce but not eliminate these hazards.

© 2000 Brian Litz

Sawmill Park Trailhead
9,940'

13d

1.80 miles to Sawmill Park Trailhead
2.20 miles to Rambouillet Yurt

3.40 miles to Sawmill Park Trailhead
0.80 miles to Rambouillet Yurt
4.45 miles to Colorado Trail Friends Memorial Yurt

Rambouillet Yu
11,680'

2.80 miles to Camp Trail Trailhead
1.20 miles to Colorado Trail Friends Memorial Yurt

14a

14b

14c

Camp Trail Trailhead
9,250'

Colorado Trail Friends
Memorial Yurt
11,800'

3.30 miles to Fawn Lakes Yurt
0.90 miles to Colorado Trail Frienc
Memorail Yurt

15a

1.70 miles to Fawn Lakes Yurt
2.50 miles to Colorado Trail Friends Memorial Yu

Fawn Lakes Yurt
12,100'

LAKE SAN CRISTOBAL

U.S.G.
QUAD

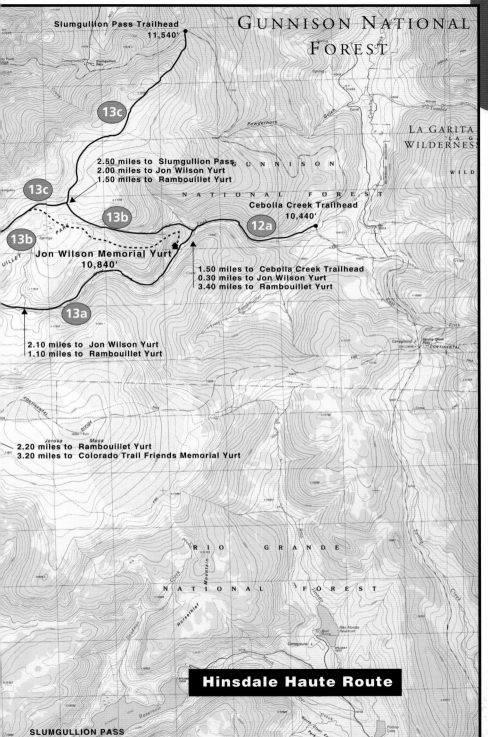

Slumgullion Pass Trailhead
11,540'

GUNNISON NATIONAL
FOREST

13c

2.50 miles to Slumgullion Pass
2.00 miles to Jon Wilson Yurt
1.50 miles to Rambouillet Yurt

13c

13b

13b

Cebolla Creek Trailhead
10,440'

12a

Jon Wilson Memorial Yurt
10,840'

1.50 miles to Cebolla Creek Trailhead
0.30 miles to Jon Wilson Yurt
3.40 miles to Rambouillet Yurt

13a

2.10 miles to Jon Wilson Yurt
1.10 miles to Rambouillet Yurt

2.20 miles to Rambouillet Yurt
3.20 miles to Colorado Trail Friends Memorial Yurt

LA GARITA
WILDERNESS

Hinsdale Haute Route

SLUMGULLION PASS

San Juan Independent Huts

This section of *Colorado Hut to Hut, Volume II,* offers a mixed bag of backcountry huts spread across the whole of the San Juan Mountains from east to west. Since the last edition of this book, the San Juans have seen the most new hut construction. These new shelters are mostly in new hut systems that are still too small to warrant their own section in this book or are simply stand-alone huts.

Of the huts now included in this independent hut section, most are yurts—and most of these are in the eastern and southeastern San Juans. The new Spruce Hole Yurt sits near the Southwest Nordic Center on the northern end of the area referred to as Cumbres Pass in the southeastern San Juans, and it well represents this trend toward yurts. The hut is ideal for beginning skiers. And just above Creede to the north are the Phoenix Ridge Yurts. These two upscale yurts sit almost side by side, separated by a short, five-minute walk.

Anyone familiar with Colorado skiing knows that the Wolf Creek Pass area is ground zero for powder skiing with its annual state record for snowfall. Most skiers arrive to ride the lifts at the resort, but a savvy cadre of skiers knows intimately the freakishly excellent backcountry skiing to be had in all directions from the summit of the pass.

East of the resort is the new Pass Creek Yurt. Like the Creede yurts and huts, this is the first, I hope, of a series of yurts that will provide access to the terrain east of the ski area.

On a sad note, the old International Alpine School Hut burned down several years ago and the promising Scotch Creek Yurt was closed for operation in 1999. This closure speaks to the difficulty of running backcountry shelters, and to the amount of tenacity required to take a hut system from the conceptual stage to the long-term operational stage. It would be great if someone would take over and re-open the Scotch Creek Yurt.

The Saint Paul Lodge continues its third decade of successful operation. Red Mountain Pass was the center of extensive mining during the late 1800s and early 1900s. While the age of the lodge itself is not known, the small cabin nearby was built in 1887. Owned and operated by Christopher George, the lodge is one of the old-timers in Colorado hut country and remains a unique experience for all skiers and a jumping-off point for sensational alpine ski-touring.

Bob Moore busts it in U.S. Basin above the Saint Paul Lodge and the Million Dollar Highway (Red Mountain Pass).

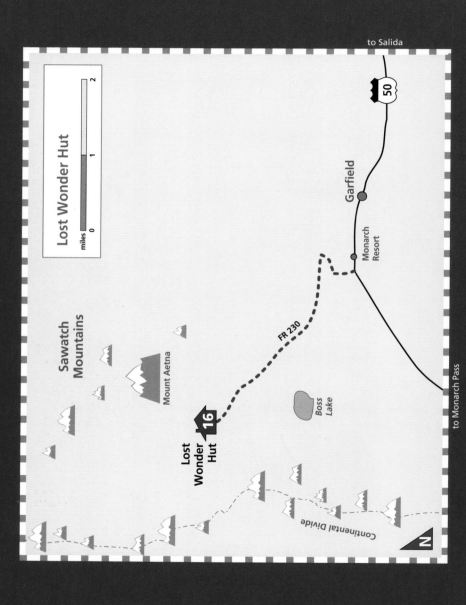

Lost Wonder Hut

miles
0   1   2

Sawatch
Mountains

Mount Aetna

Lost
Wonder
Hut 16

Boss
Lake

Continental Divide

FR 230

Monarch
Resort

Garfield

50

to Salida

to Monarch Pass

N

Lost Wonder Hut (Sawatch Range)

HUT ELEVATION	10,900'
DATE BUILT	Original building mid-1950s; renovations throughout 1990s
SEASONS	Year-round
CAPACITY	8 to 10
HUT LAYOUT	2-story wood hut with 2 private bunkrooms upstairs; 1 double bed in loft, 3 twin beds in upstairs community room, 3 twins downstairs
HUT ESSENTIALS	Wood-burning stove for heat, propane stove and oven, photovoltaic lights, all kitchenware, mattresses and pillows, adjacent outhouse
OTHER GOODIES	Spring water (directions in hut)

Anyone driving over Monarch Pass under clear conditions can't help but notice the distinctive profile of Mount Aetna to the north. Lost Wonder Hut sits at the foot of this 13,743-foot mountain in the Middle Fork of the South Arkansas River drainage. This drainage is quiet during the winter and sees few skiers or snow-mobilers, although the presence of the hut will undoubtedly encourage more people to visit this high-country valley.

Named after the Lost Wonder Mine, this new hut is an old mining cabin that has been "pop-topped." The original first floor now houses the kitchen, dining room, and community area. The new second floor has two bedrooms, a loft, and a large community and sleeping area with tall, south-facing windows that gather copious amounts of solar energy, making this a great place to take a nap, read a book, or just enjoy the mountain panorama. There is a new deck off the south side for sun-worshippers and a new mudroom for ski storage under the second-story deck.

The Lost Wonder Hut is fully equipped with all the necessary amenities. It sleeps 8 to 10 comfortably. Book reservations through the Continental Divide Hut System, LLC (see Appendix A).

RECOMMENDED DAY TRIPS:

Once at the hut, you can tour to the head of the valley or explore the surrounding glades and burns. Watch out for hazardous avalanche terrain. You can also head up the valley and over the pass at the northern end and drop down to Saint Elmo. You will have to leave a shuttle car up in the valley for this extended tour. Or you can hike or ski back down to Boss Lake.

In the springtime, the steeper walls of the valley offer unlimited options for spring descent and peak climbs after the snowpack has stabilized.

TOUR 16a
Garfield Trailhead to Lost Wonder Hut
SEE MAP PAGES 116 AND 119

INTERMEDIATE

TIME	2 to 4 hours
DISTANCE	3 miles
ELEVATIONS	TRAILHEAD: 9,660' HUT: 10,900' GAIN: +1,240'
AVALANCHE	Route crosses avalanche runout zone; can be dangerous during high-hazard periods
MAPS	USGS 7.5': Garfield, 1982
	National Forest: San Isabel
	Trails Illustrated: Map #130 (Salida/St. Elmo/Shavano Peak)

TOUR OVERVIEW: The route to the Lost Wonder Hut follows a summer four-wheel-drive road. Except for a few intersections and a crossing at the bottom of an avalanche runout zone, this route is straightforward and, for the most part, quite safe.

$\sum$ breakfast being a function of:
$\geq (f)\,\frac{M_1 \cdot M_2}{R}$ x Velocity^2
$3^2 \cdot 2y)\,/\,2\pi R - 0.5$ [mass of yolks]
$E=mc^2 + (4k)$ Earth's rotation =
tasty hotcakes 4 me!

"Dr. Flapjack," Mike O'Brien calculates a trajectory.

DIRECTIONS TO TRAILHEAD: Drive on U.S. 50 to the tiny town of Garfield, which is roughly 4 miles below the summit of Monarch Pass. Park across the street from the Monarch Lodge, just to the north, at a plowed area for highway maintenance vehicles, making sure you don't block the post with electrical outlets. To find the trail, walk uphill along the northern shoulder of the highway, past the snowmobile rental business. Immediately on the western edge is a forked trailhead/road with a sign to Boss Lake.

THE ROUTE: Take the right fork, following the route to Boss Lake, and begin climbing a steep, south-facing road. Within minutes the trail intersects a flat, low-angled, abandoned railroad grade that looks like a road. Do not turn here. Cross the grade and begin to climb again, then head to the northeast (right) toward a switchback. Follow the switchback around to the left and start the climb into the valley along a steep, open trail that is often sun-hardened.

The trail eventually enters a forest, and from here the route simply follows a road, bypassing small cabins, mines, the occasional side road, and the turnoff to Boss Lake near the 1.7-mile mark. Continue climbing until the road enters an obvious treeless area that marks the lower reaches of a huge, avalanche-prone gully on the southern flank of Mount Aetna. Be careful, for you can easily start a snowslide. From here it is possible to see the Sangre de Cristo Mountains to the southeast.

Once you enter the forest again, the hut is not much farther. Travel past two ancient Forest Service cabins on the right, drop down slightly, and cross a small creek, then follow the road up a slight incline to the two-story Lost Wonder Hut.

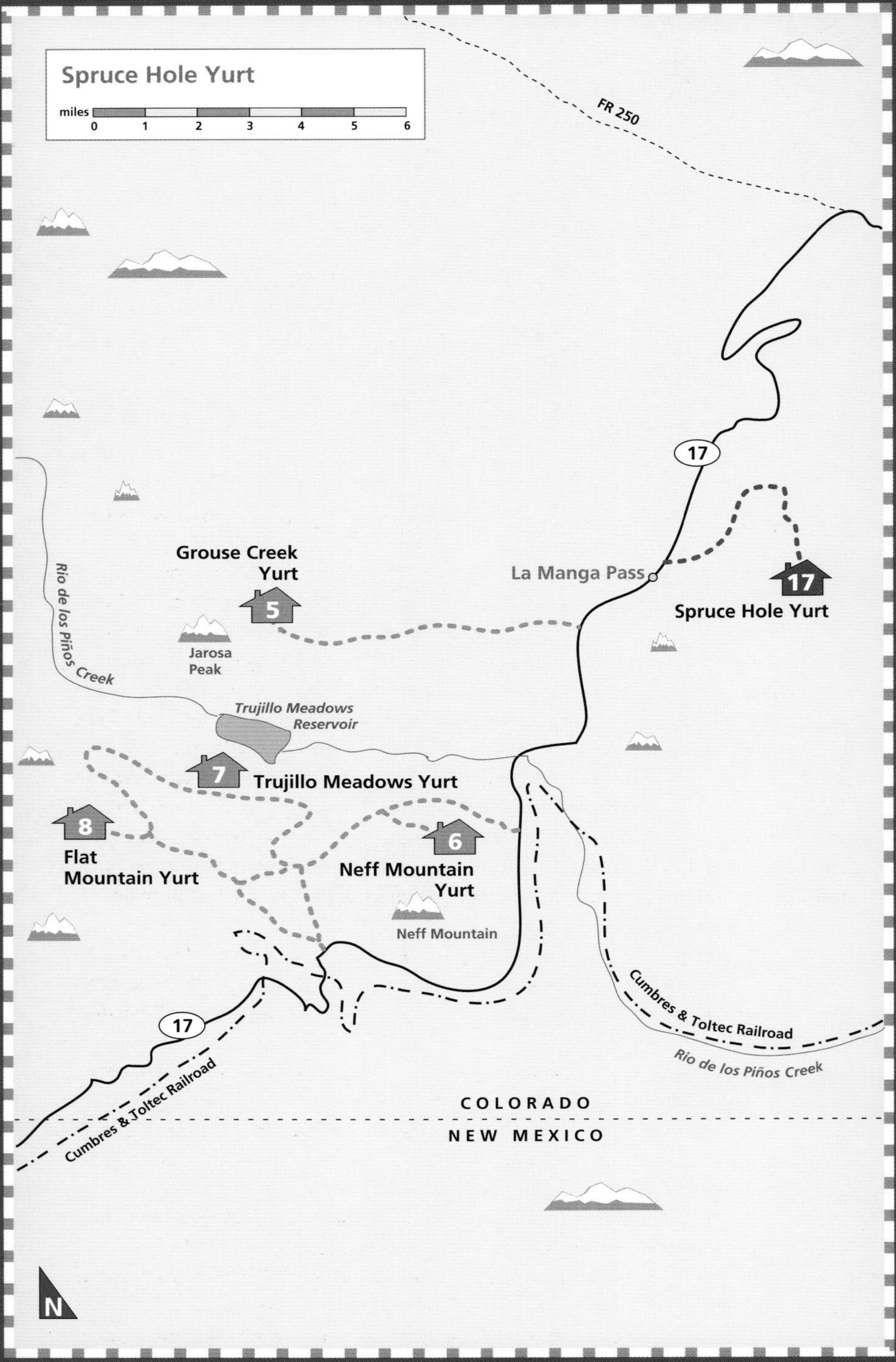

Spruce Hole Yurt

miles
0 1 2 3 4 5 6

FR 250

to Antonito

17

Grouse Creek
Yurt

5

La Manga Pass

17

Spruce Hole Yurt

Jarosa
Peak

Rio de los Piños Creek

Trujillo Meadows
Reservoir

7 Trujillo Meadows Yurt

8

Flat
Mountain Yurt

6 Neff Mountain
Yurt

Neff Mountain

Cumbres & Toltec Railroad

17

Cumbres & Toltec Railroad

Rio de los Piños Creek

COLORADO

NEW MEXICO

N

17 Spruce Hole Yurt

HUT ELEVATION	10,600´
DATE BUILT	1998
SEASONS	November 1 through April 30 (depending on snowpack)
CAPACITY	6
HUT LAYOUT	20-foot yurt with single bunk beds over a double bed and a queen-sized bed
HUT ESSENTIALS	Wood-burning stove for heat, propane cookstove, propane lights, all kitchenware and seasoning
OTHER GOODIES	Observation tower for stargazing; full bedding (no sleeping bags needed)

Spruce Hole Yurt is owned and operated by Cumbres Nordic Adventures. It sits across the road from the Southwest Nordic Center yurts on the northern end of the uplift commonly referred to as Cumbres Pass. The Cumbres Pass area straddles a southern-extending arm of the San Juan Mountains and is notable for its consistent and deep snowpack. Actually, though, Cumbres "Pass" is a long plateau with twin highpoints. The highpoint named "Cumbres Pass" lies on the southern end of the plateau, and La Manga Pass, the other highpoint, lies on the northern end.

The entire plateau is dominated by topography that is ideal for cross-country Nordic skiing. Rolling mountains and ridges gently separated by wide-open meadows and creek drainages abound. This is kick-and-glide country, where waxable touring and lighter-weight telemark gear rule. Around the hut lie thousands of acres for touring, and the steep, forested gradients hidden uphill above the hut provide ample and sweet telemark terrain.

Spruce Hole Yurt is easy to reach, yet its short, 2-mile, moderately pitched approach road offers even neophyte skiers incredible views throughout its length. And even if your downhill technique is limited to the snowplow, you will be able to master the return trip easily.

The yurt itself is unusual and especially comfortable. Standing in the center is a handmade table supported by three beams. Jutting straight up through the center of the table is an old, peeled tree trunk upon which sits an antique swiveling desk chair directly under a clear dome at the apex of the roof. Climb aboard this stargazing observation tower and catch up on your astronomy.

Also unusual—and welcome—are the supremely comfortable futons and the fully stocked linens and bedding. No need for a sleeping bag here!

Spruce Hole Yurt is an ideal place to introduce anyone to hut life. Its approach is easy and scenic. And though it is only a short ski from the trailhead, it is far from large metro areas—which limits nighttime light pollution while maximizing the magical effects of a starry night.

RECOMMENDED DAY TRIPS:

You can continue south along the road in front of the yurt, contouring along the gentler eastern flank of Pinorealosa Mountain until you reach Spruce Hole Yurt. Return to the fork in the road and the locked gate via an easterly forest road that runs north-south just west of the rounded Elevation Point 10,624'. Frankly, though, you can create your own route throughout this secluded basin.

Skiers looking for vertical or a bit more arduous exercise can pick a route up onto Pinorealosa Mountain for stunning views in every direction. On a clear day, you can even pick out the Blanca Peak group and Culebra Peak of the southern Sangre de Cristo Mountains to the northeast and east, respectively. If you want turns, you can ski off the northwest slopes of the mountain and crank-turn back down to the approach road. Or ski back down to the yurt via the steeper terrain behind the hut. The eastern slopes have lots of less demanding slopes to ski, too. Once you're on top of Pinorealosa, consider a long tour south along the ridge-crest.

Mary Ann DeBoer greets the world from the deck of Spruce Hole Yurt.

NOVICE

TOUR
17a La Manga Summit Trailhead to Spruce Hole Yurt
SEE MAP PAGES 58, 61, 120, AND 124

TIME	1 to 3 hours
DISTANCE	2.25 miles
ELEVATIONS	TRAILHEAD: 10,200' YURT: 10,600' GAIN: +400'
AVALANCHE	Minimal danger
MAPS	USGS 7.5': Cumbres, 1967; Osier, 1967
	National Forest: Rio Grande

TOUR OVERVIEW: Presently the one route to the yurt is via Spruce Hole Road. This route is very straightforward, with minimal route-finding complications, avalanche hazard, and elevation gain. It has the added benefit of great views across the northern skyline.

DIRECTIONS TO TRAILHEAD: To reach the trailhead from Chama, New Mexico, drive north on Hwy 17 from Chama over Cumbres Pass. Continue north—passing several parking areas for the Southwest Nordic Systems trailheads en route—until you pass the La Manga Summit sign. The signed turnoff to Spruce Hole is roughly 0.25 mile north of this sign, with a total driving distance from Chama of 20 miles.

From the Colorado side, drive west and south from Antonito in the San Luis Valley on Hwy 17 for 28 miles. Again, the signed turnoff to Spruce Hole is 0.25 mile north of the La Manga Pass sign. If you reach the La Manga Pass sign, you've gone too far. Turn around and drive back 0.25 mile. Normally there is a plowed parking area on the east side of the road at the beginning of Spruce Hole Road. If, for some reason, this area is not plowed, park near the La Manga Pass sign and walk back to the trailhead.

Unique to Spruce Hole Yurt is its "observatory."

THE ROUTE: Head east on Spruce Hole Road and follow the obvious road around the northern extension of Pinorealosa Mountain. Make a short, gliding descent heading south along the eastern flank of the ridge, veer east along the road, and arrive at a fork in the road. Turn right (southeast) and continue into an old logging area. Bypass a locked gate and continue through a clearing dotted with small, sparse, secondary-growth trees until you arrive at the yurt, which sits in the meadow tucked to the base of a high, northeast-facing, forested hill.

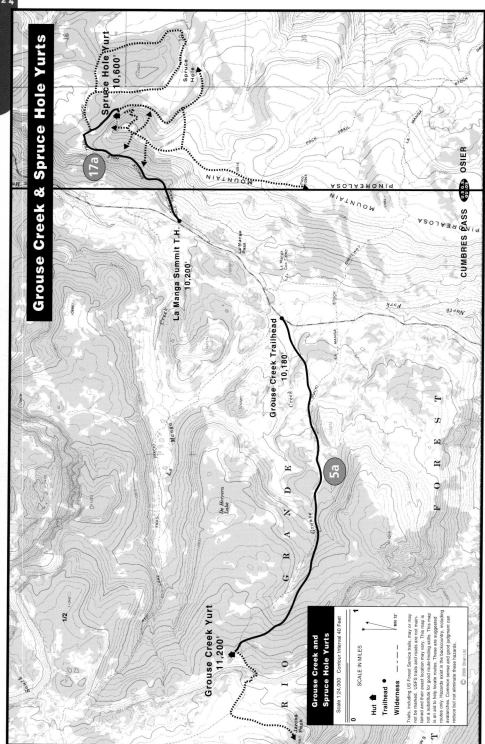

Grouse Creek & Spruce Hole Yurts

Spruce Hole Yurt
10,600'

Spruce Hole

17a

PINOREALOSA MOUNTAIN

MOUNTAIN

OSIER

CUMBRES PASS

PINOREALOSA

U.S. GAS GUIDES

La Manga Summit T.H.
10,200'

La Manga Pass

Grouse Creek Trailhead
10,180'

5a

R I O   G R A N D E   F O R E S T

Grouse Creek Yurt
11,200'

Grouse Creek and Spruce Hole Yurts

Scale 1:24,000   Contour Interval 40 Feet

SCALE IN MILES

0   1/2   1

Hut
Trailhead
Wilderness

MN 12°

Trails, including US Forest Service trails, may or may not be marked. USFS trails and roads are not maintained and their exact location may vary. This map is not a substitute for good route-finding skills. This map is an aid to help locate routes. These are suggested routes only. Hazards exist in the backcountry, including avalanches. Common sense and good judgment can reduce but not eliminate these hazards.

© 2000 Brian Litz

KELTY APPAREL. LIGHTWEIGHT, PACKABLE OUTDOOR GEAR THAT DOES EVERYTHING BUT TAKE UP SPACE.

16 oz. Helium jacket
Waterproof I Breathable I Self-stuffing

800-423-2320 I www.kelty.com
Kelty Canada 514-733-4700

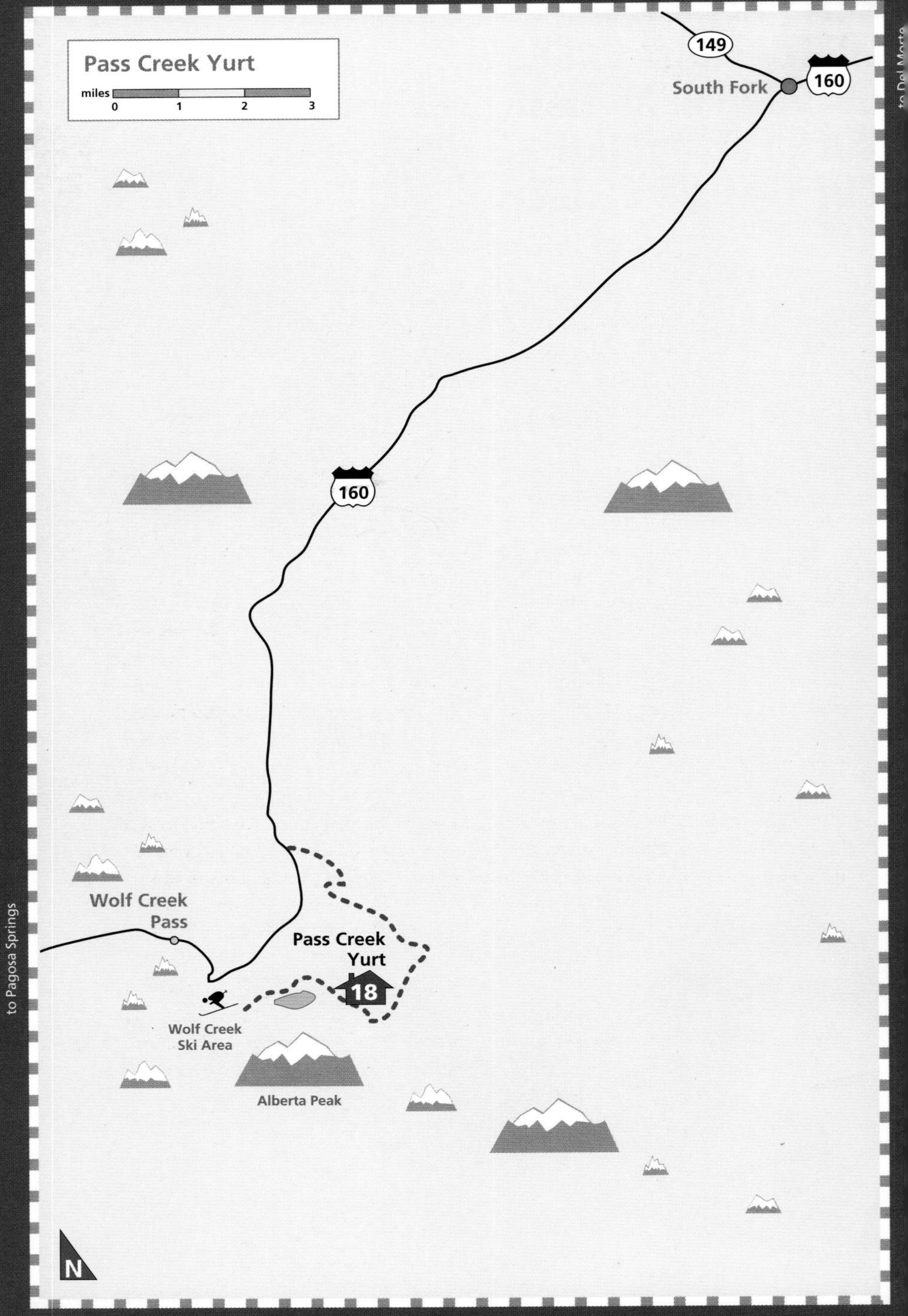

Pass Creek Yurt

miles
0   1   2   3

149

160

South Fork

to Del Norte

160

to Pagosa Springs

Wolf Creek
Pass

Pass Creek
Yurt

18

Wolf Creek
Ski Area

Alberta Peak

N

18

Pass Creek Yurt

HUT ELEVATION	10,250'
DATE BUILT	1997
SEASONS	Thanksgiving through April
CAPACITY	6
HUT LAYOUT	20-foot yurt with futon bunk beds
HUT ESSENTIALS	Wood-burning stove for heat, propane cookstove and lights, all kitchenware, outhouse; no dogs allowed

Colorado's savvy skiers are familiar with the Wolf Creek Pass area for one reason: prodigious snowfall. The pass itself snakes over a north-south appendage of the mighty San Juan Mountains. The local topography is such that this little southern Colorado sub-range sucks moisture out of the prevailing westerlies at an alarming rate. Atop the pass is the diminutive Wolf Creek ski area, which in a normal year can have double the average snow base of the major resorts to the north.

Though the backcountry skiing easily is the best pure-powder backcountry skiing and touring off any major highway in the state, few skiers—other than secretive locals—take advantage of this blizzard-born bounty. In fact, the dearth of nearby major metro areas assures skiers of copious amounts of purebred powder.

In 1997, the area's first backcountry hut—the Pass Creek Yurt—opened southeast of the pass and the resort. This conventionally appointed, six-person canvas cupcake resides an easy 3-mile tour away (to the east/southeast) from the resort parking area, yet it provides access to heretofore rarely visited and ideal freeheel tele bowls and glades. Lower down on the east side of the pass is the road to the summer Forest Service campground known as Tucker Ponds. This road was the primary route devised for getting to the yurt. The route from the ski area, however, probably will prove to be the most popular over time because of its shorter length and minimal elevation gain.

The yurt is tucked into a beautiful (though logged) basin offering easily a week's worth of steep shots and tree skiing with lots of elbowroom. With much terrain a snowball's throw away from the front deck, mornings can be latte-lazy and afternoons filled with short skin ascents and invigorating descents. For freeheelers of any ilk, the Pass Creek Yurt is truly paradise found.

RECOMMENDED DAY TRIPS:

Pass Creek Yurt sits below ideal free-heel backcountry terrain. The north-facing terrain west of the yurt has nice, lower-angled runs that can be skied down toward Pass Creek and the Tucker Ponds Road. Take the main road back around the last ridge, then climb south to gain more vertical. The small drainage southwest of the yurt is a nice, quiet area for a short tour. And, of course, any of the terrain south of the hut can be plundered. Simply head up through the logged terrain and follow the path of your choosing.

Dave Waltz-ing through a backcountry ballroom near Wolf Creek Pass.

TOUR
18a

Wolf Creek Ski Area Trailhead to Pass Creek Yurt
SEE MAP PAGES 126 AND 132

TIME	2 to 4 hours
DISTANCE	2.8 miles
ELEVATIONS	TRAILHEAD: 10,600' YURT: 10,250' GAIN/LOSS: +357'/-717'
AVALANCHE	Minimal danger
MAPS	USGS 7.5': Wolf Creek Pass, 1984; Elwood Pass, 1966 National Forest: Rio Grande

TOUR OVERVIEW: This is the shortest, most direct tour to the yurt. For the most part, the route follows old Forest Service logging roads the entire distance. Because the roads are buried under snow and are rarely skied or snowmobiled, the tour maintains a nice backcountry air. Though mostly a traverse, this route actually has a net loss of elevation because of the initial descent through the Nordic area to the Alberta Park Reservoir Spillway and dam. After that, the tour rolls along, gaining and losing minimal elevation while providing extensive views to the north and west.

Overall, this is an enjoyable line that offers just enough moderate backcountry route-finding challenges to hold your attention and keep you on your toes. You'll also encounter fewer snowmobiles on this route, compared to the Tucker Ponds route.

Note: The ski area has put in a new lift just east of the parking lot, which has displaced the trail in Alberta Park ever so slightly to the north.

DIRECTIONS TO TRAILHEAD:
Trailhead parking is at the Wolf Creek Ski Resort. The turnoff to the resort is off U.S. 160 roughly 1 mile east (the San Luis Valley/Del Norte side, not the Pagosa Springs/Durango side) of the summit of Wolf Creek Pass. Pull

Pass Creek Yurt

off the highway to the south and drive through the resort parking area, aiming for the very end of the lower parking terrace. Park close to the end, and as unobtrusively as possible. Wolf Creek Backcountry will issue you a parking permit to display in your window.

THE ROUTE: Leave your car and walk or ski off the eastern terminus of the parking area. Immediately begin a gradual descent east, then southeast, following the Nordic trails until you glide out into the Alberta Park Meadow. Here you will encounter the new lift. Again on trails, pass around to the left (north) of the chairlift base facilities. Now follow an obvious road along the northern edge of the meadow east until you reach the dam at the diminutive Alberta Park Reservoir.

Ski across the dam and make a steep, short climb up the west-facing hillside immediately east of the dam. Switchback up the short climb until the angle levels off. Continue an easterly course on a gently ascending traverse cross-country through tiny clearings. Eventually you will begin to enter old logging areas and meadows.

In the area west of Elevation Point 10,615' and north of Railroad Pass at an elevation of roughly 10,120 feet, the route traverses this moderate terrain, aiming for the pass just north of Elevation Point 10,615'. As you ascend toward the pass, the trail eventually gains a logging road running east-west. This is the road you will follow to the yurt. Ski east and then contour slightly to the northeast, aiming for the prominent ridge to the east. This ridge has two "knobs," and the road passes between them. The

Mark Mueller skis above Pass Creek Yurt.

crest of the ridge forms a nice promontory with unobstructed views from west to east across the northern horizon, where the road passes over it.

Once past the ridge-crest, the road veers sharply south (right) for a short distance and then contours east/northeast through more logging areas on the last gradual traverse before rounding another north-running ridge. Head south slightly downhill along the still-prominent road until you reach the yurt, which sits just off the road on a small, obvious shelf.

NOVICE/INTERMEDIATE

TOUR
18b
Tucker Ponds Trailhead to Pass Creek Yurt
SEE MAP PAGES 126 AND 132

TIME	3 to 6 hours		
DISTANCE	5.5 to 6.8 miles		
ELEVATIONS	TRAILHEAD: 9,206'	YURT: 10,250'	GAIN: +1,044'
AVALANCHE	Minimal danger		
MAPS	USGS 7.5': Wolf Creek Pass, 1984; Elwood Pass, 1966		
	National Forest: Rio Grande		

TOUR OVERVIEW: This route follows an obvious, snow-covered summer road (Forest Road 390) up through the Pass Creek Valley. While it provides summer access to the campground, the road continues well toward the head of the valley. The road was once used to access logging roads higher up the valley; one of these roads takes you to the yurt.

Today the route is a gentle, multi-use trail for skiing and snowmobiling. You will find the occasional blue or orange diamond marking the road. Although you may encounter a few snowmobiles, they typically translate into minimal trail-breaking and a solid, supportive base for touring. If you follow the road continuously, the route is approximately 6.8 miles. If you take advantage of shortcuts, the length is more like 5.5 miles.

DIRECTIONS TO TRAILHEAD: The parking area is 6 miles east of Wolf Creek Pass and 12.5 miles southwest of South Fork. There is a plowed parking area on the east side of the road.

THE ROUTE: Leave the cars and ski along the gently inclined road. After passing the Tucker Ponds campground, the road contours around the base of Elevation Point 9,775'. On the south side of this hill, you can cut straight across the flat area to shortcut a switchback. A similar maneuver can be executed near Elevation Point 9,800', where the road makes two clean switchbacks as it ascends away from the creek along the southern slopes of the valley.

Near the 9,940'/5.5-mile mark, a drainage comes in from the right (south). Here you can ski up through the drainage on either side, or cut uphill southeast to one of the side logging roads that leads directly to the hut. You can also reach this side logging road by simply following the main road to the road intersection a bit farther up the valley at 10,040 feet.

This side logging road is distinct and traverses south up this side drainage on the eastern (left) side. As you near the yurt, the road switchbacks sharply to the north/northwest (right), climbing steadily, though moderately, to the yurt. Note that the upper part of this road near the yurt does not show up on the current USGS topos.

132

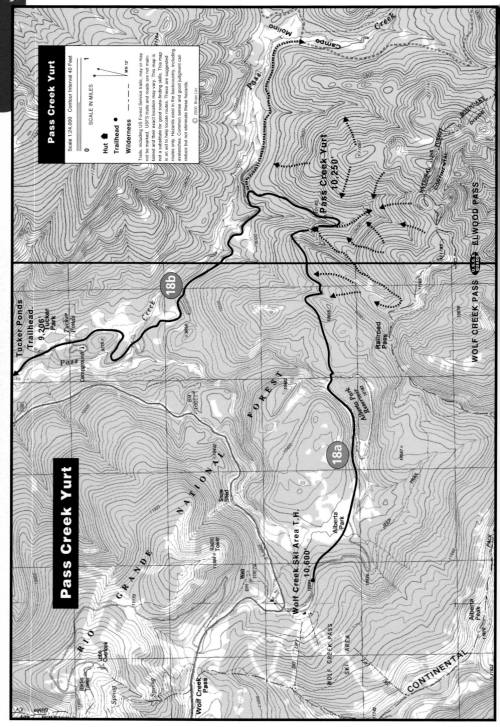

Mark Mueller basks in the "Divine Lite" at Wolf Creek Pass.

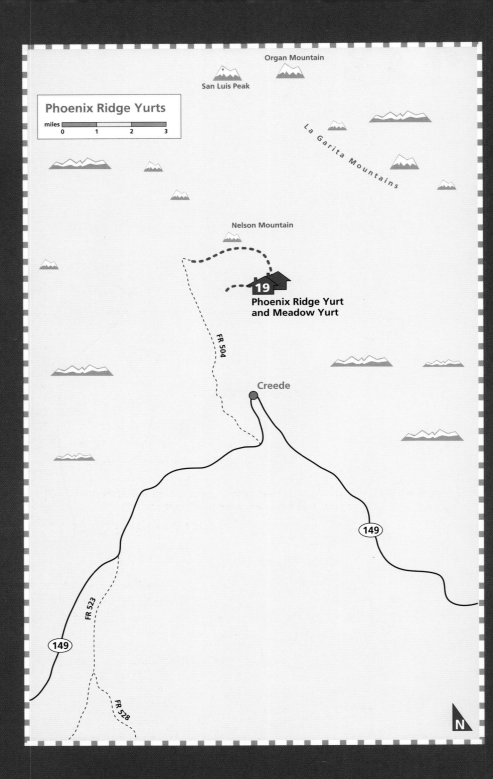

19 Phoenix Ridge Yurts

PHOENIX RIDGE YURT	
HUT ELEVATION	10,500'
DATE BUILT	1998
SEASONS	November 15 through April 1 (winter), June 15 through October 10 (summer)
CAPACITY	6
HUT LAYOUT	20-foot yurt with 1 queen-size futon, 1 full sofa bed, and 2 cots
HUT ESSENTIALS	Wood-burning stove for heat, propane cookstove and oven, all kitchenware, photovoltaic lights
OTHER GOODIES	Attached 12-foot yurt that is a heated bathroom, shower, composting toilet; large deck (with killer views); signed and groomed Nordic trails
MEADOW YURT **HUT ELEVATION**	10,500'
DATE BUILT	1998
SEASONS	November 15 through April 1 (winter), June 15 through October 10 (summer)
CAPACITY	6
HUT LAYOUT	20-foot yurt with 1 queen-size futon sofa bed, 1 bunk, and 2 cots
HUT ESSENTIALS	Wood-burning stove for heat, propane cookstove and oven, all kitchenware, photovoltaic lights
OTHER GOODIES	Attached heated bathroom with propane-incinerating toilet, shower, large deck, signed and groomed Nordic trails

Rising out of the historical ashes of Creede's heyday as a booming mining mecca are the twin shelters of the Phoenix Ridge Yurts. Much overlooked as a place to play in the winter, Creede has long been a popular summer destination and is the home of a renowned repertory theater and the Wheeler Geologic Area. Creede is starting to gain recognition for summer mountain biking as well as winter skiing. No matter what time of year you visit, Creede offers much uninhabited terrain for non-motorized recreationists to explore.

The two yurts—Phoenix Ridge Yurt and Meadow Yurt—sit on a forested bench north of town near Campbell Mountain. The site of some of the area's earliest mining activity, Campbell Mountain is really more like a ridge, whose monolithic prow cleaves the east and west Willow Creek drainages at the edge of town. You can kick back on the deck of the Phoenix Ridge Yurt and take in the view across East Willow Creek to the rampart of the La Garita (spanish, "lookout") Mountains to the northeast. Since the area is an old mining site, it is dotted with historic cabins, ruins, and even a few open vertical mine shafts of which you should be wary.

What is unique about these two yurts is that even though they are in a gorgeous, remote locale, they are much like a backcountry destination resort. There are no other huts to tour to (yet), and by their shortest approach, the huts are only a mile from the trailhead via an easy road—though there are more difficult alternatives. The yurts themselves are standard kit yurts with every conceivable option added on—and then some.

Inside these comfy shelters are real beds and origami-like futon couches that open up into equally soothing nests. Each hut is fitted with private shower units fueled by water heated on the stove. It is hard to find a more upscale, portable backcountry abode. This is a perfect spot to just get away.

The yurts sit a quick five-minute walk apart and can be reserved individually or together. All in all, the Phoenix Ridge Yurts are inviting, unusual, and worth a look.

RECOMMENDED DAY TRIPS:

Around the yurts is a cornucopia of potential activities and tours. Using the yurts as a base camp, you can kick-and-glide around the yurts on the systems marked "Nordic trails," tour out to the spectacular Hobbit, climb 12,038-foot Nelson Mountain or other unnamed peaks, downhill terrain directly to the north, or, for the most ambitious, plan a surgical spring strike to ski 14,014-foot San Luis Peak.

The Hobbit is the rocky buttress at the south end of the ridge, just above town. The ridge immediately behind the Hobbit, on the yurt side, can be reached via a 1.5-mile tour through the woods followed by a safe, but airy, exposed traverse along the ridge. From the yurts, ski south and follow these marked trails around and then south from Campbell Mountain: Holy Moses Road, HM2 Trail, Ski Bowl Trail, South Campbell Mountain Loop, and Hobbit Connector. Eventually the Hobbit four-wheel-drive road leads out onto the ever-narrowing and ever-rockier ridge.

Continue out as far as you feel comfortable. Some stretches of the ridge may require you to do some easy scrambling and use your hands for balance. This route will keep you on your toes. There are some skiable shots off the ridge, but be sure to assess them for avalanche hazards first.

To climb Nelson Mountain, leave the yurts and climb back up the La Garita Stock Driveway/North Campbell direct-approach tour (Tour 19b, see pages 138–139) until you regain the stock driveway trail. Cross it and climb cross-country, heading northwest up to the summit following the flagged route. Watch out for potential slide terrain near the summit. This is a roughly 1.5-mile tour one way.

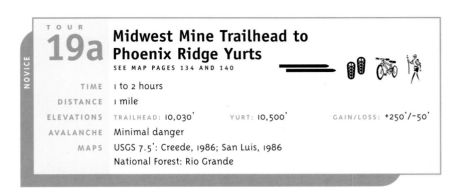

NOVICE

TOUR

19a

Midwest Mine Trailhead to
Phoenix Ridge Yurts

SEE MAP PAGES 134 AND 140

TIME	1 to 2 hours
DISTANCE	1 mile
ELEVATIONS	TRAILHEAD: 10,030´ YURT: 10,500´ GAIN/LOSS: +250´/-50´
AVALANCHE	Minimal danger
MAPS	USGS 7.5´: Creede, 1986; San Luis, 1986
	National Forest: Rio Grande

TOUR OVERVIEW: This is the quickest and most direct—though least scenic and adventurous—trail to the yurts. The route follows a well-worn summer road.

DIRECTIONS TO TRAILHEAD: Drive on CO 149 toward Lake City. On the south end of Creede (as you begin to head toward Lake City and Slumgullion Pass), a gravel road heads west from near the ballpark. This road, Forest Road 504, is marked with a yellow cemetery sign. (It is not marked with a Forest Route number sign, although it is marked sporadically with "Bachelor Loop Historic Tour" signage.) Follow this primary road 6 miles north to "Allen's Crossing," where the road switchbacks to the southeast over West Willow Creek. After the switchback, continue southeast for roughly 1 mile to the end of the plowed road (7 miles total from Creede) at the Midwest Mine.

Although the County plows this road, it does not have "high priority" status. Consequently, four-wheel drive or chains are recommended. Inquire with the hut system about current conditions.

THE ROUTE: Leave your car and follow Forest Road 502 to the northeast on a 1-mile, 250-foot climb to a saddle on the north side of Campbell Mountain. Drop off the saddle and

Phoenix Ridge Yurt has a satellite shower yurt.

glide 0.25 mile to the entrance to the Phoenix Ridge property on the right (south). This turnoff is marked, as is the rest of the route at critical junctures.

TOUR

19b Emerald Ranch/Nelson Mountain Road Trailhead to Phoenix Ridge Yurts

SEE MAP PAGES 134 AND 140

TIME	2 to 3 hours
DISTANCE	2.5 miles
ELEVATIONS	TRAILHEAD: 10,400' YURT: 10,500' GAIN/LOSS: +850'/-750'
AVALANCHE	Minimal danger
MAPS	USGS 7.5': Creede, 1986; San Luis, 1986 National Forest: Rio Grande

TOUR OVERVIEW: This is a delightful trail marked by a nice, gradual climb and traverse followed by a descent along a titillating ridge to the yurts. Some short, easy scrambling or walking may be required, depending on snowpack. This route has glorious views and is highly recommended.

Robert Sullivan, Mark Richter, and Cully Culbreth chill at Meadow Yurt.

DIRECTIONS TO TRAILHEAD: Follow the directions for the Midwest Mine Trailhead to Phoenix Ridge Yurts (Tour 19a, see page 137) to "Allen's Crossing" and the switchback over West Willow Creek. After the switchback, continue southeast for roughly 0.25 mile to an intersection with a road coming in from the left (north) that is marked with a stone gate. Park along the sides of the road and leave space for plows.

The county plows this road, but it does not have "high priority" status. Consequently, four-wheel drive vehicles or chains are recommended. Inquire with the hut system about current conditions.

THE ROUTE: From your parked car, ski or walk uphill through the gate. This is the Nelson Mountain Road. Follow it for 0.25 mile until you come to another intersection. Avoid the gated road that goes straight ahead, and instead turn right onto a narrower, four-wheel-drive road. Pass several beaver dams and climb steeply past a cabin on the left before reaching an area filled with scattered stumps. Ski upward about 300 feet until Nelson Mountain Road heads north (left). Take the La Garita Stock Driveway Trail (Forest Road 787) east up through more scattered stumps and even some bristlecone pines. The route along the stock driveway is marked with blue diamonds.

Eventually the trail begins to level off. Look for markers where the trail enters a stand of spruce and fir trees. Continue rolling along through the woods for 0.3 mile until you reach some clearings on the south shoulder of Nelson Mountain at 11,250 feet.

Descend along a four-wheel-drive road, then via the open swath of the stock driveway. Where the trail veers to the northeast (left) on an aspen shoulder, the La Garita Mountains come into view. As the stock driveway turns northeast, look for blue diamonds marking a four-wheel-drive road descending to the south (right). Follow this road to a saddle, where the road turns and descends to the southwest. Leave the road and follow the ridge straight ahead out and up to a promontory (a great photo spot!). If you look hard, you can see Phoenix Ridge Yurt below, tucked into trees overlooking the East Willow Creek chasm on the left side of a large, forested bench to the south.

Drop off the highpoint and descend steeply (this may require walking on the south-facing slope) to another four-wheel-drive road heading south along the ridge-crest. Descend another 0.5 mile on the road to a saddle and the intersection with the Midwest Mine route (Forest Road 502). Turn left and ski a few hundred feet to the entrance of the Phoenix Ridge property.

Mark Richter and Robert Sullivan on the spectacular overlook day tour near the Phoenix Ridge Yurts; 14,014-foot San Luis Peak is in the distant background.

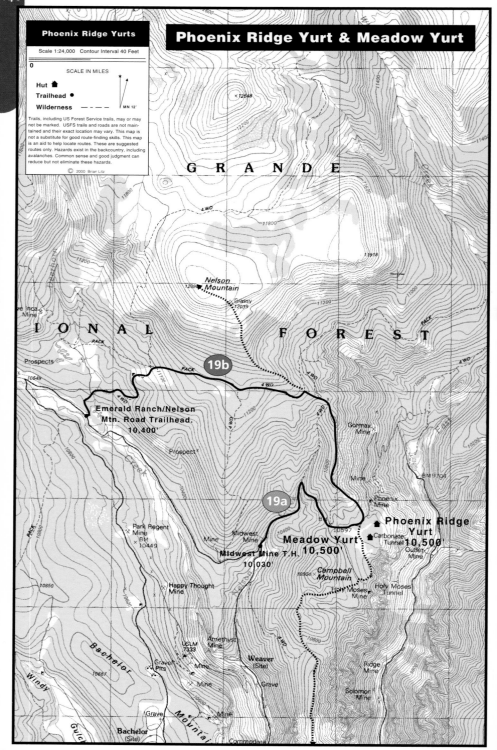

Phoenix Ridge Yurts

Phoenix Ridge Yurt & Meadow Yurt

Scale 1:24,000   Contour Interval 40 Feet

0
SCALE IN MILES

Hut
Trailhead
Wilderness — — — —   MN 12°

Trails, including US Forest Service trails, may or may
not be marked. USFS trails and roads are not maintained and their exact location may vary. This map is
not a substitute for good route-finding skills. This map
is an aid to help locate routes. These are suggested
routes only. Hazards exist in the backcountry, including
avalanches. Common sense and good judgment can
reduce but not eliminate these hazards.

© 2000 Brian Litz

GRANDE

NATIONAL   FOREST

Nelson Mountain

Emerald Ranch/Nelson
Mtn. Road Trailhead.
10,400'

Gormax Mine

Phoenix Mine

Phoenix Ridge Yurt
10,500'

Meadow Yurt 10,500'

Midwest Mine T.H.
10,030'

Campbell Mountain

Holy Moses Mine

Weaver (Site)

Bachelor (Site)

Saint Paul Lodge

HUT ELEVATION	11,400'
DATE BUILT	1880s
SEASONS	Thanksgiving through April (depending on snowpack)
CAPACITY	22 (6 to 8 in cabin)
HUT LAYOUT	Massive, rambling, multi-storied wooden building featuring a communal dining area on the main floor and a south-facing deck and library/reading room on the second floor; many sleeping rooms with bunks
HUT ESSENTIALS	Operates like a bed-and-breakfast with full kitchen facilities and a sauna
OTHER GOODIES	Library, rental equipment, excellent food served family-style, and the owner himself!

Saint Paul Lodge is less than a mile from the summit of Red Mountain Pass on U.S. 550, between Ouray and Silverton. The route into this old mining structure is short, steep, and manageable by most skiers.

From the lodge, you can ski into U.S. Basin and McMillan Basin for scenic and challenging day trips. Because the trailhead and lodge are at such a high altitude, this route offers less experienced skiers the kind of true alpine backcountry skiing that's usually available only to more advanced skiers. This is not a beginner's area. You should be in good shape, have solid touring abilities, and be able to assess avalanche hazard if you ski sans guide.

Saint Paul Lodge is on Red Mountain, which was the center of prolific mining activity in the late 1800s and early 1900s. Historically, the lodge served as the "tipple house," where buckets of ore were raised and tipped to unload their cargo. The 800-foot main shaft is still there—plummeting directly below the dining table!

The lodge offers a variety of packages for guests, including board and lodging, guide services, and instruction, as well as medical and avalanche seminars. It sleeps 22 and is well-suited to large groups. An old cabin on the property can be rented on a weekly basis. The cabin sleeps six to eight and is open all year. In summer it is accessible by car. Owner and operator Christopher George, a colorful English gent, bakes a mean apple pie and has stories to fill many a winter night. George taught Colorado Outward Bound winter mountaineering courses for 10 years, taught with the American Avalanche Institute, co-directed three local Work Speed Skiing events, and was a guide with the British Mountaineering Association before moving to the United States about three decades ago. He has operated the lodge since 1974.

Because the lodge lies at such a high elevation, it has a long ski season. Springtime skiing can be superb in this area, especially during the transition season when lower-elevation trailheads are muddy and bar access to other ski areas.

Contact the lodge to make reservations (see Appendix A).

RECOMMENDED DAY TRIPS:

Skiing around the lodge is as bountiful as it is varied. South of the hut are top-notch glades with many aspects—be careful of avalanche pockets and terrain traps—that drop down toward the highway. You can climb directly east of the lodge toward McMillan Peak for turns. The classic medium-length tour in the area heads east up U.S. Basin to the pass that overlooks Silverton, the Gladstone mining town area, and the jagged Needle and Grenadier Mountains of the Central San Juans and the Weminuche Wilderness.

This makes an excellent, safe tour and a nice introduction to high-altitude skiing. Returning to the lodge down through the open valley, you'll have lots of elbowroom for turns. Remember to remain well away from the avalanche-prone, cornice-guarded walls that form the southern wall of U.S. Basin.

Of course, all the skiing here is fantastic in late spring, including the steeper slopes on the peaks.

Skiers six-pack a trail outside of Saint Paul Lodge—truly one of the most incredible locations in Colorado.

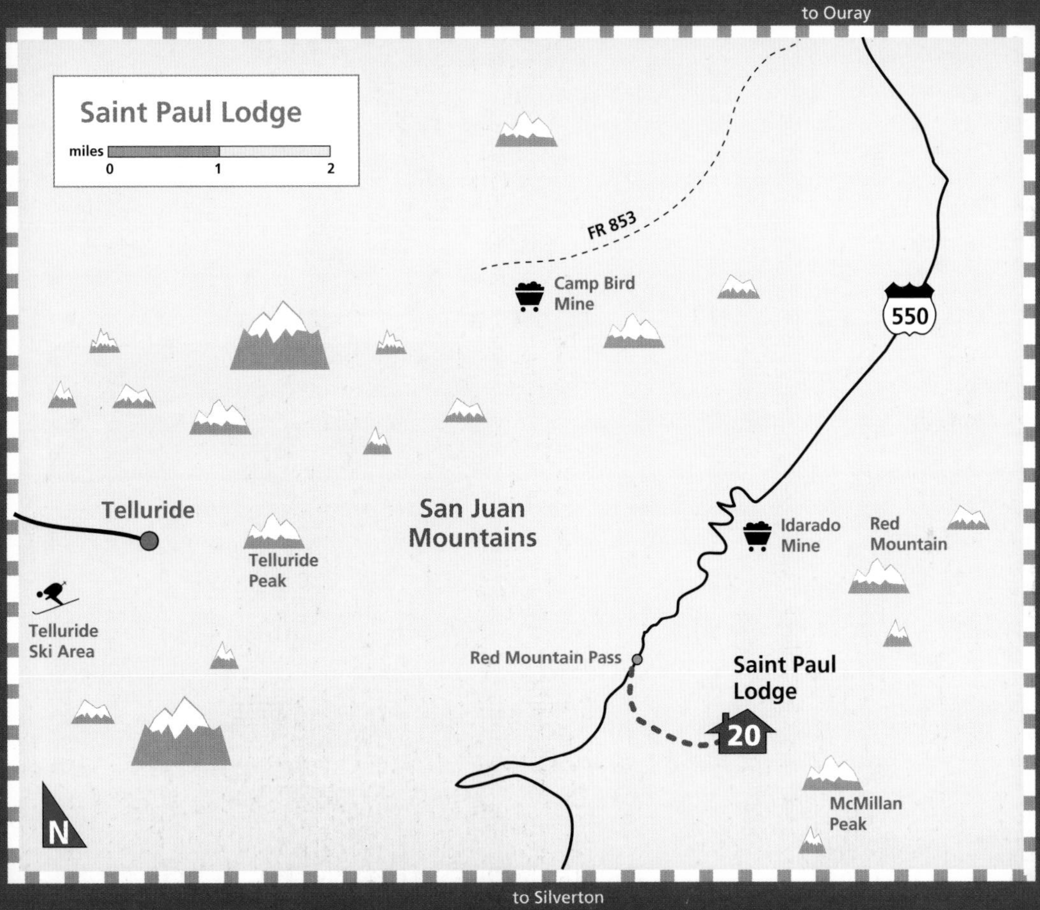

Saint Paul Lodge

miles
0 1 2

to Ouray

550

FR 853

Camp Bird
Mine

Idarado
Mine

Red
Mountain

Saint Paul
Lodge

McMillan
Peak

20

San Juan
Mountains

Red Mountain Pass

to Silverton

Telluride

Telluride
Peak

Telluride
Ski Area

N

TOUR

INTERMEDIATE

20a Red Mountain Pass Trailhead to Saint Paul Lodge

SEE MAP PAGES 143 AND 146

TIME	1 to 2 hours
DISTANCE	1 mile
ELEVATIONS	TRAILHEAD: 11,060' LODGE: 11,400' GAIN: +340'
AVALANCHE	Some avalanche terrain encountered; easily avoided
MAPS	USGS 7.5': Ironton, 1972
	National Forest: San Juan
	Trails Illustrated: Map #141 (Silverton/Ouray/Telluride/Lake City)

DIRECTIONS TO TRAILHEAD: Drive to the summit of Red Mountain Pass on U.S. 550. Immediately south of the summit is a small, plowed parking area on the east side of the highway. Park here.

THE ROUTE: Ski south/southeast along a snow-covered road, passing several old mining buildings. Ski around a steep knob and up into a small drainage.

Continue up the north side of the creek along a steep road. After gaining about 160 feet of elevation, the road abruptly crosses a creek and begins a traversing ascent out of the creek bed to the Saint Paul Lodge. Be careful that you do not remain in the creek bed or you will miss the turn and end up heading north onto a small bench.

Chris George, proprietor of Saint Paul Lodge and alpine raconteur, dishes up the evening meal at the lodge.

Saint Paul Lodge is a bastion in the night.

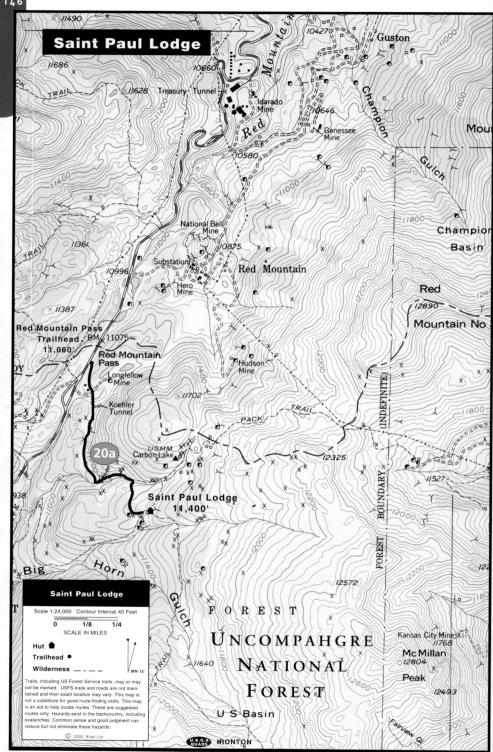

Saint Paul Lodge

11490

11686

11660

TRAIL

11628 Treasury Tunnel

Idarado
Mine

10646

10427

Guston

1000

Red Mountain

Champion Gulch

Mou

11600

Genessee
Mine

10580

11000

11400

11400

11800

Champion

Basin

National Bell
Mine

11361

10875

Substation

Red Mountain

11200

Red

12890

Mountain No

10996

Hero
Mine

Red Mountain Pass
Trailhead BM 11075
11,060'

11387

Red Mountain
Pass

Longfellow
Mine

11702

Hudson
Mine

1400

12000

11800

Koehler
Tunnel

12000

DY

20a

USMM
Carbon Lake

PACK TRAIL

12325

11527

938

Saint Paul Lodge
11,400'

12200

FOREST BOUNDARY (INDEFINITE)

12000

11000

11400

Big Horn Gulch

12572

12000

12200

12200

124

1180

Saint Paul Lodge

Scale 1:24,000 Contour Interval 40 Feet

| 0 | 1/8 | 1/4 |

SCALE IN MILES

Hut 🏠

Trailhead ●

Wilderness – – – –

MN 12°

FOREST

UNCOMPAHGRE

NATIONAL

FOREST

Kansas City Mine
11768

McMillan
12804

Peak

12493

11640

11800

12600

2000

U S Basin

Fairview Gl

Trails, including US Forest Service trails, may or may
not be marked. USFS trails and roads are not maintained and their exact location may vary. This map is
not a substitute for good route-finding skills. This map
is an aid to help locate routes. These are suggested
routes only. Hazards exist in the backcountry, including
avalanches. Common sense and good judgment can
reduce but not eliminate these hazards.

© 2000 Brian Litz

U.S.G.S.
QUADS IRONTON

POINT AND CHUTE.
committed to the core

patagonia®

San Juan Hut System—Winter/Ski

During the mid-1980s, two Telluride-area residents, Mike Turrin and Joe Ryan, concluded that the San Juan Mountains of southwestern Colorado would be an ideal spot for a winter and summer hut system. Though several independent backcountry lodges catered to telemark skiers, no true hut-to-hut routes existed.

The San Juan Mountains, Colorado's largest range, have long been a favorite arena for summer mountaineers, rock climbers, and winter ice climbers, as well as downhill and backcountry skiers. The vertical relief is enormous, however, and the topography has presented unique challenges to backcountry skiers and hut planners alike.

The ridgelike San Juans tower above tree line, with few skiable passes. There are also numerous avalanche paths throughout the area. Consequently, natural hut routes are uncommon. After considerable exploration, Turrin and Ryan were able to piece together a 38-plus-mile linear route from Telluride to Ouray. By judiciously situating the shelters along a network of trails and old logging roads, they provided access to some of the most incredible wilderness skiing in the West.

The hut system lies in the shadow of the Sneffels Range, a unique subrange of the San Juans that runs east to west. The castellated summits and ridges present a formidable wall to the north. Below the steep, alpine towers, thick spruce and aspen forests sweep down to piñon- and juniper-covered foothills and some of North America's most scenic ranches. This is one of the most beautiful of the backcountry skiing areas—not just in Colorado but in all of North America.

San Juan Hut System skiing is always adventurous and at times extremely challenging. Some trails are easy-to-follow roads and others are old summer trails obscured by winter snow. Trails are not consistently marked, although a new blue-diamond marker system is gradually being introduced. Navigating on these trails can be the greatest challenge, often requiring astute route-finding through thick forests or across open meadows. Trail-breaking on the less frequently traveled routes can be physically taxing. The entire region is laced with secondary trails and roads that do not appear on the most recent USGS topo maps; consequently, competent navigation and route-finding skills are essential for safe, efficient travel.

You should be relatively fit, for many of the trails are long and strenuous. As a general rule, skiing to the Blue Lakes and Burn Huts is suitable for strong novice skiers, the routes to the Ridgway and Last Dollar Huts are suitable for strong intermediate skiers, and the West Dallas Creek Trail to the North Pole Hut should be left to advanced skiers who have good route-finding skills. The inter-hut trails, with the exception of the Ridgway-Burn route, are appropriate only for strong intermediate and advanced skiers.

The vast, rarely skied slopes around these high alpine huts offer endless hours of recreation. Day telemark skiing is usually exceptional, but it does require knowledge of backcountry snow conditions, as well as avalanche terrain and how to use avalanche safety equipment. Less experienced groups should consider guided trips. It is safe to say that the powder skiing in the San Juan Hut System is, if not the best, at least unsurpassed in Colorado.

Five shelters make up the system. These huts are cozy and uncomplicated, and they have everything you need to live comfortably in the backcountry. Each hut sleeps about eight people, with the optimum group size being five to seven. Skiers pay a per-person rate. Presently, the huts are open only in winter for skiing.

Huts and trails from Telluride to Ridgway are described. You can reach each hut from its own trailhead or via the hut-to-hut trails. To make reservations or arrange for a guided trip, call the San Juan Hut System (see Appendix A).

Jordan Campbell and John Fielder ascend Last Dollar Road above Telluride, with Silverton West Group of San Juan Mountains in the background.

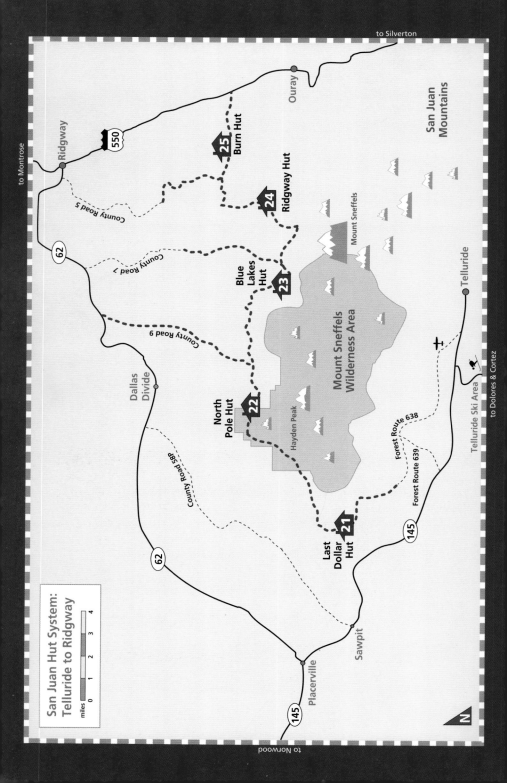

San Juan Hut System:
Telluride to Ridgway

miles

0   1   2   3   4

to Silverton

to Montrose

Ridgway

550

62

Ouray

San Juan
Mountains

County Road 5

25
Burn Hut

24
Ridgway Hut

County Road 7

Mount Sneffels

Blue
Lakes
Hut

23

County Road 9

Mount Sneffels
Wilderness Area

Telluride

Dallas
Divide

North
Pole Hut

22

Hayden Peak

County Road 58P

Forest Route 638

Forest Route 639

Telluride Ski Area

to Dolores & Cortez

62

21
Last
Dollar
Hut

145

145

Sawpit

Placerville

to Norwood

145

N

Last Dollar Hut

HUT ELEVATION	10,980'
DATE BUILT	1987
SEASONS	Thanksgiving through late April; open in summer for biking (see page 193)
CAPACITY	8
HUT LAYOUT	16 x 16 wood hut with built-in bunks along 2 walls
HUT ESSENTIALS	Wood-burning stove for heat, propane cookstove, propane lights, all kitchenware, foamies, minimalist outdoor toilets

The Last Dollar Hut, which sleeps eight, was one of the first two huts built in the San Juan Hut System. The hut has one of the most spectacular panoramic vistas in the state—the view overlooking the Silverton West Group of the San Juans, the Wilson Peaks, and the La Sal Mountains in Utah.

The closest hut to Telluride, the Last Dollar Hut is a fine destination for an overnight or long weekend trip. Consequently, this is one of the most popular of the San Juan Hut System huts and more than one group often books it. Less experienced skiers can simply take in the beautiful surroundings or they can ski the more limited moderate terrain.

RECOMMENDED DAY TRIPS:

Experienced backcountry skiers will find an abundance of day telemark skiing beyond the hut to the east—far to the east. Unfortunately, most of the steep terrain directly behind the hut is not great for skiing. Rather, you need to make the approximately one-hour climb along the ridge to above tree line and then carefully ski the avalanche chutes and slopes that plunge off the broad north face of the ridge. Many of these avalanche runs do not appear on the USGS topo maps, but they are there, they are obvious, and, under the wrong conditions, they are dangerous. Under safe conditions (in spring) these 1,000- to 2,000-foot runs provide superb skiing for experienced, advanced skiers. Separating these gullies and chutes are thick woods with generally tight, steep, technical tree skiing.

For an even better view of southwestern Colorado, an ascent to the ridge at tree line to the east makes a nice day trip. In addition, the hut has plenty of "front yard" for just sunning and enjoying the view.

INTERMEDIATE

TOUR
21a Deep Creek Mesa Trailhead to Last Dollar Hut

SEE MAP PAGES 150 AND 174–175

TIME	3 to 4 hours
DISTANCE	3.0 miles
ELEVATIONS	TRAILHEAD: 9,593' HUT: 10,980' GAIN/LOSS: +1,467'/-80'
AVALANCHE	Route crosses avalanche runout zones; can be dangerous during high-hazard periods
MAPS	USGS 7.5': Grayhead, 1953; SAMS, 1982
	National Forest: Uncompahgre
	Trails Illustrated: Map #141 (Silverton/Ouray/Telluride/Lake City)

TOUR OVERVIEW: In summer, Last Dollar Road is a favorite of mountain bikers and wildflower photographers. Unplowed and closed in winter, it is the shortest route to the Last Dollar Hut. Route-finding is easy, though the trail climbs 1,500 feet in 3.0 miles. The steepest part of the climb is onto Last Dollar Pass near the end of the tour. Less experienced skiers can also enjoy this trail—just leave early, bring skins, and take your time.

DIRECTIONS TO TRAILHEAD: Drive on CO 145 to the Deep Creek turnoff, marked "Lime" on the USGS maps. This turn is near mile marker 75, which is 9.4 miles east of Placerville or 3.4 miles west of "Society Corner" which is the intersection of the road into town and the continuation of CO 145 towards Lizard Head Pass and Dolores in Telluride. Turn northeast into the narrow Deep Creek canyon. Drive up along Deep Creek until you intersect Last Dollar Road. Making a sharp left onto Last Dollar Road, drive through a group of barns, cabins, and fences to the parking area at the end of the plowed public road. The trailhead has now moved closer to the hut as a result of development of the Grayhead subdivision. Though the actual distance varies according to local road conditions, the new trailhead should be just beyond the National Forest boundary at about 9,600 feet. (Do not take the west-running road that drops downhill to a gully and then back up to Grayhead Mountain, where a repeater sits.) The total distance from CO 145 is roughly 5.5 miles. In the spring, this road can be slick and muddy.

THE ROUTE: From the parking area, ski along the snow-covered road up to the summit of Last Dollar Pass, on the northeast corner of Last Dollar Mountain near Elevation Point 10,663' on USGS topo maps. Most of the ascent is up south-facing terrain through meadows and stands of aspens on moderate and steep hills that maintain a good cover of snow. The route crosses below several avalanche paths just prior to Summit Creek. These hazards are easily seen and avoided by dropping down off the road to the southwest and rejoining the road after several hundred feet.

Just before Summit Creek, you'll see several old cabin ruins off to the left. The grueling part of the climb begins after you cross Summit Creek, where the road switchbacks up a steep, treeless slope. If the snowpack is unstable, you can bypass the large switchback by climbing directly up Summit Creek, regaining the road where the left-turning switchback makes the final ascent to the top of the pass.

From the pass, near a brown Forest Service sign (Alder Creek/Trail 510), the hut is 0.25 mile and 400 vertical feet north/northeast up the ridge. Directly ascend the ridge next to the trees on the slope to the south, or follow the indistinct Whipple Mountain Trail (419), which climbs through trees along the forested, northern aspect of the ridge. This trail is 50 to 100 feet north of the apex of the ridge and switchbacks just prior to reaching the hut. The Last Dollar Hut is at the edge of a huge, treeless, south-facing slope, hidden in a group of spruce trees, and can be hard to find until you run right into it.

Josh Weinstein skis the avalanche runs near Last Dollar Hut under unusually soft and stable late-winter conditions.

ADVANCED/EXPERT

TOUR
21b

Last Dollar Hut to North Pole Hut

SEE MAP PAGES 150 AND 174–175

TIME	7 to 11 hours
DISTANCE	9.0 to 9.5 miles (depending on exact route)
ELEVATIONS	LD HUT: 10,980' NP HUT: 9,960' GAIN/LOSS: +500'/-1,700'
AVALANCHE	Route crosses avalanche slopes; prone to skier-triggered avalanches during high-hazard periods
MAPS	USGS 7.5': SAMS, 1982
	National Forest: Uncompahgre
	Trails Illustrated: Map #141 (Silverton/Ouray/Telluride/Lake City)

TOUR OVERVIEW: The ski route from the Last Dollar Hut to the North Pole Hut is one of the most difficult and potentially dangerous trails covered in this guidebook. The route follows the Alder Creek Trail, a well-worn summer path marked with occasional tree blazes, which crosses a small section of the Mount Sneffels Wilderness. The trail is long and strenuous, is not skied regularly, and does not appear on the most recent USGS 7.5-minute topo map. An "Alder Creek Trail" appears on the Trails Illustrated map, but it is just a rough approximation of

A crisp mid-winter day engulfs Last Dollar Hut.

the route. Essential for this tour are a good sense for route-finding, a willingness to ski off-trail, and map, compass, and altimeter skills.

In recent years Joe Ryan has skied the route, clearing downed logs and cutting tree blazes to help delineate the path for skiers. But it remains a committing endeavor.

Note: Several large gullies and avalanche slide paths, which are easy to cross in summer, do not appear on the USGS map. These are dangerous in winter. Therefore, the San Juan Hut System changes portions of the route near these slides throughout the ski season in an effort to avoid avalanche hazards. Skiers planning to travel from the Last Dollar Hut to the North Pole Hut should call the System to verify the route and conditions.

THE ROUTE: From the Last Dollar Hut, return to Last Dollar Pass and the brown Forest Service sign. Once you are back on the road, head north (right) and then west as you begin descending. Avoid the new Alder Creek Trailhead (it's off to the right and marked by a large trailhead sign). Cruise along the road on a fun drop until the road bends. Here, near a small clump of aspens and willow bushes, is a right fork — this is approximately 200 yards down the road. The fork is marked with blazes on both sides of the trail. It is easy to miss,

Jennifer Pratt fries sopapillas at Last Dollar Hut.

though. Take this "truck-width" fork and continue dropping down this road/trail until it cranks noticeably around a corner to the right (east/northeast).

As soon as you round the corner, slow down and look for a rusty, white metal "T" stake on the right. This is the turnoff to the Alder Creek Trail. From here, the road drops precipitously while the "horse-width" trail launches off into the forest and heads east/northeast on a 1.5-mile traverse across a steep, forested slope, remaining at roughly 10,600 feet.

Finally the trail climbs over a small ridge before making a steep descent into a large, scenic basin southwest of Hayden Peak. This is near the "GRE" in "UNCOMPAHGRE" on the topo maps. In this area the trail crosses several small avalanche-prone sloughs. Cross one at a time and be careful. Just past the "E," one particular slide path sits below a rock outcrop.

The trail enters a small clearing at about 10,640 feet on the floor of this basin, just northwest of a creek with flowing water. This clearing is a good lunch spot, with views of high ridges to the east and south. Consequently, with these unobstructed views, it is also a good spot for orienteering. Once across the creek, climb into a larger meadow with a roofless trappers' cabin on the southwest side. The trail exits the northeast corner of this small meadow near a tiny creek and begins a long traverse north. This stretch poses the hardest route-finding of the journey. The stretch from here to the north side of North Pole Peak is difficult to follow at times.

Continue forging ahead and try to remain at roughly 10,800 feet. Cross another large avalanche gully where the trail passes near the bottom of the runout zone. Continue, passing through several other sloughs that can be hazardous under the right conditions. Eventually you will cross another slide path with a starting zone far up the ridge. All of these paths are the lower extensions of avalanche gullies marked on the USGS topo maps (easily visible as creek drainages); the portions that the trail crosses do not appear on the map. They are obvious, however, and make useful navigation points. The trained map-and-compass user can identify them using triangulation off the ridges and peaks above. Many of these slide paths drop into hazardous, textbook terrain traps, so exercise extreme caution when crossing them. If need be, drop off the trail and pass underneath them.

The third major gully, which is directly west of the summit of Hayden Peak, is the Alder Creek slide path. It is deep and dangerous, and often has water running through it. The trail crosses directly below a cliffband in the gully, where you will see a small waterfall (or frozen waterfall, as the case may be). Exercise extreme caution when crossing these gullies—cross one person at a time and turn on your transceivers. If you find any hint of potential slide activity, drop way down and cross under the end of the runout zones, regaining the trail after safe passage.

If you must drop down below the Alder Creek path, look for blazes on trees on the south side of the gully. Drop downstream along the gully for about 100 yards. Pick your way down into and across the gully, then climb the sun-baked south-facing side of the path again. Climb back uphill along the gully and regain the trail.

After crossing the third gully, the trail heads west/northwest a short distance up onto a distinct benchlike shoulder west of Hayden Peak. Enter an area of wind-fallen trees. Ski along the eastern edge of these trees and eventually regain the trail. New blazes will help throughout this difficult section; altimeters can be helpful, too.

If all goes according to plan, you will eventually reach a four-way trail intersection, marked with an old trail sign, in the middle of a stand of huge aspens. This intersection is roughly 2.75 miles from the Alder Creek slide path. Overall, this passage of trail is marked and easier to follow. En route to the four-way inter-section, you must cross two aspen stands, which can be tricky under poor visibility. In both instances, the trail enters the clearings from the south near the tops and exits on the north at lower elevations. Keep an eye out for new blazes.

Note: Back at the four-way intersection: To the north, an obvious trail/road descends steeply, eventually into the San Juan Vista Estates (not on the USGS topo); another road heads uphill to the south/southeast (also not on USGS topo); and what is now the Dallas Trail heads off into the woods to the east. Groups that are considerably off the route sometimes drop too far down to the north as they approach the four-way intersection. If you do find yourself skiing down into large aspen woods, meadows, fences, and some houses, you are near San Juan Vista Estates. Climb back uphill and search for the trail.

Ski east from the intersection, following the now relatively easy-to-follow trail, which is marked by occasional blazes. The trail rolls in and out of several drainages, passing a wilderness boundary sign en route. You can usually locate free-running water in the Middle Fork of Leopard Creek. Beyond this creek, a sustained climb takes you to the final highpoint. The top of this ridge is also where day skiers begin the ascent to Hayden Peak by leaving the trail and skiing uphill to the south. From the highpoint, descend into a large wetland meadow at 10,000 feet.

Immediately after the trail reaches the valley floor and a clearing, you come to a fork. Turn north and tour along the western perimeter of the meadow, passing under several large spruce trees. Beyond these trees, a smaller, distinct clearing is bounded by tall aspens on the west and north. The North Pole Hut sits in this clearing.

Wilson/El Diente massif as seen from the front lawn of the Last Dollar Hut.

22

North Pole Hut

HUT ELEVATION	9,960′
DATE BUILT	1991 (yurt), 1995 (current cabin)
SEASONS	Thanksgiving through late April
CAPACITY	8
HUT LAYOUT	16 × 16 wood cabin with built-in bunks along 2 walls
HUT ESSENTIALS	Wood-burning stove for heat, propane cookstove, propane lights, all kitchenware, foamies, minimalist outdoor toilets

Of the shelters in the San Juan Hut System, the North Pole Hut is the most remote. You will not see day skiers here. The cabin rests in a small, aspen-lined clearing on the western edge of a large meadow, in the shadow of a wall of towering, rocky peaks. This location, with views of the peaks to the south, is one of the most breathtaking hut sites in all of the San Juans.

A canvas-topped yurt once sat here, but a sturdier wooden structure has replaced it. The new hut is on par with the other winter shelters in the system and it makes for a rustic, warm, and cozy base camp for exploring the backcountry. Make reservations through the San Juan Hut System (see Appendix A).

Previously, this backcountry shelter was reached via a direct 5.5-mile tour from a trailhead on Hastings Mesa. That route is no longer available because of private-property closures. You must now approach the hut from the northeast, via a long, complicated route up the West Dallas Creek Road (County Road 9) and the Dallas Trail. This change has doubled the

Heading out for Hayden Peak from the North Pole Hut. Though out of sight, its lower northeastern ridge can be seen at the left.

distance and drastically increased the commitment necessary—which is unfortunate, as some skiers will be discouraged from visiting the North Pole Hut and consequently will miss the superb skiing above it on Hayden Peak.

Much of the difficulty lies not in the elevation gain but, rather, in the distance and the complexity of route-finding during the final 3 miles of the approach trail. This challenging stretch of trail comes at the end of what is already a long day. If you dillydallied at the trailhead and got a late start, you may end up with the added factor of darkness. Reaching the hut from the Last Dollar Hut is no easier and presents its own set of challenges. For the strong, experienced route-finder, though, the powdery reward lying above the hut easily outweighs the high "grunt factor" on the approach.

RECOMMENDED DAY TRIPS:

Ski mountaineers can tackle the north ridge of Hayden Peak (under appropriate conditions), while powderhounds can explore the many ridges and slopes found below tree line. Whether you want to climb Hayden Peak or ski the powder runs off the ridge above and south of the hut, begin by heading out on the trail to the Last Dollar Hut. After you have climbed onto the first ridge to the west, leave the trail and ascend, straight south, the narrowing ridge-crest toward tree line. This ascent gets steeper the higher you get, but it is a safe route, protected by trees. As you approach tree line, the angle begins to lessen until you reach a flat scree shoulder (a good lunch spot) above the trees and below the steeper talus slopes of Hayden Peak's north ridge.

Powder skiers can drop back down north anywhere along the ridge for some unbelievable skiing. Just be careful of the large avalanche bowl (near the mine symbol on the USGS topo maps) tucked under the cliffs on the north wall of Hayden Peak's north ridge. These tempting slopes can be skied, but only by knowledgeable skiers. This is very serious terrain.

Mountaineers can tackle the steep, loose talus above the lunch spot. Though loose and often covered by drifts of unconsolidated snow, it is generally wind-scoured and straightforward for seasoned peak-baggers. Once you're on top of the ridge, a gentle walk takes you to the final summit pyramid. The last, short, east-facing summit slope is often very hard and a bit dicey for a few feet. Above this final obstacle, hand-and-foot scrambling takes you onto the magnificent apex of the peak. The large, amazingly low-angled hanging snowfield on the eastern aspect of the long, low-angled upper ridge often has great skiing.

Intermediate cross-country skiers will find nice touring on the old roads and trails south of the hut and moderate tele skiing on the lower slopes above the hut to the south.

TOUR
22a West Dallas Creek Trailhead to North Pole Hut

SEE MAP PAGES 150 AND 174–175

ADVANCED/EXPERT

TIME	6 to 10 hours
DISTANCE	8 to 11 miles (normally about 9)
ELEVATIONS	TRAILHEAD: 7,640' (varies) HUT: 9,960' GAIN: +900' (depending on trailhead)
AVALANCHE	Some avalanche terrain encountered; easily avoided
MAPS	USGS 7.5': Mount Sneffels, 1987; SAMS, 1982
	National Forest: Uncompahgre
	Trails Illustrated: Map #141 (Silverton/Ouray/Telluride/Lake City)

TOUR OVERVIEW: This tour begins at, or south of, the intersection of CO 62 and County Road 9 (West Dallas Creek Road) and travels south up along the West Dallas Creek Road through truly beautiful ranches and oak shrublands to a stunning meadow known as Box Factory Park. The area is so picturesque that much of the motion picture *True Grit* was filmed here. From the meadow, the trail heads west to the hut via an old summer trail (the Dallas Trail), a section that requires advanced route-finding skills and can be strenuous if not broken.

High-definition TV: Rick Leonidas dials in the high peaks above and south of the North Pole Hut.

The Dallas Trail is posted with a variety of markers, including blue diamonds, old silver diamonds, tree blazes, and small, red metal flags nailed to trees. You will have to pay attention to these markers. Maps, compasses, and particularly altimeters are useful in navigating the last several miles to the hut. Make sure all members of the group have headlamps with fresh batteries.

This tour is recommended only for physically strong groups of expert backcountry navigators. The San Juan Hut System recommends that the route be attempted only by large groups of skiers who can share trail-breaking duties, that groups be on the trail by no later than 8 a.m., and that each group carry bivouac gear and flashlights or headlamps.

Despite all this ominous talk, this is a stunningly scenic tour throughout, especially along the lower road, where you ski along a valley rimmed with sandstone cliffs on a trail that glides through silent aspen forests in the shadow of high peaks. Make sure you plan enough time to fully enjoy this tour. Less experienced groups should hire one of the herculean San Juan Hut guides as a trail breaker. There is nothing these mountain goats would love more!

DIRECTIONS TO TRAILHEAD: Drive on CO 62 to the turnoff, which is 6 miles west of Ridgway and 13.5 miles east of Placerville. A word of warning about the trailhead: Because winter snowstorms or spring mud can entrap automobiles, exercise caution after turning off CO 62. Depending on current road and weather conditions, the trailhead can vary by up to several miles. Usually you can park up the road roughly 2 miles around on the south side of the small, forested "peak" (a point approximately 8,160 feet high and directly west of Elevation Point 7,796') immediately south of the ranch houses that you pass on the road. Sometimes you can even drive another mile up the road (3 miles total) to park. If you are worried about getting snowed in, you can shuttle loads a mile or two up the road, leaving the car parked down by the highway.

To be absolutely safe, or if you own a passenger car, you should park just off CO 62 beyond the "Double RL" ranch sign. The sign marks a private road into Ralph Lauren's ranch, but County Road 9 is a public road, so don't worry about parking here. Also, don't confuse the East Dallas Creek Road (CR 7, marked as "Dallas Creek") with West Dallas Creek Road (CR 9).

THE ROUTE: Begin skiing or walking south on CR 9 and follow it over West Dallas Creek, then up and around the eastern side of a hill. Pass through a flat

Another day, another sunset, in the San Juans.

clearing and begin climbing southwest into shrubland. (The clearing is the one mentioned earlier as an alternate parking area and works well as a gear drop-off point when road conditions dictate a car shuttle.) Keep climbing for about a mile as you gradually approach one of the most spectacular portions of the lower road—the sandstone canyon overlook. At 3 miles, the road runs along the cliffs. Pass an "Entering Public Lands" sign at 3.2 miles. *Note:* Mileages are measured from the highway.

The road follows the canyon and then veers slightly away from it, heading due south. At 4.5 miles, the road goes over a little rise as it bends east, passing a quaint log cabin and a sulfur spring on the left. Then it contours sharply around a switchback to the southwest. Continue uphill on the road toward spruce/fir forests; the landscape gradually narrows along a ridge. Ski past two roads on the left (behind a metal gate) at 5.2 miles, a cattle guard, a gate at 5.3 miles, and a National Forest boundary sign at 6.5 miles. *Note:* According to a sign near the beginning of the road, this Forest Service boundary should be 7.5 miles. According to Mike and Joe, it is more like 6.5.

You will know you are within half a mile of the Dallas Trail intersection when the road enters deeper woods and traverses steep eastern slopes above the West Fork of Dallas Creek. Then, as you make the final approach, the road reaches flatter, more open terrain with views of the high cirque above Box Factory Park. Keep an eye out for a "Dallas Trail #200" sign (the route to Blue Lakes) just off the road to the left (east), near aspen trees at the base of a low north-south ridge or hill. Continue to the south/southwest on the road (now the Dallas Trail), passing the trail sign, and descend to the creek.

Cross the creek (probably with your skis off), climb the west bank, and turn south (left) into Box Factory Park. A barbed wire fence runs north-south through the park; pass through a red gate and head west toward a hillside, aiming for the trail, which traverses north through aspens. The spot where the trail enters the aspens is about 200 feet from the fence and is marked with blue diamonds. From here, the trail diagonals up toward the north and then contours around a forested ridge, following a trail marked by occasional blue diamonds. The trail descends to the southwest off the ridge and enters the eastern edge of a large clearing (marked by diamonds for skiers heading back to the trailhead or to the Blue Lakes Hut) in a broad, basinlike creek drainage.

Head west across the drainage, then northwest across the creek. Climb diagonally northwest up the large, treeless, south/southeast-facing slope, which has aspens on top. The ridge or plateau you climb onto confines or delineates this basin to the west and north, forcing the creek to drain out of the northeast corner of the basin. Although there are a number of red-flag trail markers, the exact route up this slope is not critical—in fact, the recommended route deviates from the Dallas Trail printed on the USGS topo map. As you near the crest of the ridge at 9,600 feet, turn west, then southwest. Pass through aspens and then spruces and pick up a road (shown on the topo map) that runs uphill to the southwest along

Joe Ryan, Rick Leonidas, and Jordan Campbell stand between heaven and heaven on Hayden Peak, with Utah and the La Sal Mountains in the distance.

the edge of the ridge (overlooking the basin you just crossed). Pass a wooden sign on the left en route as you ski through aspens and up into spruces.

At a fork in the road, go to the right (blue diamond) and follow the Dallas Trail to a creek that is normally running. Cross the creek, and continue on the trail as it veers north. Climb through aspen trees until the trail breaks into a large clearing on a steep slope with unobstructed views to the north and east, including 14,150-foot Mount Sneffels, which provides an opportunity for map-and-compass orientation. As you traverse this clearing, keep an eye out for small, red metal flags on aspen trees and one that marks the entrance back into the forest.

After re-entering the woods, the trail continues west on a gently ascending traverse across steep, heavily forested, north-facing slopes until it reaches a road running north-south. This entire stretch is marked sporadically with blue diamonds and old metal trail-marker "flags."

The 1.2 miles of trail between the two roads is probably the most difficult section in terms of route-finding. The key is to routinely take the time to stop, look around for trail markers, and get your bearings. An altimeter can be helpful here to keep you on a slightly rising traverse from roughly 9,800 feet at the trail intersection to just under 10,000 feet at the second road. Occasional blue diamonds, tree blazes, and red metal flags mark the route here. This is not a good stretch of trail to be skiing at night!

Once you reach the second road, cross to the trail on the west side, which is now a summer logging road. Blue diamonds mark this intersection. Contour west, passing another road to the left en route. There is a silver diamond on the correct road (as well as silver diamonds all over the place). Head southwest until you reach another logging-road intersection along the eastern edge of a wetland meadow. You'll see another north-south road here, and a number of silver trail markers. Cross the road and continue west as it begins to contour around the southern edge of the meadow, through stands of evergreen trees marked with the occasional trail blaze. After crossing a creek (marked with blazes on two large spruces), the trail contours slightly to the west/northwest and climbs a steep but short hill (about 15 feet high) to a clearing on the southwest perimeter of the meadow. To the south and west are thicker woods and steeper slopes, and high above the forest rises Hayden Peak and other lofty ridges. The meadow rolls away to the north.

The North Pole Hut sits on the western edge of the meadow, hidden in a little clearing lined with aspens on the west and north. The turnoff to the hut is where the Last Dollar Hut Trail begins to climb noticeably to the west, up and over the forested north ridge of Hayden Peak. Turn to the north/northwest (right) and ski along the edge of the forest, passing under large, isolated stands of spruce trees, and continue another couple hundred yards across the clearing to the hut.

TOUR
22b
North Pole Hut to Blue Lakes Hut
SEE MAP PAGES 150, 174–175, AND 188–189

ADVANCED/EXPERT

TIME	6 to 10 hours
DISTANCE	7.5 miles
ELEVATIONS	NP HUT: 9,960' BL HUT: 9,380' GAIN/LOSS: +1,020'/-1,410'
AVALANCHE	Some avalanche terrain encountered; easily avoided
MAPS	USGS 7.5': Mount Sneffels, 1987; SAMS, 1982
	National Forest: Uncompahgre
	Trails Illustrated: Map #141 (Silverton/Ouray/Telluride/Lake City)

TOUR OVERVIEW: The trail between these two huts follows the Dallas Trail, an old pack trail that is now a well-traveled summer hiking route traversing the aspen- and evergreen-blanketed foothills of the Sneffels Range. Skiers on this route enjoy close-up views of Hayden Peak, Mears Peak, Wolcott Mountain, and, of course, Mount Sneffels. (Jules Verne used the name "Mount Sneffels" in his classic tale *Journey to the Center of the Earth.*)

This long tour requires expert route-finding skills. The trail is sinuous, often winding through nondescript woods, and is marked with a variety of trail markers, including old overgrown trail blazes, wooden signs, blue diamonds, posts, and silver metal strips tipped with red paint and nailed to trees. Skiers should study the map before departing and always keep an eye out for markers.

The route follows the Dallas Trail closely and is, for the most part, free of avalanche danger. But you will encounter several small slide paths and sloughs at various points throughout the tour. Cross these carefully or bypass them if conditions warrant. Get an early start, especially if you'll be breaking trail!

Ace Kvale gets physical with problematic wind-deposited snow below Hayden Peak.

THE ROUTE: From the North Pole Hut, return south through the spruce stand to the next clearing, which sits below the steeper timbered slopes to the south and west. The Dallas Trail runs east-west here along the southern edge of the wetland/beaver pond area. Turn east onto the trail marked by a diamond. Immediately climb onto a small hill, cross a creek, and begin contouring to the northeast—bypassing a road to the south and one to the north as you pass through a four-way intersection.

Ski along a faint, snow-covered road through interspersed stands of spruce trees and small clearings, all the while following the southern and eastern perimeter of a large wetland meadow. Contour around a low ridge, eventually heading east. Intersect a north-south road (shown on the USGS maps and marked by silver diamonds) on the eastern edge of the meadow. Cross this intersection and continue east to another north-south road (also shown on the USGS maps), which is marked with blue diamonds. The Dallas Trail continues across the road to the east.

The trail now enters the forest and begins a 1.2-mile traverse east across tributaries of Stough Draw. This entire passage provides some difficult route-finding. En route, the trail crosses a large meadow on the northeast aspect of a ridge. Circled with aspens, this meadow drops down to ranch country and is a scenic spot, with great views north and east toward Mount Sneffels. The trail through here makes a slightly descending traverse heading directly to the south/southeast—you do not lose too much elevation here. Eventually the trail veers east again into spruces. Cross a flowing creek and continue east until you arrive at a north-south ridgetop road above the West Fork of the West Fork of Dallas Creek (marked by a wooden Forest Service sign). This intersection is in a spectacular spot overlooking Mount Sneffels and the high peaks and basin to the south. (See Tour 22a for more information on this route.)

Craig Gaskill and Kurt Lankford take to the trail near North Pole Hut.

After you reach the road, turn northeast and descend along the eastern edge of the ridge, along the right edge, until you break out of the forest into a ridgetop clearing surrounded by aspens and even more panoramic views of the Sneffels Range. Just before you enter the clearing, a sign shows where the trail descends into the large, treeless basin of Dallas Creek. The terrain here is open, and it is easy to choose your own route down to the creek. Often, this descent negotiates sun-baked crust—so take your time.

Once at Dallas Creek, cross it (at about 9,300 feet) and ski east/northeast across the clearing toward the eastern edge of the small basin. Keep the thick woods on the southern side of the basin to your right. As you approach the spot where the trail re-enters the woods to the east, the woods along the southern edge of the clearing should be close by and you should be nearing the southeast corner of the meadow that dominates the drainage bottom. Do not follow the natural descent line along the creek that runs sharply to the north/northeast. Locating the trail into the woods can be a bit tricky, so pay attention even though it is marked. Once you're back in the woods, follow the trail around a small, wooded ridge to the east, where you make a quick, gliding descent southeast through aspens into Box Factory Park, a magnificent lunch spot below massive alpine cirques and precipitous walls.

To exit the park, pass through a red gate in a barbwire fence by a Dallas Trail sign, and drop down to Dallas Creek. Cross the creek to a small clearing on the eastern side, then turn north and make a short climb onto a tiny bench. On top of this bench is a "Dallas Trail #200" sign marking the spot where the trail exits West Dallas Road to continue east. If you miss this turn, you will know it, as West Dallas Road heads steeply downhill to the north/northeast and eventually reaches shrublands en route to the standard trailhead for the North Pole Trail.

Begin a short, steep climb. Cross what appears to be a road (actually an aqueduct), and continue climbing east over a small ridge. Drop south off the eastern side of the ridge and rejoin, but do not follow, the aqueduct. Near a small creek drainage that runs north-south, leave the aqueduct and enter the forest heading east/northeast via a gently inclined, indistinct trail. Here you begin the long 2.5-mile traverse eastward to Cocan Flats.

Pass through several clearings, including a sloping meadow, after another 0.5 mile. The trail between here and Vance's Creek is well-marked and easier to follow. Continue traversing across steep, forested slopes, crossing two deep drainages. From the bottom of the second gully (Vance's Creek), you'll see a treeless, shrub-covered hill to the north. Climb out of the creek, heading northeast. Cross over a buried fence, then follow a road upward and east to a treeless saddle south of the aforementioned shrub-covered hill.

Descend across the creek, then turn upstream (still skiing away from the shrub-covered hill, heading south/southeast), following an indistinct road up and over a low, forested pass and then down along a creek into Cocan Flats, which also offers great views of Mount Sneffels. Ski across the flats on a southeasterly course, intercept the road into East Dallas Creek, and begin the descent to the hut. This road is easy to follow, but it does cross a few, steep, normally inactive, avalanche-prone gullies — so be careful!

Coast down the road to a point roughly 80 feet above East Dallas Creek, where a small road forks south onto a tiny bench below an old logged-over area. Turn onto the road and follow it for a few hundred feet to the Blue Lakes Hut, which is on the left, overlooking the creek.

23 Blue Lakes Hut

HUT ELEVATION	9,380'
DATE BUILT	1989 (original tent); 1991 (current hut)
SEASONS	Thanksgiving through late April
CAPACITY	8
HUT LAYOUT	16 x 16 wood cabin with built-in bunks along 2 walls
HUT ESSENTIALS	Wood-burning stove for heat, propane cookstove, propane lights, all kitchenware, foamies, minimalist outdoor toilets

Blue Lakes Hut lies below Mount Sneffels on a small bench above East Dallas Creek. One of the simplest of the San Juan huts to reach, Blue Lakes Hut is a good beginner destination. Nice skiing is available close to the hut; the surrounding hillsides are great for telemarking; and Cocan Flats and the East Fork of Dallas Creek make fine touring areas.

Skiing from Blue Lakes Hut to the North Pole Hut or the Ridgway Hut requires much more experience and stamina than is required to reach this hut from the trailhead.

Book reservations through the San Juan Hut System (see Appendix A).

RECOMMENDED DAY TRIPS:

The large, convoluted slopes and log cuts to the southwest of the hut are loaded with all levels and types of skiing. Many of these runs push up to near tree line. Feel free to explore.

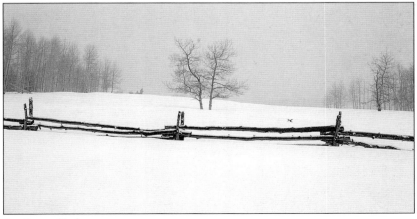

San Juan solitude.

Opposite: Mark Kelley skis through open country from North Pole Hut to Blue Lakes Hut under the watchful eye of Mount Sneffels.

SEE MAP PAGES 150, 174–175, AND 188–189

TOUR

23a East Dallas Creek Trailhead to Blue Lakes Hut

NOVICE

TIME	4 to 6 hours
DISTANCE	5.2 miles
ELEVATIONS	TRAILHEAD: 8,200' HUT: 9,380' GAIN: +1,180'
AVALANCHE	Some avalanche terrain encountered; easily avoided
MAPS	USGS 7.5': Mount Sneffels, 1987
	National Forest: Uncompahgre
	Trails Illustrated: Map #141 (Silverton/Ouray/Telluride/Lake City)

DIRECTIONS TO TRAILHEAD: Drive on CO 62 to East Dallas Creek Road (County Road 7). This turnoff is marked by a National Forest access sign 4.9 miles west of the U.S. 550 intersection in Ridgway. Turn south onto this dirt road and follow National Forest signs approximately 4 miles to the end of the plowed road. You will drive through two intersections heading into the trailhead. At the first, follow the National Forest sign, and at the second—marked "7A"—take the righthand turn. Watch carefully for these signs, as it is easy to turn onto private ranch roads.

THE ROUTE: From the trailhead, ski south along the forest access road up the East Fork of Dallas Creek. Pass a National Forest boundary en route. Be sure to remain on the main road above the creek until you contour to the south/south-west into a large, willowy meadow. Ski due south up the slowly narrowing valley through increasingly forested terrain until the road nears the Blue Lakes Trailhead (approximately 9,320') and climbs around a hairpin turn, heading sharply back

to the north/northwest. Stay on the road past this switchback. After several hundred feet, you can see the hut on the left. Continue upward for a short distance, keeping an eye out for a lefthand turn onto a small, knoblike bench. Eventually a small fork veers left (south) to the hut.

Shelter from the storm at Blue Lakes Hut.

TOUR
23b Blue Lakes Hut to Ridgway Hut

SEE MAP PAGES 150, 174–175, AND 188–189

TIME	5 to 7 hours
DISTANCE	5.0 to 5.5 miles
ELEVATIONS	BL HUT: 9,380' R HUT: 10,200' GAIN/LOSS: +2,040'/-1,200'
AVALANCHE	Route crosses avalanche slopes; prone to skier-triggered avalanches during high-hazard periods
MAPS	USGS 7.5': Mount Sneffels, 1987
	National Forest: Uncompahgre
	Trails Illustrated: Map #141 (Silverton/Ouray/Telluride/Lake City)

TOUR OVERVIEW: This is another challenging stretch of trail in the San Juan Hut System. Although it is only 5 to 5.5 miles long, the trail is not marked and the ascent over the ridge between the huts gains and loses considerable elevation.

Descending to the Ridgway Hut requires intermediate downhill ski techniques and good route-finding skills, as the thick forest around the hut has few obvious landmarks. In addition, there are several old logging roads that do not appear on the USGS topo map. Navigating to the hut can be confusing if you wander off the route.

Skiing this route in reverse (east to west), from the Ridgway Hut to the Blue Lakes Hut, can be even more difficult, as the descent consists of even steeper, more demanding tree skiing. With no powder snow, this descent can test the best. Skiers attempting this tour must be skilled at wilderness navigation, route-finding, and tree skiing. The tour described here is modified from the route described in previous editions and is the recommended path. It maximizes the quality of snow while trying to minimize the exposure to avalanche hazard in Wilson Creek.

THE ROUTE: Leave the Blue Lakes Hut and return to the road, then drop down to East Dallas Creek Road. The best spot for this streamcrossing varies throughout the winter, depending on snow conditions, but the recommended route goes like this: Once back on the East Dallas Creek Road, turn upstream (south) and ski up to the end of the road at the summer parking area for the Blue Lakes Trailhead. The Blue Lakes Trail leaves the south end of the parking area and is marked "Do not take this trail."

Instead, look for a "truck-width" road going down east to the creek and a log bridge. This trail is the Wilson Creek Trail #203 that goes up into Blaine Basin. Crossing the creek is a bridge that still supports skiers. *Important note:* Across the bridge is an old log-cut above you to the right that has seen serious avalanche activity during periods of high snowpack instability. When conditions are hazardous, do not follow the trail across the bridge and under this path. Instead, devise a crossing of the creek downstream (north) via downed logs and snowbridges where cover is provided by the forest.

Once across the creek, climb up the steep, timbered slopes to the east and regain the trail/road beyond the slide path. Of course, if conditions are stable, cross the bridge and follow the trail past the slide area. Either way, after you are past the slide area, ski past several switchbacks that take you up and over a low, angled ridge. Just past the ridge, ski past a smaller trail leading up to the right and continue southeast into the Wilson Creek drainage following the main trail.

The next stretch of trail essentially follows the Wilson Creek drainage, flirting with potential avalanche hazard throughout—so keep an eye out. After the trail has crossed the creek, cross an irrigation ditch, then switchback up to a road that heads southeast up-valley on the northeast side of Wilson Creek.

Ski to a small clearing that runs along the left side of the trail. This is the old recommended ascent trail to the ridge. It is not used anymore, though it may still be marked with silver diamonds. Continue up-valley until you reach a small, thermal spring that runs year-round and flows down into Wilson Creek. Proceed past this spring and cross the creek via snowbridges and/or downed logs. You will now be southwest of the creek.

Follow the trail along the creek until the summer route crosses back to the east/northeast side of the creek. The best winter crossing is just before this summer route crossing and before you reach the dangerous, steep slide paths that come down off Peak 12,910' (called "Blaine Peak"). Throughout this portion of drainage are steep-walled creek banks that form terrain traps. Look for a lower-angled path up and out of the creek.

Now the grunt portion of the tour begins as you make the ascent north-east to the top of the ridge via a cross-country route. Begin heading east/northeast, aiming for the area that corresponds to the 10,600' printed contour elevation on the USGS topo maps. Compass bearings, an altimeter, and, of course, the map are all-important here.

Note: You do not want to begin heading too directly north on the beginning of the climb. This takes you to the large, flat bench that sits due west of the pass over the ridge and is separated from the pass by a steep, sun-baked (at times snow-less), aspen-covered slope.

The recommended route makes the best use of forest cover and, consequently, the best snow for touring uphill and downhill for skiers coming over from the Ridgway Hut. Once you have arrived at 10,600', contour north up along a lower-angled bench that leads to a depression at 10,740'. This depression is a small wetland, or sink, in summer and is marked on the topo maps with a closed, amoeba-shaped contour line with "spokes" pointing toward the center.

Ski north over this depression, or bench, and begin climbing slightly north/northwest up the final ascent to the top of the ridge. If you do this correctly, you should arrive at the pass that lies between two knobs on top of the ridge. Don't forget to turn around and peer across the chasm you just climbed out of and take in one of the finest mountain vistas to be seen in Colorado!

Now for the final stretch. Cross over the ridge and ski east down into the dark north-facing forest through nicely spaced spruce trees. After losing 400 feet, begin looking for a logging road that traverses east from the shallow creek drainage that you have been shadowing. This road extends east out of the taller trees and onto a bench scattered with small post-logging second-growth trees. There are also views to the higher peaks above. The hut is directly below you here. You can either drop down to the hut or circle around to the east and north before skiing back west a few hundred feet to the hut.

The key to this closing descent is not to drop too far down—especially when you are euphorically skiing through the trees—and miss the logging road.

Joe Ryan and the late, great Rags the Dog tour above the Ridgway Hut. Behind is the enormous north face of Cirque Peak that separates Blaine and Yankee Boy Basins.

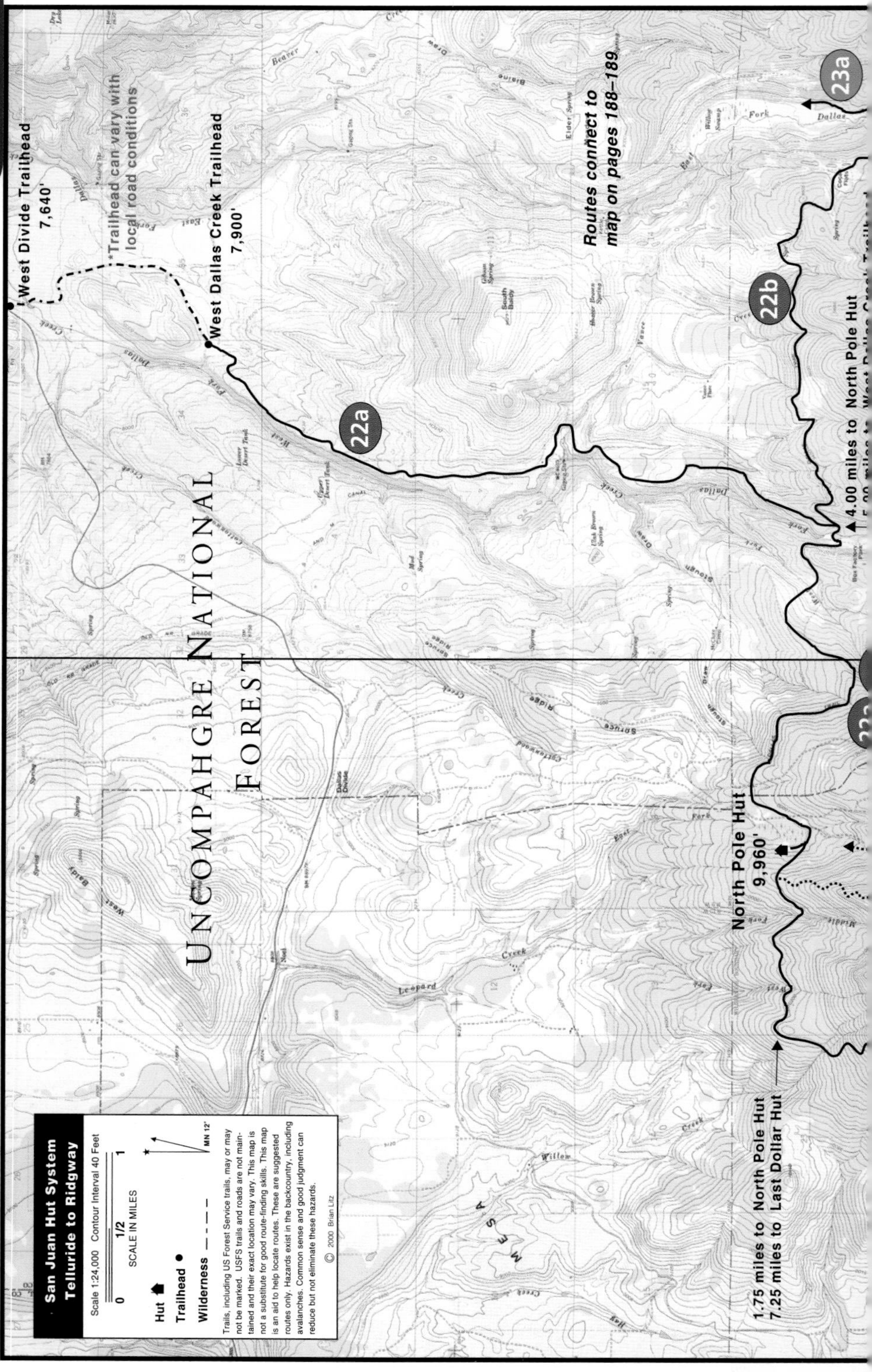

San Juan Hut System
Telluride to Ridgway
Scale 1:24,000 Contour Interval 40 Feet
0
1/2
1
SCALE IN MILES
Hut
Trailhead
Wilderness
MN 12°
Trails, including US Forest Service trails, may or may not be marked. USFS trails and roads are not maintained and their exact location may vary. This map is not a substitute for good route-finding skills. This map is an aid to help locate routes. These are suggested routes only. Hazards exist in the backcountry, including avalanches. Common sense and good judgment can reduce but not eliminate these hazards.
© 2000 Brian Litz
West Divide Trailhead
7,640'
*Trailhead can vary with local road conditions
West Dallas Creek Trailhead
7,900'
Routes connect to map on pages 188–189
22a
22b
23a
UNCOMPAHGRE NATIONAL FOREST
North Pole Hut
9,960'
4.00 miles to North Pole Hut
1.75 miles to North Pole Hut
7.25 miles to Last Dollar Hut
M E S A
Dallas Divide
Leopard Creek
Willow Creek
Hay Creek
Spruce Ridge
Cottonwood
West Baldy
South Baldy
Uncompahgre
Beaver Creek
Dallas Creek
West Fork
East Fork
Vance Creek
Blaine Draw
Elder Spring
Slough Draw
Mud Spring

Last Dollar, North Pole, & Blue Lakes Huts

175

24 Ridgway Hut

HUT ELEVATION	10,200'
DATE BUILT	1998
SEASONS	Thanksgiving through late April
CAPACITY	8
HUT LAYOUT	16 x 16 wood cabin with built-in bunks along 2 walls
HUT ESSENTIALS	Wood-burning stove for heat, propane cookstove, propane lights, all kitchenware, foamies, minimalist outdoor toilets

Ridgway Hut, which sleeps eight, was the second hut erected in the San Juan Hut System. To this day, this premier ski hut remains popular. The route to the hut follows one of the most beautiful and scenic trails in the state, touring past rustic wooden fences and tall aspens (many covered with bear-claw marks), up into the forest below Mount Ridgway.

Backcountry skiing around the Ridgway Hut is like tree skiing at a downhill area—minus the lifts, crowds, and draft beer. The skiing above the huts is best suited

to intermediate and expert skiers. To fully enjoy the skiing above the hut, you must have at least intermediate downhill skills, as well as a solid understanding of backcountry safety and avalanche procedures. Be cautious of several large avalanche gullies south of the hut, and bear in mind that you will encounter serious wilderness skiing around this hut—so come prepared with the proper safety equipment and the proper mindset.

All a-bored in the Ridgway Hut.

RECOMMENDED DAY TRIPS:

The telemark skiing above the hut is absolutely incredible. Either climb directly south from the hut or, better, head south up onto the bench with small post-logging trees. Find the logging road that heads west into the thicker forest. After a few hundred feet you will reach a small drainage heading up to the left. Ascend this to the top of the ridge (this is the beginning of the route to the Blue Lakes Hut). You can traverse along the top of the ridge north and drop off to the right (east). For the best skiing, though, traverse left (southeast) up the ridge-crest and drop off at will onto the northeast side back down to the logging approach road and the hut. The skiing off this timbered ridge is superb—and safe—with telemark runs of up to 1,400 vertical feet. With a full day you can make several runs through this area, exploring the great snow.

Expert skiers can continue up the ridge, past a high, rocky outcrop and up the wind-scoured ramp that gives access to the highest, above–tree-line ridge. This ramp is to the left (north) of the prominent, west-facing massive rock buttress that tops out at Elevation Point 11,786' on the topo maps. From atop the ramp, steep tree skiing leads back down north and northeast to the hut. Also, the large, distinctive avalanche gully with the intermittent creek that is directly east of Elevation Point 11,786' is skiable under absolutely safe conditions. Approach this with extreme caution. You can ski along its western edge in the trees for some fantastic tree glade skiing. Ski at your own risk!

In addition to the great telemark skiing, those willing to climb to the ridge will be treated to **intimate views of Blaine Basin and the north faces of Mount Sneffels and Cirque Mountain.** This is one of my favorite lunch spots in Colorado!

Skiers can explore above the hut to the south as far as tree line and spend hours, if not days, telemark skiing. Although there are no exact routes, skiers who are comfortable with off-trail backcountry skiing can wander all over, exploring the glades of the upper Beaver Creek drainage.

Extreme skiing is available in the avalanche gullies, chutes, and basins above the hut near tree line. Many of these appear on the topo maps. In fact, an almost unlimited number of adrenaline-inducing lines drop down off the ridgelike wall south of the hut. These routes are not covered in this book because of their capricious nature. For information on these thrilling routes, and to reserve the hut, call the San Juan Hut System (see Appendix A).

TOUR
24a

Girl Scout Camp Road Trailhead to Ridgway Hut

SEE MAP PAGES 150 AND 188–189

INTERMEDIATE

TIME	5 to 7 hours
DISTANCE	7.0 to 7.5 miles
ELEVATIONS	TRAILHEAD: 8,720'　　HUT: 10,200'　　GAIN/LOSS: +1,980'/-450'
AVALANCHE	Minimal danger
MAPS	USGS 7.5': Mount Sneffels, 1987
	National Forest: Uncompahgre
	Trails Illustrated: Map #141 (Silverton/Ouray/Telluride/Lake City)

TOUR OVERVIEW: This distinctly Colorado trail gets my vote as one of the most beautiful trails anywhere, with its ranch-country ambiance, silent, monochromatic aspen woods, and the rugged Sneffels Range on high. All in all, this is a solid intermediate trail that is not too difficult to follow, though you need to pay attention at a few critical intersections. In addition, its upper half follows distinct trails and roads, none of which appear on the most recent revision of the USGS 7.5-minute topo map. The upper section, too, is the most physically demanding and comes at you near the end of the day and the tour—so pace yourself.

When leaving the hut, less proficient skiers would be wise to use skins on their skis to slow the descent to Beaver Creek, for the trail drops down a forested ridge via a steep, twisting road. Well-traveled and scenic, this is a recommended trip for skiers who have limited time to spend in the San Juan Hut System.

DIRECTIONS TO TRAILHEAD: Drive on CO 62 to County Road 5 (Girl Scout Camp Road). This turnoff is on the western edge of Ridgway, 0.8 mile west of U.S. 550. Turn south onto CR 5, contour sharply right after 0.2 mile, then drive to a fork in the road and a barbed wire fence, a total of 5.5 miles from CO 62. The left fork goes to the Elk Meadows Development, which is private property (you'll see a line of mailboxes). The right fork crosses a cattle guard and is marked by a "Leaving Ridgway Fire Protection" sign. This is the public access route, which crosses private property for several miles. Park off the road to the right after crossing the cattle guard, or park along the road just before the fork. Local conditions (mud and snow) may dictate where you park.

THE ROUTE: Leave the cars and ski along the road in an ascending traverse across the north aspect of Elevation Point 9,204'. Contour around this point, then ascend south across a very wide, treeless drainage. Gain the south edge of a bluff that overlooks the vast Beaver Creek drainage, where you will have an unobstructed panorama of the Sneffels Range, and then ski down the bluff to the southeast on a long, traversing road through scrub oak.

Superb Ridgway Hut is base camp for some of the best hut powder skiing in Colorado.

Tour south along this gentle road toward the forest. Soon aspen trees and occasional fences hem the trail. Continue along the road, passing green metal signs reading "Beaver Creek Wildlife Preserve—No Hunting." Follow the road south, down across an east-facing slope and across Coal Creek, then double-pole east on the road past a yellow metal gate that marks the National Forest boundary. Do not continue straight ahead but, rather, make a sharp right turn south onto a road and begin a steady, moderate climb for roughly 0.4 mile to a tiny clearing below aspens—a critical route landmark. From this clearing, which may be marked by several small pieces of orange flagging, the most obvious trail heads due east into

Joe Ryan skis above Ridgway Hut during a spell of rock-solid snowpack conditions.

the trees. This route is the Dallas Trail to the Burn Hut and Ouray, and at times it is buzzing with snowmobilers. Do not take this trail.

Turn sharply west and follow a narrow trail, marked with blue diamonds and trail blazes, up over a small ridge. Descend off the ridge via a steep drop along a barbed wire fence, cross a creek, then ascend onto a wide ridge that is topped by a large, secluded meadow at 9,453' in the middle of an aspen forest. (The section of trail from this meadow to the hut follows roads and trails that are not on the USGS topo map.)

Cross to the west side of the meadow, passing another north-south road en route, then continue west down a short, steep drop, crossing another creek. Climb out of this small drainage, ski down a subtle ridge, and cross a wide, shallow basin covered with aspen trees. Follow this trail west through the aspens, then slightly north, until the trail reaches a tiny creek. The trail immediately inter-sects the road that descends left (south) to Beaver Creek. This intersection, marked with orange flagging tied to a small evergreen tree, is easy to miss. Turn south onto this road and climb slightly before dropping into the Beaver Creek drainage. Follow the road on a northwesterly course up onto a forested ridge, cross another creek to the west, then begin the last steep ascent. This climb heads directly south up a thickly forested ridge via a sharply switchbacking road. After gaining roughly 600 feet in elevation, the road traverses off the west side of the ridge to a gully. Cross the shallow drainage and follow the trail along a gentle traverse west through immature trees until you reach the Ridgway Hut.

Note: Remember that the road from Beaver Creek to the hut does not appear on the latest 7.5-minute quads.

TOUR 24b
Ridgway Hut to Burn Hut
SEE MAP PAGES 150 AND 188–189

INTERMEDIATE

TIME	2 to 4 hours
DISTANCE	4.75 miles
ELEVATIONS	R HUT: 10,200' B HUT: 9,880' GAIN/LOSS: +900'/-1,160'
AVALANCHE	Some avalanche terrain encountered; easily avoided
MAPS	USGS 7.5': Mount Sneffels, 1987; Ouray, 1983
	National Forest: Uncompahgre
	Trails Illustrated: Map #141 (Silverton/Ouray/Telluride/Lake City)

THE ROUTE: From the Girl Scout Camp Road Trailhead, the Burn Hut Trail and the Ridgway Hut Trail overlap for the first 4 miles until they reach a small clearing at 9,400 feet. From that spot, the trails split into a Y. The trail between the Ridgway and Burn Huts follows the upper arms of the Y, dropping from one hut to the meadow and then climbing back to the other. The information summary above gives the trail data for skiers traveling west to east from the Ridgway Hut to the Burn Hut. Obviously, it can be, and often is, skied from east to west.

Because this tour covers terrain discussed within other trail descriptions, refer to the two Girl Scout Camp Road Trailhead tours (Tours 24a and 25a, see pages 178 and 184) for specific directions to each hut from the clearing where the trail splits.

John Fielder, sans his omnipresent camera, nears the bottom of the spectacular avalanche run above Ridgway Hut. Skiing terrain like this should be done only under the most stable conditions and by those who know what they're doing.

25 Burn Hut

HUT ELEVATION	9,880'
DATE BUILT	1989
SEASONS	Thanksgiving through late April
CAPACITY	8
HUT LAYOUT	16 x 16 wood cabin with built-in bunks along 2 walls
HUT ESSENTIALS	Wood-burning stove for heat, propane cookstove, propane lights, all kitchenware, foamies, and minimalist outdoor toilets

The Burn Hut is a fine destination for beginning and intermediate skiers, mixed groups, and aspiring backcountry skiers who may not be ready to cope with serious avalanche hazards and complicated route-finding. The route to the hut is somewhat long for a novice-level tour, but overall it is very moderate. The trail follows a low-gradient road, which is challenging but not overwhelming, and you get the beautiful panoramas associated with harder tours in the area.

The original Burn Hut was moved slightly, to a better location, and was replaced with a nicer, yet still simple, structure. The current hut is down the hill to the east from the old location, just across Coal Creek in a stately stand of aspens. Now all of the high peaks to the south are visible, framed through the pale limbs of the trees. For all intents and purposes, this move does not affect the nature of the approach. The final mile of the tour is still the steepest. The cabin, which sleeps eight, is surrounded by meadows, forests, and rolling hills that are ideal for all levels of skiers to explore. For reservations, call the San Juan Hut System (see Appendix A).

RECOMMENDED DAY TRIPS:

One quick trip proceeds along the road that is just to the north of the hut, climbing to the northeast up and over a ridge. The views only get better the farther you go. Once over the ridge, the trail just barely enters a clearing before exiting to the south into the woods again. Look around a bit if you don't immediately find the trail into the woods.

Once you have found the trail, follow it east across a creek drainage and another clearing. From here, follow the creek upstream east/southeast for a few hundred feet until you crest a small saddle, where the treeless Moonshine Park rolls down to the east. There is superb skiing here. Far below is Ouray and, to the east, the ragged summits and needles of the Cimarron Group of the San Juans. This is the only spot in the San Juan Hut System where this view can be seen. It is truly incredible!

Gene White, Mike O'Brien, and David Harrower kick-and-glide through sublime aspen forests common to San Juan Hut System.

TOUR

25a Girl Scout Camp Road Trailhead to Burn Hut

SEE MAP PAGES 150 AND 188-189

TIME	3 to 6 hours
DISTANCE	5.5 miles
ELEVATIONS	TRAILHEAD: 8,720' HUT: 9,880' GAIN/LOSS: +1,420'/-230'
AVALANCHE	Minimal danger
MAPS	USGS 7.5': Mount Sneffels, 1987; Ouray, 1982
	National Forest: Uncompahgre
	Trails Illustrated: Map #141 (Silverton/Ouray/Telluride/Lake City)

TOUR OVERVIEW: This trail shares the trailhead and the first several miles of the Girl Scout Camp Road Trailhead to the Ridgway Hut tour. Refer to Tour 24a (see page 179–180) for directions to the small clearing at 9,400 feet.

THE ROUTE: From the small clearing, follow the road east through a stand of spruce trees and begin the 1.3-mile climb to the hut. Travel up the road 0.4 mile on a moderately steep climb until you break into a small meadow along a creek drainage. Proceed past a gray, fenced-in, water-gauging station and continue up through a switchback onto a ridge.

Burn Hut with Whitehouse Mountain above.

Climb through the forest until you enter a large meadow ("the burn"). Continue east into and across the meadow. Head slightly east and southeast, veering just to the right of the road. Aim for a thick stand of aspens across the creek. The Burn Hut sits in the center of these aspens and is obscured by the trees.

ADVANCED/EXPERT (WAY GNARLY)

TOUR
25b Burn Hut to Ouray Trailhead

SEE MAP PAGES 150 AND 188–189

TIME	4 to 7 hours
DISTANCE	5.6 miles
ELEVATIONS	HUT: 9,880' TRAILHEAD: 7,600' GAIN/LOSS: +340'/-2,600'
AVALANCHE	Some avalanche terrain encountered; easily avoided
MAPS	USGS 7.5': Mount Sneffels, 1987; Ouray, 1982
	National Forest: Uncompahgre
	Trails Illustrated: Map #141 (Silverton/Ouray/Telluride/Lake City)

TOUR OVERVIEW: This stretch of trail follows the Dallas Trail to its eastern terminus down in the valley south of the town of Ouray. Officially, this trail is the final leg of the San Juan Hut System route from Telluride to Ouray. The problem is that few people ever ski it, and I have been hesitant to include it in prior editions of *Colorado Hut to Hut* for a variety of reasons. Foremost is the fact that it is probably the most difficult winter "hut" trail in the state. Its menu of challenges offers up a hearty blend of technical skiing, tricky route-finding, poor snow on

Above Ridgway Hut, Gene White looks at 14,150-foot Mount Sneffels' North Face.

the lower stretches, vast amounts of elevation gain or loss (depending on direction of travel — though I suggest this as only an egress route), and, last but not least, the possibility of deadly falls off slick, exposed switchbacks down through cliffbands near the bottom end of the trail. Co-owner of the system Joe Ryan describes this trail as "extreme Nordic."

I have done this route, though, and with good snow conditions, expert skiers can manage it. For those with a taste for adventure, it is an unforgettable journey. Most of the trail is quite nice and offers up good skiing. If you try to use this as an approach route to the Burn Hut, get a pre-dawn, "alpine" start. If I have whetted your perverse appetite, read on. I will give you only a slight overview of the route and leave the details of this trip for the experienced to discover.

DIRECTIONS TO TRAILHEAD: Drive to a point roughly 2 miles north of Ouray. Cross a beige-colored bridge to the west and gain the frontage road. Turn right (north), and drive along the Uncompahgre River for 0.25 mile. Look for a small post and a Dallas Trail sign. The best parking is back by the bridge to the south. Park between the frontage road and the river. If you end your trip by skiing out from the Burn Hut, this is the place to leave end-of-trip shuttle cars.

THE ROUTE: From the Burn Hut, continue on the Dallas Trail (the road) heading to the northeast up and over the ridge to the east. This leads you to the top of Moonshine Park and the Cimarron vista. Drop east through Moonshine Park. Do not ski all the way to the bottom. Rather, about two-thirds of the way down, look for a trail and marker exiting the park to the right (south). Follow the trail into the woods and continue the journey downward. From here on down, the route follows the summer trail directly and is marked with a variety of trail markers and blazes.

As you drop in elevation, snow conditions can and will deteriorate, as much of the lower aspects have eastern and southern exposures, and because of the relatively low elevation. Remember that as you make the final descent through the cliffs (beware of the potential for 100-foot falls), the snow can be almost nonexistent or might consist of packed ice. You can always walk and carry your skis through here. Joe Ryan has skied the entire length on several occasions.

Ski areas cover less than
one tenth of one percent of the
skiable terrain on earth.

Cool.

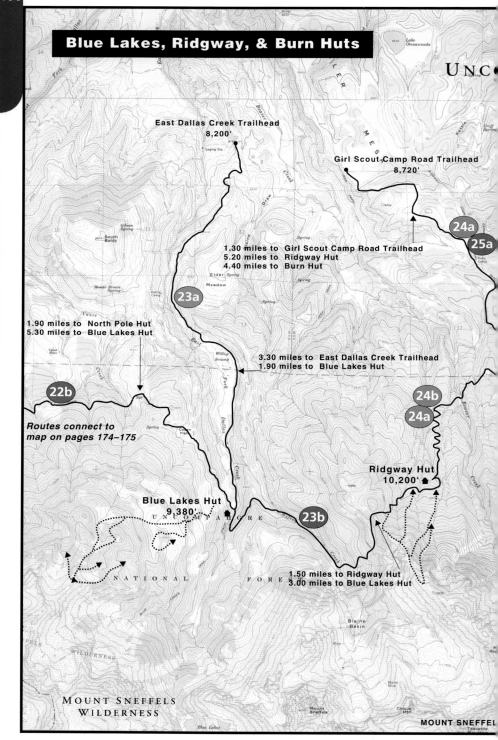

Blue Lakes, Ridgway, & Burn Huts

UNC

East Dallas Creek Trailhead
8,200'

Girl Scout Camp Road Trailhead
8,720'

24a

25a

1.30 miles to Girl Scout Camp Road Trailhead
5.20 miles to Ridgway Hut
4.40 miles to Burn Hut

23a

1.90 miles to North Pole Hut
5.30 miles to Blue Lakes Hut

3.30 miles to East Dallas Creek Trailhead
1.90 miles to Blue Lakes Hut

22b

24b

24a

*Routes connect to
map on pages 174–175*

Ridgway Hut
10,200'

Blue Lakes Hut
9,380'

23b

1.50 miles to Ridgway Hut
3.00 miles to Blue Lakes Hut

MOUNT SNEFFELS
WILDERNESS

MOUNT SNEFFEL

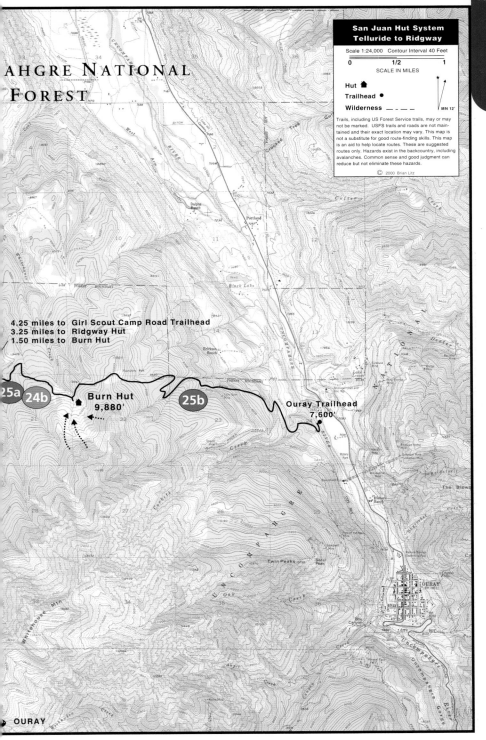

AHGRE NATIONAL
FOREST

San Juan Hut System
Telluride to Ridgway

Scale 1:24,000   Contour Interval 40 Feet

0   1/2   1
SCALE IN MILES

Hut ⌂
Trailhead ●
Wilderness — — — —   MN 12°

Trails, including US Forest Service trails, may or may
not be marked. USFS trails and roads are not maintained and their exact location may vary. This map is
not a substitute for good route-finding skills. This map
is an aid to help locate routes. These are suggested
routes only. Hazards exist in the backcountry, including
avalanches. Common sense and good judgment can
reduce but not eliminate these hazards.

© 2000 Brian Litz

4.25 miles to Girl Scout Camp Road Trailhead
3.25 miles to Ridgway Hut
1.50 miles to Burn Hut

25a   24b

Burn Hut
9,880'

25b

Ouray Trailhead
7,600'

OURAY

San Juan Hut System—Summer/Bike

The journey from Telluride to Moab, Utah, is as much an exploration into the geology and ecology of the American West as it is a mountain-biking adventure. Islands of alpine peaks float in a sea of piñon/juniper forests and sandstone mesas. The lonesome and seemingly desolate lands of western Colorado and southeastern Utah are home to a wealth of plants, animals, and people as colorful as the polychromatic countryside.

From Telluride, a Victorian mining town cradled high in a picturesque canyon in the San Juan Mountains, Last Dollar Road climbs up and over the western corner of the Sneffels Range. The road then strikes off to the north and west across the fascinating Uncompahgre Plateau. Formed 10 to 40 million years ago, the San Juans tell a story of volcanic mountain building and glacial sculpting, and the Uncompahgre Plateau exhibits massive uplift caused by internal disturbances of the earth's crust.

The broad expanse of the Colorado Plateau sweeps west across southern Utah. Formed from ancient dunes, tidal flats, and riverbeds compressed over eons into a complex layer cake of sedimentary rocks, Utah's high desert contains some of North America's most compelling and beautiful topography. Deeply etched by water and wind, this environment is a moisture-starved labyrinth of dead-end arroyos, impassable gorges, and delicate rock towers.

Mountain biking through this country is not easy, but it is highly rewarding. Sweet, aromatic sagebrush, crimson sunsets, and an overwhelming sense of solitude create an experience that will leave you with a feeling of accomplishment and satisfaction. The 215-mile tour is described from Telluride to Moab, which is the only feasible direction of travel, as Moab is several thousand feet lower than Telluride. Because the trip is a one-way journey, shuttles must be arranged for the end of your tour.

The route requires more stamina than technical riding skill, as nearly the entire tour travels over well-maintained forest roads. Riding to the Last Dollar Hut and the La Sal Hut represents the most difficult time. Most of the trip, however, is through rolling countryside amid thick evergreen forests interspersed with panoramic vistas.

Mike Turrin and Joe Ryan and the staff of the San Juan Hut System will work with your group to custom-tailor a trip to your requirements. The huts are open from June 1 through October 1, with pleasant touring all summer long. Daytime temperatures in August and into September can soar. Early summer and autumn, with warm days and brisk evenings, are perhaps the best times to cover the route. Remember that western skies are notorious for turning inky black with violent thunderstorms throughout the summer. Carry rain clothes and be prepared to sit out short storms. Early- and late-season riders may also experience light snow at higher elevations, so plan accordingly. Whenever you go, be sure to carry several water bottles.

Each shelter is equipped with propane lights and a cookstove, a wood-burning stove for heat, cookware and utensils, a water supply, an outdoor toilet, and even sleeping bags, pads, and bunks. During the summer months, riders are encouraged to sleep under the stars—to experience the expansive heavens that have inspired so many western artists, Native American storytellers, and singing coyotes.

A few rules to remember when using the huts: Conserve water, shut off propane, burn paper, sweep and clean, put out the fire in the woodstove, and fasten and lock all doors and windows. Currently, all huts are supplied with two metal refuse cans—one for trash and one for food scraps. Also, the Gateway and La Sal Huts no longer have wood-burning stoves for heat because of the potential fire hazard they present in this arid country.

The Telluride-to-Moab mountain-bike tour is becoming very popular, so plan your trip early! Book reservations through the San Juan Hut System (see Appendix A).

Bernice Notenboom soaks up rays near Telluride.

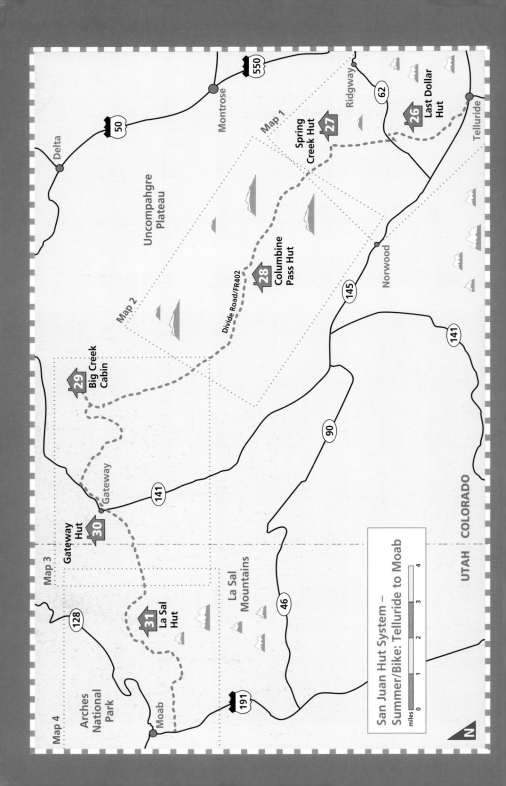

San Juan Hut System –
Summer/Bike: Telluride to Moab

26

Last Dollar Hut

HUT ELEVATION	10,980'
DATE BUILT	1987
SEASONS	June 1 through October 1 (summer biking); open in winter for skiing (see page 151)
CAPACITY	8
HUT LAYOUT	16 x 16 wood cabin with built-in bunks along 2 walls
HUT ESSENTIALS	Propane cookstove and lights, water, all kitchenware, fully stocked food supply

The Last Dollar Hut, which sleeps eight, is the highest-elevation hut on the Telluride-to-Moab route. The road to the hut is steep and scenic. The first day of riding is relatively short with respect to mileage, but it is at a high elevation with continual climbing during the final portion of the ride. Last Dollar Road is one of the most scenic and most photographed backroads in Colorado. For reservations, call the San Juan Hut System (see Appendix A).

A biker enjoys the scenery on Last Dollar Road.

TOUR

26a DAY 1: **Telluride to Last Dollar Hut**

SEE MAP PAGES 192 AND 195

TIME	3 to 6 hours
DISTANCE	14.9 miles

ELEVATIONS   TRAILHEAD: 8,800'   HUT: 10,980'   GAIN/LOSS: +2,700'/-550'

MAPS   National Forest: Uncompahgre

TOUR OVERVIEW: This tour overlooks the La Sal Mountains and the state of Utah to the west, the Wilson Peaks to the south, and the Silverton West Group of the San Juan Mountains to the east. Whether your trip is planned during the summer when the wildflowers are in bloom or in the autumn when the mountains are awash with golden aspen, you will enjoy the finest mountain scenery that Colorado and Utah have to offer.

THE ROUTE: The tour begins in Telluride. Head west out of town to Society Turn, where CO 145 turns south to Ophir, Lizard Head Pass, and Dolores. From Society Turn, turn north onto the airport road (Forest Road 638) at mile 4.1. Leave the pavement at a stop sign and go right at mile 6.2 on a dirt road. The airport runway and hangars will be in view. Descend 400 feet into the Deep Creek Valley, and cross the creek via a bridge at mile 8.4 (do not take a left here!).

Continue up this road until you see a sign for Willow Creek at mile 11.1. Pass an Uncompahgre National Forest sign at mile 12. Ride past an old homestead, fallen-down cabins, and some beaver ponds, then cross the creek and begin ascending switchbacks at mile 13.1. Pass the Whipple Mountain Trail (sign 419) at mile 14.4, and continue to Last Dollar Pass at mile 14.7.

The hut is 0.25 mile and 300 vertical feet up the ridge to the east/northeast. Pedal directly up the steep and rocky path to a point where it becomes too steep to ride. Walk your bike to the hut, which can be seen when you are roughly 70 feet away.

MAP 1: San Juan Hut System – Summer/Bike:
Last Dollar Hut and Spring Creek Hut

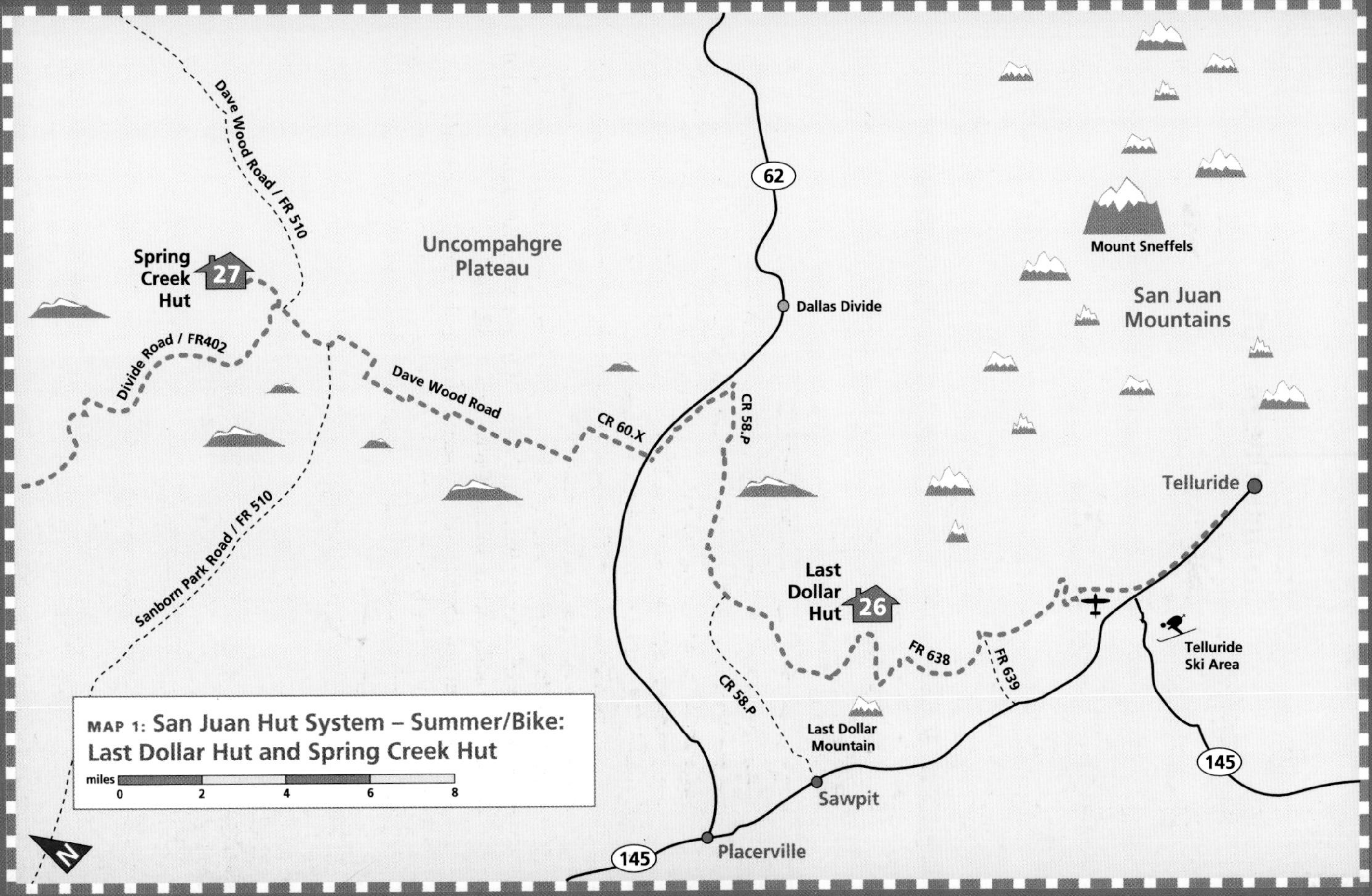

to Dolores

145

Telluride

Telluride Ski Area

FR 639

FR 638

Last Dollar Mountain

Sawpit

Mount Sneffels

San Juan Mountains

Last Dollar Hut

26

Dallas Divide

62

CR 58.P

CR 58.P

Placerville

145

to Ridgway & U.S. 550

CR 60.X

to Norwood

Uncompahgre Plateau

Dave Wood Road

Dave Wood Road / FR 510

Spring Creek Hut

27

Divide Road / FR402

Sanborn Park Road / FR 510

N

miles
0   2   4   6   8

Connect Map 2

27 Spring Creek Hut

HUT ELEVATION	9,200'
DATE BUILT	1988 (nearby ranch house), 1990 (current hut)
SEASONS	June 1 through October 1
CAPACITY	8
HUT LAYOUT	16 x 16 wood cabin with built-in bunks along 2 walls
HUT ESSENTIALS	Propane cookstove and lights, water, all kitchenware, fully stocked food supply

The second leg of the journey to Moab begins with a massive loss in altitude as you leave the Last Dollar Hut and descend to Dallas Divide. From Dallas Divide the route climbs onto the Uncompahgre Plateau and begins a traverse that lasts 2½ days across this impressive geological feature. The roads in this area are secondary dirt roads characterized by technically easy riding.

Bernice Notenboom views Utah's canyon country from the La Sal Mountains in the San Juan Hut System.

INTERMEDIATE

TOUR
27a

DAY 2: **Last Dollar Hut to Spring Creek Hut**
SEE MAP PAGES 192 AND 195

TIME 4 to 6 hours

DISTANCE 26.3 miles

ELEVATIONS LD HUT: 10,980' SC HUT: 9,200' GAIN/LOSS: +1,600'/-3,000'

MAPS National Forest: Uncompahgre

THE ROUTE: Pick up the route from near the front door of Last Dollar Hut and descend on foot to the north (this is not the route taken to the hut!). To control erosion, walk your bike for 250 feet to a point where the trail is wide enough to drive a truck. From here, return down to the summit of Last Dollar Pass (Forest Road 638) at mile 0.25.

Descend the north side of the pass to Alder Creek at mile 4.2. Climb out of Alder Creek onto Hastings Mesa to County Road 58P (Last Dollar Road). Near here you will pass Sawpit Road intersecting from the left at mile 5.8; this road is marked by old corrals and livestock-loading chutes and is to be avoided.

Continue on CR 58P, passing San Juan Vista on your right. You will eventually reach an intersection with CO 62 (paved) at mile 11.0. Turn west for a rapid ride down to County Road 60X (passing County Road 62X on the right). Leaving CO 62 near an abandoned ski cabin at mile 13.6, turn north onto CR 60X and ascend into Buck Canyon.

Climb 400 feet out of Buck Canyon and enter Howard Flats at mile 14.6. This was the site of an old Ute Indian horseracing track. From here, the route stair-steps through a series of 90-degree turns. Continue north to mile 15.7, where the road turns west at a small intersection. Go west (CR Z.60) until the main road turns north (CR 59.Z). Stay on the main road as it again makes a turn west on the Montrose/San Miguel county line. Turn north (CR JJ58) at mile 19.1. Stay on CR JJ.58 until you turn west onto CR 11, then make a final 90-degree turn onto Dave Wood Road at mile 20.9. Ride under power lines, descend to a broad valley, and cross Horsefly Creek at mile 23.4.

At a marked intersection with the Sanborn Park Road on the left (west) at mile 23.9, turn right onto Forest Road 510 and begin the second 400-foot ascent of the day. Pass Johnson Spring on the right at mile 25.4 (potable water flows from a black hose), then turn left onto Forest Road 402 at mile 25.6. The Dave Wood Road and FR 402 (Divide Road) intersect near a sign for Columbine Pass.

Follow FR 402 until you reach a firewood area, and turn right onto a small secondary road with a cattle guard at mile 25.8. Cross the first cattle guard, then two additional cattle guards. After passing the last cattle guard, ride to the third water-bar ditch running out to the left. Near the ditch is a large Douglas fir stump marking the spot where a path leads from the road to the hut. Spring Creek Hut is 150 feet away in the woods at mile 26.3.

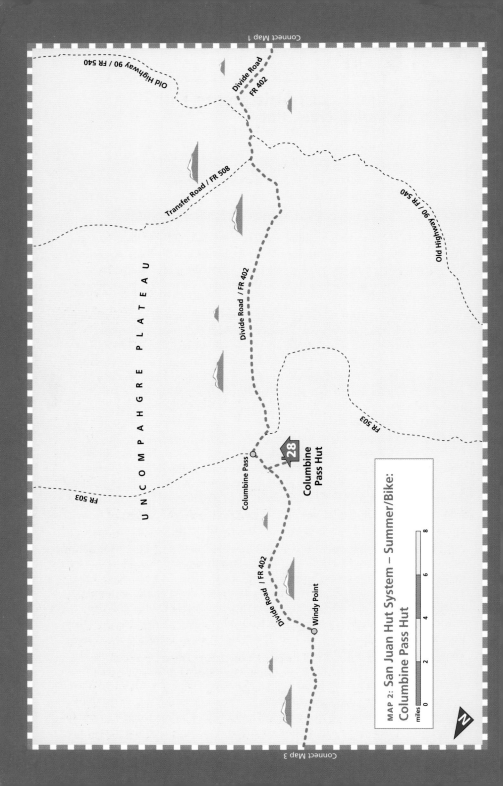

Old Highway 90 / FR 540

Divide Road
FR 402

Transfer Road / FR 508

Old Highway 90 / FR 540

U N C O M P A H G R E   P L A T E A U

Divide Road / FR 402

FR 503

FR 503

Columbine Pass

28

Columbine
Pass Hut

Divide Road / FR 402

Windy Point

MAP 2: San Juan Hut System – Summer/Bike:
Columbine Pass Hut

miles

0   2   4   6   8

N

28 Columbine Pass Hut

HUT ELEVATION	9,205'
DATE BUILT	1988 (tent); 1990 (nearby ranger station); 1991 (current hut)
SEASONS	June 1 through October 1
CAPACITY	8
HUT LAYOUT	16 x 16 wood cabin with built-in bunks along 2 walls
HUT ESSENTIALS	Propane cookstove and lights, water, all kitchenware, fully stocked food supply

The route connecting Spring Creek Hut and Columbine Pass Hut follows good secondary roads over gently rolling terrain. It is nontechnical, and mountain bikers of all abilities will be able to enjoy this stretch. Keep an eye out for vehicles traveling over these roads. Potable water is available at Columbine Campground.

TOUR 28a DAY 3: Spring Creek Hut to Columbine Pass Hut

SEE MAP PAGES 192 AND 198

INTERMEDIATE

TIME	5 to 7 hours
DISTANCE	34.3 miles
ELEVATIONS	SC HUT: 9,200' CP HUT: 9,205' GAIN/LOSS: +1,800'/-1,800'
MAPS	National Forest: Uncompahgre

THE ROUTE: Leave Spring Creek Hut and retrace the route to Forest Road 402 (Divide Road). Leave the firewood cutting area, and at mile 1.1 head right (north) along FR 402 toward Columbine Pass. Pass the Spring Creek Trailhead on the right at mile 8. Go past the intersection at FR 540 (the intersection is also marked by an "Old Highway 90" sign), and turn left here at mile 15.3. Continue west along FR 402 toward Columbine Pass, bypassing Old Highway 90, which is now on the left.

Pedal past Transfer Road East on the right at mile 16. At a cattle guard, head left toward Antone Spring, bypassing the second Transfer Road (Forest Road 508) on the right at mile 17.1. Ride past Houser Flats (Forest Road 603) on the left at mile 20.1 and past Tabeguache Overlook at mile 31.2, also on the left.

When you reach Columbine Pass at mile 32, go right on Forest Road 503. Columbine Campground is at mile 32.7 (stop here if you need water). Ride past the now-defunct Columbine Ranger Station to the intersection of FR 402 and FR 503 at mile 32.9. Head west following FR 402 toward Windy Point, the second left turn, at mile 34.2. Turn and ride approximately 200 yards to the Columbine Pass Hut.

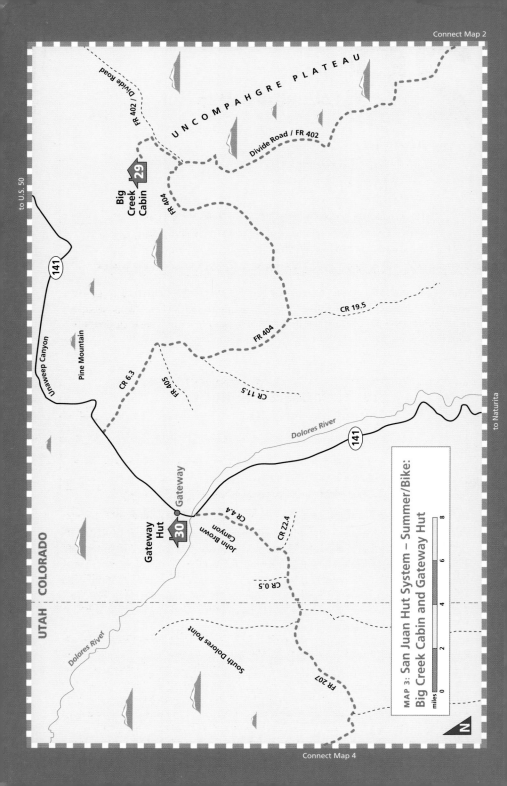

to U.S. 50

to Naturita

UTAH

COLORADO

U N C O M P A H G R E   P L A T E A U

Divide Road / FR 402

FR 402 / Divide Road

FR 404

FR 404

CR 19.5

CR 11.5

FR 405

CR 6.3

Pine Mountain

Unaweep Canyon

Dolores River

Dolores River

South Dolores Point

John Brown Canyon

CR 4.4

CR Z2.4

CR 2.4

CR 0.5

FR 207

Gateway

Gateway Hut

Big Creek Cabin

141

141

29

30

MAP 3: San Juan Hut System – Summer/Bike: Big Creek Cabin and Gateway Hut

miles

0   2   4   6   8

29 Big Creek Cabin

HUT ELEVATION	8,300'
DATE BUILT	Built 1930s; opened for hut use 1988
SEASONS	June 1 through October 1
CAPACITY	8
HUT LAYOUT	16 x 16 wood cabin with built-in bunks along 2 walls
HUT ESSENTIALS	Propane cookstove and lights, water, all kitchenware, fully stocked food supply

This is a spectacular leg of the journey to Moab. The road clings to the western edge of the Uncompahgre Plateau, rolling over undulating terrain. To the west, riders can see the incredible vistas of the La Sal Mountains and the high desert of southeastern Utah.

TOUR 29a DAY 4: Columbine Pass Hut to Big Creek Cabin
SEE MAP PAGES 192 AND 200

NOVICE/INTERMEDIATE

TIME	5 to 7 hours		
DISTANCE	37.2 miles		
ELEVATIONS	CP HUT: 9,205'	BC CABIN: 8,300'	GAIN/LOSS: +1,600'/-2,200'
MAPS	National Forest: Uncompahgre		

THE ROUTE: Begin the day by retracing the route back to Forest Road 402 (Divide Road), and ride toward Windy Point. Bypass Windy Point at mile 9.5, stopping to enjoy the great views of the La Sal Mountains to the west. Leave Montrose County and enter Mesa County at mile 14. Continue past Club Cow Camp on the left at mile 15.4 and past a Monument Hill sign on the right at mile 17. Pass Campbell Point on the right at mile 20.6 and Cold Springs Ranger Station on the right at mile 29.3. Begin to descend at mile 31.8 and then start climbing when the road veers to the right at mile 33.1.

You will arrive at Divide Forks Campground at mile 33.5. The campground has potable water, so stop here if you need to refill your water bottles. At the intersection of FR 402 and FR 404, turn to the right at mile 33.8 and head toward Grand Junction.

Descend along this road to a cattle guard and a sign for Telephone Trail at mile 36.9. Turn left here and leave the main road to follow a two-track road along a zigzag pole fence. Continue following the fence (which soon becomes a wire fence) as it corners 90 degrees to the left. Ride for another 400 feet and climb over a small hill to the cabin. Big Creek Cabin is a log building on the edge of a meadow. It is situated in a group of aspen. A road now leads directly to the hut.

Gateway Hut

HUT ELEVATION	4,600'
DATE BUILT	1988
SEASONS	June 1 through October 1.
CAPACITY	8
HUT LAYOUT	16 x 16 wood cabin with built-in bunks along 2 walls
HUT ESSENTIALS	Propane cookstove and lights, water, all kitchenware, fully stocked food supply

Riding to Gateway Hut involves some serious fun, exciting descents, and knuckle-cramping braking as you drop 4,400 feet from the cool forests of the Uncompahgre Plateau into the Dolores River Valley. This is an exciting day, with minimal climbing and maximum downhill road action. Tune your brakes!

TOUR 30a — DAY 5: Big Creek Cabin to Gateway Hut

SEE MAP PAGES 192 AND 200

TIME	4 to 7 hours
DISTANCE	30.4 miles
ELEVATIONS	BC CABIN: 8,300' G HUT: 4,600' GAIN/LOSS: +2,100'/-4,900'
MAPS	National Forest: Uncompahgre

NOVICE/INTERMEDIATE

THE ROUTE: Return to the intersection of Forest Roads 402 and 404 and turn right (northwest) onto FR 404 (Uranium Road) at mile 3.5. Ride past Rim Trail at mile 6.5, and at mile 8.1 begin the first major descent of the day (2,000 feet!) to Indian Creek. A gate and cattle guard mark the bottom of the descent at mile 14.3.

At a sign marking the turnoff to the town of Gateway at mile 14.6, turn right onto County Road 6.3/FR 405 toward Pine Mountain Road. Begin an arduous climb at mile 16.8. At mile 19.6 you will come to a four-way intersection. Turn right here (remaining on CR 6.3/FR 405). Proceed straight through the intersection with CR 10.8/FR 405 at mile 23.2, and continue your descent along CR 6.3 toward Gateway.

Cross a cattle guard at mile 23.4 and enter a flash-flood zone at mile 26.8. You will intersect CO 141 (paved) at a stop sign at mile 28.6. Turn left (west) and head toward the town of Gateway. Continue on through the town of Gateway. The road to the hut is just before the bridge over the Dolores River. Take this dirt road right (north), and follow it for 0.25 mile to the hut under the cottonwood trees beside the Dolores River.

Bernice Notenboom and Mike Turrin visit outside Big Creek Cabin, Uncompahgre Plateau.

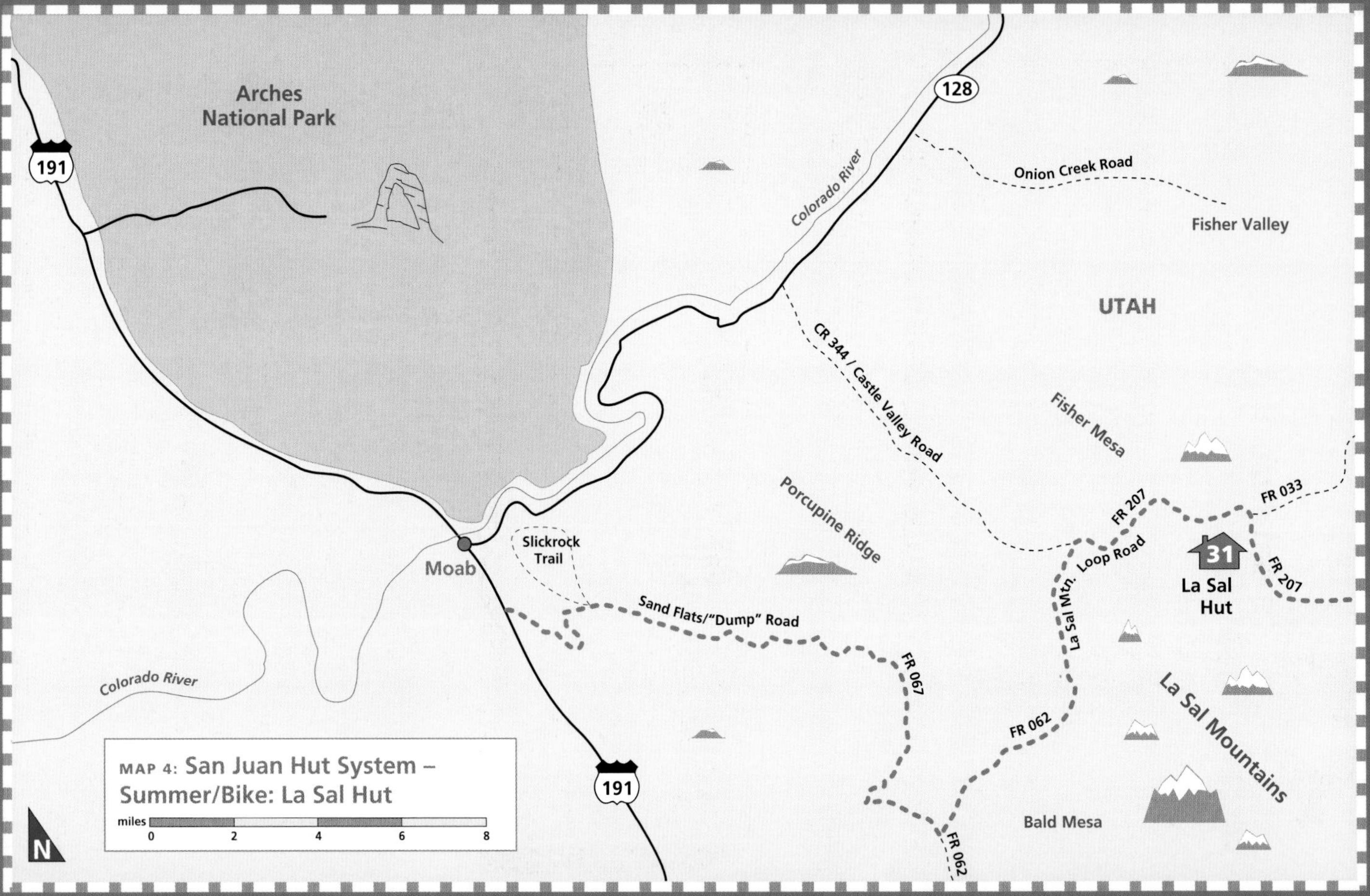
Arches
National Park
191
128
Colorado River
Onion Creek Road
Fisher Valley
UTAH
CR 344 / Castle Valley Road
Fisher Mesa
Porcupine Ridge
FR 207
FR 033
31
La Sal
Hut
FR 207
La Sal Mtn. Loop Road
Slickrock
Trail
Moab
Sand Flats/"Dump" Road
FR 067
FR 062
FR 062
La Sal Mountains
Bald Mesa
Colorado River
191
MAP 4: San Juan Hut System – Summer/Bike: La Sal Hut
miles
0
2
4
6
8
N

Connect Map 3

31 La Sal Hut

HUT ELEVATION	8,200'
DATE BUILT	1988 ("hobo camp" tarps); 1989 (Mountainsmith Mountain Shelter); 1990 (yurt); 1995 (present cabin)
SEASONS	June 1 through October 1
CAPACITY	8
HUT LAYOUT	16 x 16 wood cabin with built-in bunks along 2 walls
HUT ESSENTIALS	Propane cookstove and lights, water, all kitchenware, fully stocked food supply

The ascent from Gateway Hut to the La Sal Hut is far and away the most difficult leg of the Telluride-to-Moab tour. With more than 3,600 feet of elevation gain, this is not a ride for the faint of lung.

TOUR 31a — DAY 6: Gateway Hut to La Sal Hut

ADVANCED

SEE MAP PAGES 192 AND 204

TIME	6 to 10 hours
DISTANCE	25.5 miles
ELEVATIONS	G HUT: 4,600' LS HUT: 8,200' GAIN/LOSS: +4,400'/ -700'
MAPS	National Forest: Manti-La Sal

TOUR OVERVIEW: Gateway Hut is located deep in the Dolores River Valley, and summertime temperatures can easily soar to above 100 degrees. Because of this, proper planning is essential to having a successful day. Leave as early as possible to take advantage of the cooler morning temperatures, take a break during the hottest part of the afternoon, and drink lots of water.

THE ROUTE: Return to CO 141, cross the Dolores River, and follow the road as it bends to the left. At the turnoff for John Brown Canyon, turn right into the canyon at mile 3.3. Proceed past a mining equipment yard to the end of the pavement. You will begin ascending at mile 4.3 and at mile 9.9 will see a sign that reads: "Warning— Entering Uranium Mining Area." Turn right at the intersection at mile 10.

At mile 11.7 you will reach another intersection with a gate to the right. Turn left! Cross the Utah state line at mile 12.4. Cross a cattle guard at mile 14.2, turn left at an intersection, and cross two more cattle guards at miles 16 and 17.7. When you reach the La Sal Mountain State Forest sign at mile 18.4, continue in the direction of the mountains. Do not turn left!

Ride past the Taylor Ranch (red gate and cattle guard) at mile 18.7, and proceed past a turnoff on the left at a sign reading "5 Bar A, Sally's Hollow, Kirk's Basin" at mile 20.3. Do not turn left! Descend across a stream. You will pass a "Leaving State Land" sign, some old corrals, a cattle guard, and a sign for the Taylor Livestock Company. Continue climbing.

At mile 22.7, pass a road on the left at a sign reading, "Don's Lake, Beaver Basin, Sally's Hollow, Gateway, and Hidden Lake." Stay right, ride under power lines, and begin to descend at mile 23.5. Pass the Manti–La Sal National Forest sign, a cattle guard, and a gravel site at mile 25. Pass a red stake and a 6-foot-wide, clear-cut corridor (running up the hillside into the forest) that mark the boundary between private land and National Forest land.

You will arrive at a T intersection at mile 25.4, marked with a sign reading "Moab/North Beaver Mesa." From this intersection, retrace your route south about 500 feet toward the large ponderosa pines. On the west side of the road is a small, grassy pull-off with an old fire ring. From the southwest corner of the clearing, a four-wheel-drive road enters a dense oak thicket. Follow this road approximately 400 feet to a clearing and the tan-colored yurt.

The La Sal Hut is well-hidden and can be difficult to locate if you do not find the proper trail. The oak forest here is also full of game trails that resemble footpaths.

Bernice Notenboom looks down upon Castle Valley on final leg of journey to Moab.

TOUR
31b
DAY 7: **La Sal Hut to Moab, Utah**
SEE MAP PAGES 192 AND 204

TIME	5 to 7 hours		
DISTANCE	38.4 miles		
ELEVATIONS	LS HUT: 8,200'	MOAB: 4,200'	GAIN/LOSS: +1,700'/-5,500'
MAPS	National Forest: Manti–La Sal		

TOUR OVERVIEW: The leg of the trip from La Sal Hut to Moab is a fitting finale to this 207-mile journey. From the high forests of the La Sal Mountains, the route overlooks western Colorado and eastern Utah. Good secondary roads allow you to concentrate on the scenery rather than on boulders during the incredible 5,000-foot-plus descent to the surreal canyonlands of Utah.

THE ROUTE: From the La Sal Hut, return to the road, proceed back to the T intersection, and turn west toward Moab. At mile 2.1 begin a 2,000-foot-plus descent. When you reach gravel piles on the right, follow a small dirt road on the north into the woods to the cliffs at Fisher Valley Overlook at mile 2.4.

Pavement begins at mile 4.4, ends at mile 5.1, and begins again at mile 5.4. Cross a cattle guard and a stream at mile 6.5, then exit the Manti–La Sal National Forest at mile 7.5. At the head of Castle Valley, you'll see a sign reading "Moab, La Sal Mountain Loop Road" and "Oowah Lake, Warner Campground, Moab." Turn left onto the La Sal Mountain Loop Road at mile 8 and begin ascending. There is a spectacular view of Castleton Tower at mile 9.2.

Pass Manti–La Sal National Forest and Harpole Mesa signs at mile 9.9 and begin switchbacking at mile 10.5. Pass a sign reading "Miner's Basin/Pinhook Battleground." Stay on the pavement, which ends at mile 13.5. Pass communications towers on the left and ride under power lines at mile 16.6, where the descent begins.

When you reach Forest Road 67 (Sand Flats Road) on the right at mile 17, turn right and ride through a T intersection under power lines at mile 17.6. Leave Manti–La Sal National Forest at a cattle guard at mile 20.5 and proceed through a right turn near a blue-roofed house, which is across a shallow rock canyon. Stay on the main road, paralleling the canyon on the left, and re-enter the National Forest.

Descend a steep switchback, and cross a cattle guard at mile 22.5. Leave the National Forest again at mile 23.9. Enter a canyon via a shelf road at mile 24.2. You will reach pavement at mile 34.2 and pass the Slickrock Trail at mile 34.6. You've done it! Moab!

APPENDIX A: Reservations and Information

Crested Butte Area

10th Mountain Division Hut
Association (Friends Hut)
1280 Ute Avenue
Aspen, CO 81611
970-925-5775
www.huts.org

Adventures to the Edge
(Cement Creek Yurt)
P.O. Box 91
Crested Butte, CO 81224
970-349-5219
www.adcn.com
(AdventureConsulting.com,
an online booking service)
www.atedge.com
E-mail: atedge@adcn.com

Crested Butte Nordic Center
(Gothic Cabin)
P.O. Box 1269
620 Second Street
Crested Butte, CO 81224
970-349-1707

Elkton Cabins (Elkton Cabin,
Silver Jewel, Miner's Delight)
P.O. Box 3128
Crested Butte, CO 81224
970-349-1815
E-mail: elkton@rmi.net

San Juan Mountains

Southwest Nordic Center (Grouse
Creek Yurt, Neff Mountain Yurt,
Trujillo Meadows Yurt, Flat Mountain
Yurt, Bull of the Woods Yurt)
P.O. Box 3212
Taos, NM 87571
505-758-4761
E-mail: yurt@newmex.com

San Juan Snowtreks (Fisher Mountain
Hut, Lime Creek Yurt)
539 Paige Loop
Los Alamos, NM 87544
505-892-2926, 505-672-3042

San Juan Mountains (continued)

Hinsdale Haute Route (Jon Wilson
Memorial Yurt, Rambouillet Yurt,
Colorado Trail Friends Memorial Yurt,
Fawn Lakes Yurt)
P.O. Box 771
925 Ocean View Drive
Lake City, CO 81235
Phone and fax: 970-944-2269
www.hinsdalehauteroute.com

Continental Divide Hut System, LLC
(Lost Wonder Hut)
c/o Colman
28310 Pine Drive
Evergreen, CO 80439
303-670-1082
www.lostwonder.com
E-mail: lostwonder@lostwonder.com

Cumbres Nordic Adventures, LLP
(Spruce Hole Yurt)
P.O. Box 73
Chama, NM 87520
888-660-9878 (888-660-YURT)
www.yurtsogood.com
E-mail: info@yurtsogood.com

Wolf Creek Backcountry (Pass Creek Yurt)
P.O. Box 143
Pagosa Springs, CO 81147
970-731-2486
E-mail: wcb@frontier.net

Vertical Reality, LLC (Phoenix Ridge Yurts)
P.O. Box 618
Creede, CO 81130
719-658-0216

Saint Paul Lodge
P.O. Box 463
Silverton, CO 81433
970-387-5367, 970-387-5494
www.frontier.net/~stpaul
E-mail: stpaul@frontier.net

San Juan Hut System

(WINTER/SKI: Last Dollar Hut, N. Pole Hut,
Blue Lakes Hut, Ridgway Hut, Burn Hut;
SUMMER/BIKE: Last Dollar Hut, Spring
Creek Hut, Columbine Pass Hut, Big
Creek Cabin, Gateway Hut, La Sal Hut)
P.O. Box 1663
Telluride, CO 81435
970-728-6935
www.sanjuanhuts.com
E-mail: info@sanjuanhuts.com

*"Tele-Ned" Ryerson makes it look easy
deep in the heart of "God's Country."*

APPENDIX B: Road and Weather Conditions

National Weather Service   303-494-4221
Colorado Road Conditions   303-639-1111

APPENDIX C: County Sheriffs and National Forests

In case of immediate, life-threatening emergencies, always call 911. Dialing 911 will connect you with the nearest emergency-response network. Be prepared to provide as much information as possible concerning the type of emergency and your location (huts, roads, creek names, etc.). The phone numbers listed below are non-emergency numbers that connect you with their dispatchers 24 hours a day. Use these numbers for problems such as stolen cars or to report lost skiers who have returned to safety on their own. *Note:* Conejos County (Southwest Nordic Center) is not on the 911 system at this time; call the number below for all types of emergencies.

Friend's Hut, Cement Creek Yurt, Gothic Cabin, and Elkton Cabins
Gunnison County Sheriff (Crested Butte)
                                970-641-8000
Grand Mesa, Uncompahgre, and
Gunnison NF, Gunnison
                                970-641-0471

Southwest Nordic Center
Conejos County Sheriff   719-376-5921
Rio Grande NF, Conejos Peak Ranger
District (La Jara)   719-274-8971

San Juan Snowtreks
Mineral County Sheriff   719-658-2600
Rio Grande NF, Divide Ranger District
(Creede)   719-658-2556

Hinsdale Haute Route
Hinsdale County Sheriff   970-944-2291
Grand Mesa, Uncompahgre, and
Gunnison
Gunnison Ranger Dist.   970-641-0471

Lost Wonder Hut
Chaffee County Sheriff   719-539-2596
Pike and San Isabel NF,
Salida Ranger District   719-539-3591

Spruce Hole Yurt
Conejos County Sheriff   719-378-5921
Rio Grande NF, Conejos Peak Ranger
District (La Jara)   719-274-8971

Pass Creek Yurt
Mineral County Sheriff   719-378-5921
Rio Grande NF, Divide Ranger District
(Del Norte)   719-657-3321

Phoenix Ridge Yurts
Mineral County Sheriff   719-658-2600
Rio Grande NF, Divide Ranger District
(Creede)   719-658-2556

Saint Paul Lodge
San Juan County Sheriff   970-387-5531
Ouray County Sheriff   970-325-7272
San Juan NF, Columbine Ranger District
                          970-247-4874

San Juan Hut System
San Miguel County Sheriff   970-728-3081
Ouray County Sheriff   970-325-7272
Montrose County Sheriff   970-249-6606
Mesa County Sheriff   970-242-6707
Grand County Sheriff, UT
               435-259-8115, 435-259-5541
Grand Mesa, Uncompahgre, and
Gunnison NF, Ouray Ranger District
                            970-240-5300
Manti-La Sal NF, Moab/Monticello
Ranger District, UT   435-259-7155

**For general information about
National Forests: 303-275-5350**
U.S. Forest Service
Rocky Mountain Regional Office
Box 25127
Lakewood, CO 80225

APPENDIX D: Guide Services

For information on guide services, please call the reservation number for the particular hut system you are interested in visiting.

APPENDIX E: Avalanche Training and Information

American Association of Avalanche Professionals
P.O. Box 1032
Bozeman, MT 59771
406-587-3830

American Avalanche Institute
P.O. Box 308
Wilson, WY 83014
307-733-3315
E-mail: aai@wyoming.com

Silverton Avalanche School San Juan Search and Rescue
P.O. Box 178
Silverton, CO 81433
970-387-5531

Avalanche Information Phone Numbers
Colorado Avalanche Information Center (CAIC):
Colorado Springs (statewide forecast)
                    719-520-0020
Denver/Boulder Area
(statewide forecast)   303-499-9650
Durango (regional forecast)
                    970-247-8187
Fort Collins (statewide forecast)
                    970-482-0457
Summit/Eagle County
(regional forecast)   970-668-0600

United States Forest Service Backcountry Avalanche Information:
Minturn (Vail/Eagle County regional forecast)   970-827-5687
Aspen (Aspen/Carbondale/Crested Butte regional forecast)   970-920-1664

Utah Avalanche Information:
Grand County, Utah   435-259-7669

Most ski and backcountry-equipment shops can provide skiers with information on groups and clubs offering avalanche training. In addition, many city and county recreation departments offer weekend and evening training courses.

Also, by becoming a "Friend of the Colorado Avalanche Information Center," you can receive daily e-mail updates on Colorado avalanche and weather conditions. At $25 (spring 2000), this is a steal for information critical to winter backcountry travelers. Call the CAIC office nearest you.

APPENDIX F: Recommended Equipment Checklist

It is impossible to come up with a one-size-fits-all list of clothing and equipment that will satisfy the needs of the entire population of hut visitors. Just ask Joe Ryan of the San Juan Hut System, who travels sans gloves or mittens throughout the winter, year in, year out. Much of the time, he doesn't wear a shirt, even in brisk weather! Obviously, Joe's selection of garments (or lack thereof) wouldn't suit the majority of winter travelers. Whatever your preference, many sources of information are available on how to properly outfit yourself for mountain travel throughout the seasons, and the well-worn concept of layering still applies.

If you are new to backcountry life, take time to consult with an experienced friend, a professional ski or mountaineering retailer, or a ski/climbing guide or instructor before laying out your hard-earned cash on gear. The following are the most commonly carried items.

Ski Clothing

Base long underwear layer: Moisture-transporting wool, synthetic, or blended layer worn under shell pants during warmer conditions, or under intermediate layers in extremely cold conditions and for the truly cold-blooded; examples are Capilene, polypropylene, and bi-omponent DriClime.

Intermediate lower layers: Traditional wool pants or fleece tights/pants that can be worn alone or under shell pants for average Colorado conditions; synthetics include 100-weight microfleeces or Polartec 100 stretch.

Shell pants: Laminated or coated water-proof/breathable or highly wind/weather-resistant fabrics designed for the worst wet weather and deepest snow; scuff/edge guards and internal gaiters are helpful with lower-cut boots.

Woven-fabric pants: Four-way-stretch fabrics (Scholler-type fabric pants) are replacing traditional shell pants and wool pants for less-than-severe conditions; also good in summer.

Intermediate upper layers: Midweight or expedition-weight fleece, wool, or blended shirt or pullover worn over light, long underwear; fabrics similar to lower layer.

Heavier insulating layers: 200- to 300-weight fleeces, piles, or wool sweaters, or full-zip jackets; useful in very cold conditions or for lunch breaks and trips to the outhouse.

Windbreaker or windshirt: Super-light, simple windshirt for warmer days, and in colder temperatures during aerobic workouts; new and inexpensive windshells feature weather-resistant coatings and encapsulated fibers to enhance protection.

Shell jacket: One of the most important pieces of equipment; should have a generous cut that goes over all of your layers, and has superior venting capability, pockets large enough for gear (including skins), and a hood for blizzard conditions.

Down or synthetic vest or coat: Fluffy sweater or parka layered to fit over all of your clothes for emergency situations and lunch breaks; down works well in Colorado's relatively dry climate; new synthetic insulation includes, among others, MicroLoft, PrimaLoft, and PolarGuard HV and 3D.

Lightweight gloves: Synthetic or wool glove liners for warmer winter and spring conditions.

Heavy gloves or mittens: For general skiing, modular gloves that can be pulled apart to dry.

Gaiters: Useful for deep snow in winter and wet, slushy snow in spring.

Wool or fleece stocking cap: Available in a multitude of weights and styles.

Balaclava or faceshield: A lightweight shield that fits over or under your stocking cap for additional warmth and protection; neoprene-type facemasks also deflect wind.

Sunglasses: Should be made for high-altitude conditions and protect against UV radiation and visible light.

Goggles: Should have lenses suitable for flat light and storm conditions; an absolute necessity, winter or spring.

Hat or cap: A large-brimmed hat for additional sun protection for the face; a baseball cap will do.

Sunscreen and lip balm: An SPF factor of not less than 20–25 and, preferably, 30s to mid-40s for sunscreens.

Neck gaiter or scarf: Optional additional protection for the neck.

Hut slippers or booties: Low-cut slippers for inside the hut, and taller booties or mukluks for outside; can be plastic ski boots with insulated liners and non-slip, walking soles.

Ski Equipment

Performance free-heel or alpine touring setup: Heavy-duty tele skis with shovel widths between 85 and 105 millimeters; they have shaped, single-camber designs optimized for downhill performance and for use with skins for touring and upward mobility; plastic or leather/plastic is best; used with modern cable bindings or alpine touring bindings.

Wilderness touring setup: Metal-edged, single or camber-and-a-half skis that can be used with wax or with skins; rooted in Nordic/cross-country design; excel on trails, for touring (forward motion), and moderate telemark skiing with more moderate loads; ideal for beginner-to-advanced trails, especially roads and rolling terrain. Used with boots and "system" bindings such as NNNBC or SNSBC, or most traditional cable/three-pin bindings.

Ski poles: Most popular are adjustable-length poles that convert into avalanche-probe poles; consider big powder baskets for mid-winter conditions; handy for touring.

Backpack: Capacity depends on length of trip and size of load; for most one- to three-night trips, a pack with a 2,800- to 4,000-cubic-inch volume will suffice; most compress in size for day trips and have side-straps for carrying skis. For extended trips (a week or more), consider a 5,000-cubic-inch pack or larger.

Sleeping bag: For basic sleeping purposes, a 20- to 40-degree sleeping bag; in case of emergency bivouacs—being forced to spend the night out—a zero- to –20-degree bag (+10- to –25-degree range). Yurts tend to cool off much more quickly (especially if the fire goes out), so yurt-to-yurters should carry a warmer bag, rated in the zero- to +15-degree range.

Climbing skins and/or wax kit: Used for forward and upward movement; great for breaking speeds on long downhills; can buy trimmable skins to match your exact footprint or outline of the base of your skis (the wider and more shaped, or side-cut, your skis are, the more critical it is for skins to fit "wall-to-wall," but always leave metal edges exposed). Carry skin wax for wetter conditions.

Snow shovel: Made of metal or Lexan and light enough so you will always carry it.

Avalanche transceiver: Use only transceivers that transmit on the 457 kHz frequency and never old or questionable units; know how to use your unit before you go into the field; check the transceiver each morning.

Spare batteries: Lithium, for maximum performance in cold weather; carry extras for headlamps, GPS units, and transceivers.

Avalanche probe: Far outperforms a convertible ski pole for searching for buried victims in hardened avalanche debris.

Headlamps: Small, lightweight headlamps for short trips; for groups, several larger, professional-grade headlamps (and batteries). Though halogen bulbs provide better lighting, standard bulbs are adequate for normal use.

"Hydration systems": At least two quarts of fluids per day in anything from lightweight, insulated Camelbak-type systems to water bottles; during summer, carry a water filter/pump.

Optional and Miscellaneous Equipment

*denotes possible group items

Ensolite pad: To keep your bottom warm when sitting; for use during emergency bivouacs; and to splint broken or sprained limbs.

APPENDIX F: Recommended Equipment Checklist (continued)

Day pack or fanny pack: Ultra lightweight, stuffable pack; some do double-duty as compression stuff-sacks for your sleeping bag.

Mirror: For signaling aircraft.

Stove, pot, and fuel: Essential for emergency camps and for treating hypothermic skiers trailside.

*Tarp: Lightweight tarp to construct emergency overnight shelter.

Bivouac sack: Used for simple overnight shelter; sometimes allows a lighter sleeping bag for the hut, as a bivy sack can add roughly 10 to 15 degrees to the sleeping bag's temperature rating.

Maps and guidebooks: Maps should be carried by every member of the group; guidebooks can be shared.

*First-aid kit: Build your own or purchase commercially; if using a group kit, bring a small, personal version for blisters, headaches, and the like.

*Snow kit for avalanche analysis: The popular Lifelink or another kit, used to get a snapshot of what is going on under-foot in the snowpack.

*Altimeter: An essential navigation device for each group, if not every individual in a group; though wristwatch models are the norm today, wind-gauge/thermometer weather instrument models also are available. Stand-alone Thommens model, serving skiers, guides, and mountaineers for decades, remains the professional choice.

Ski Repair Kit/Emergency Kit
High-energy snacks and drinks
Space blanket
Duct tape
Stove parts
Long-burning candles
Webbing
Lighter and waterproof matches
Hot packs
Razor blades
Screws

Ski tips
Alpine cord
Steel wool
Glue sticks
Pocket knife or Leatherman
Sewing materials
Spare bindings, baskets, and cables
Wire
Notepad and pens
Safety pins
Flexible wire saw

Bike/Hike Clothing
See winter clothing list for more detailed descriptions of some of the following items.

Biking/hiking shorts: Either road- or mountain-biking-type shorts.

Insulating bike tights or long underwear: Synthetic or wool.

Medium-weight sweater or shirt: Heavy long-underwear-weight or long-sleeved bike shirt.

Heavy sweater, jacket, or vest: Fleece, pile, wool, or synthetic insulators such as MicroLoft.

Windpants and windshell: Weather-resistant, yet highly breatheable, for high-aerobic activity.

Rainshell: Fully waterproof is recommended; waterproof breatheables work, too, but are not essential, especially if you carry weather-resistant wind-wear.

Standard biking gloves

Shell gloves: For colder temperatures or in rain and wind.

Bathing suit/running shorts: For saunas and creeks.

Cap or hat: Light, insulative stocking cap, baseball cap, or wide-brimmed hat.

Biking/hiking socks and sock liners: Wool, Polypropylene, or Capilene.

Walking shoes for day hikes

Bike Equipment
Mountain bike
Water bottles (at least 2) or hydration
  system (like Camelbak)
Biking or hiking shoes
Sunscreen and lip balm
Helmet
Bike packs
Sunglasses
Day pack or fanny pack
First-aid kit
Flashlight or headlamp
High-energy snacks/energy bars

Bike Repair Kit and Tools
Indicates group tools
Phillips and flathead screwdrivers
Extra inner-tubes
Crescent wrench

Chain oil (small bottle)
*Headset tools: 32mm, 36mm
Tire patch kit
*Hub wrenches: 13mm, 15mm
Extra brake cables
*Bottom bracket tools
Spoke nipples
*Extra tire
Duct tape
*Extra rear derailleur cable
Tire pump
*Chain lube
Allen keys: 2.5, 4, 5, and 6mm
*Large, adjustable, open-ended wrench
Tire levers (2 to 3)
*Box-ended wrench: 17mm
Spoke wrench
Notepad and pens
Chain tool

APPENDIX G: Bibliography and Recommended Reading List

The following listing is not necessarily a list of research materials. Rather, having had the opportunity to read, review, and use many books on backcountry living, I created a menu of resources that I think are most useful for anyone—novice and expert alike—who is interested in becoming a safer, more fit, more competent adventurer. Each of these resources, organized by topic, is followed by the publisher's contact information and a brief description.

Avalanche Safety Information

Daffern, Tony. *Avalanche Safety for Climbers and Skiers,* 2nd ed. Seattle:
  The Mountaineers, 1992. (206-223-6303, www.mountaineersbooks.org)
  This book is exhaustive and comes highly recommended—an excellent starting point.

Fredston, Jill A., and Doug Fesler. *Snow Sense: A Guide to Evaluating Snow Avalanche
  Hazard,* 4th ed. Anchorage, AK: Alaska Mountain Safety Center, 1995. (907-345-3566)
  *Field-totable with a unique perspective on route selection and decision-making, this book is
  concise and informative.*

LaChapelle, Edward R. *The ABCs of Avalanche Safety,* 2nd ed. Seattle: The Mountaineers,
  1985. (206-223-6303, www.mountaineersbooks.org)
  *Ed is the elder of the avalanche tribe and a true guru; all mountaineers should carry his
  book in their pack.*

Logan, Nick, and Dale Atkins. *The Snowy Torrents: Avalanche Accidents in the United
  States 1980–1986* (Special Publications 39). Denver: Colorado Geologic Survey, 1996.
  (303-866-2611, www.dnr.state.co.us/geosurvey)
  *This detailed and analytical book from the CGS provides a fascinating look at recent
  avalanche accidents.*

APPENDIX G: Bibliography and Recommended Reading List (continued)

McClung, David, and Peter Schaerer. *The Avalanche Handbook.* Seattle: The Mountaineers, 1993. (206-223-6303, www.mountaineersbooks.org) *Based on older U.S. Forest Service publications, this is one of the most comprehensive books on the subject; extremely informative, if a bit dry.*

Moynier, John. *Avalanche Aware: Safe Travel in Avalanche Terrain.* Helena, MT: Falcon Publishing, 1998. (800-582-2665, www.falconguide.com) *A Sierra climber, snowboarder, skier, and pro guide offers his angle on safety, culled from more than two decades of serious mountain living.*

First Aid
Steele, Peter. *Backcountry Medical Guide,* 2nd ed. Seattle: The Mountaineers, 1999. (206-223-6303, www.mountaineersbooks.org) *Written by a physician, this super general-first-aid book fits easily into packs.*

Weiss, Eric. *Wilderness 911: A Step-by-Step Guide for Medical Emergencies and Improvised Care in the Backcountry.* Seattle: The Mountaineers, 1998. (206-223-6303, www.mountaineersbooks.org) *From the editors of* Backpacker *magazine, this is an easy-to-understand first-aid resource.*

Fitness
Garfield, Doug. *SkiMuscle III: The Complete Musculoskeletal Tune-up for Skiers of All Ages and Abilities,* 2nd ed. Naperville, IL: Motioneering, 1998. (800-754-8353, e-mail: inmotion@mcs.com) *Here are 100-plus pages of physics, physiology, and fitness woven into one of the most innovative, no-nonsense training programs available to skiers.*

Houston, Charles. *Going Higher: Oxygen, Man, and the Mountains,* 4th ed. Seattle: The Mountaineers, 1998. (206-223-6303, www.mountaineersbooks.org) *Houston's master work is a captivating, enjoyable read for ski-mountaineers and armchair mountaineers alike.*

Ilg, Steve. *The Winter Athlete: Secrets of Wholistic Fitness for Outdoor Performance.* Boulder, CO: Johnson Books, 1999. (303-443-9766, e-mail: books@jppublishing.com) *This volume is steeped in Ilg's unique spirituality/philosophy; no other book is so thorough or uniquely devoted to winter athletes and sports.*

Musnick, David, and Mark Pierce. *A.T.C. Conditioning for Outdoor Fitness.* Seattle: The Mountaineers, 1999. (206-223-6303, www.mountaineersbooks.org) *This comprehensive fitness overview is appropriate for all abilities and fitness levels.*

Twight, Mark, and James Martin. *Extreme Alpinism: Climbing Light, Fast & High.* Seattle: The Mountaineers, 1999. (206-223-6303, www.mountaineersbooks.org) *Though aimed at cutting-edge, high-altitude climbers, this take-no-prisoners book is chock-full of information, inspiration, hints, and tips useful for anyone heading for the high country.*

History
Dusenbery, Harris. *Ski the High Trail: World War II Ski Troopers in the High Colorado Rockies.* Portland, OR: Binford & Mort Publishing, 1991. (503-844-4960, www.binfordandmort.com) *Based on the memoirs of a 10th Mountain Division soldier, this fun book provides a frame of reference for trips into the hut system of the same name.*

Eberhart, Perry. *Guide to the Colorado Ghost Towns and Mining Camps,* 4th ed. Athens, OH: Swallow Press, 1981.
This is a good account of Colorado's early mining history and the abandoned towns left behind.

Ubbelohde, Carl, Maxine Benson, and Duane A. Smith. *A Colorado History,* 7th ed. Boulder, CO: Pruett Publishing, 1995. (303-449-4919, www.pruettpublishing.com)

Navigation

Burns, Bob, and Mike Burns. *Wilderness Navigation: Finding Your Way Using Map, Compass, Altimeter, and GPS.* Seattle: The Mountaineers, 1999. (206-223-6303, www.mountaineersbooks.org)
This instructional book covers all the bases.

Fleming, June. *Staying Found: The Complete Map & Compass Handbook,* 2nd ed. Seattle: The Mountaineers, 1999. (206-223-6303, www.mountaineersbooks.org)
A good instructional book for beginners, this handbook focuses on the map and compass only.

Letham, Lawrence. *GPS Made Easy: Using the Global Positioning System in the Outdoors,* 2nd ed. Seattle: The Mountaineers, 1999. (206-223-6303, www.mountaineersbooks.org)
The Global Positioning System (GPS) is the basis for this in-depth look at the evolving area of navigation.

Skiing Information, Instruction, and Mountain Skills Training

Brown, Nat. *The Complete Guide to Cross-Country Ski Preparation.* Seattle: The Mountaineers, 1999. (206-223-6303, www.mountaineersbooks.com).

Felkley, Dave, ed., and Gene Prater. *Snowshoeing,* 4th ed. Seattle: The Mountaineers, 1997. (206-223-6303, www.mountaineersbooks.org)
This is the best overview on contemporary snowshoeing (see also Mark Twight and James Martin's Extreme Alpinism, under "Fitness").

Gillette, Edward, and John Dostal. *Cross Country Skiing,* 3rd ed. Seattle: The Mountaineers, 1988. (206-223-6303, www.mountaineersbooks.org)
Though a bit dated, this popular book provides an enjoyable read as well as a concise overview of all aspects of skiing, from cross-country to expedition skiing.

Graydon, Don, ed. *Mountaineering: The Freedom of the Hills,* 6th ed. Seattle: The Mountaineers, 1997. (206-223-6303, www.mountaineersbooks.org)
Always fresh, this is the definitive tome on general mountain travel skills.

Masia, Seth. *Ski Maintenance and Repair.* Chicago: Contemporary Books, 1987. (847-679-5500, www.ntc-cb.com)
This is an in-depth manual for the care of modern skis.

O'Bannon, Allen, and Mike Clelland. *Allen & Mike's Really Cool Backcountry Ski Book: Traveling & Camping Skills for a Winter Environment.* Helena, MT: Falcon Publishing, 1996. (800-582-2665, www.falconguide.com)
This informative book, illustrated with great cartoons, is a classic.

O'Bannon, Allen, and Mike Clelland. *Allen & Mike's Really Cool Telemark Tips: 109 Amazing Tips to Improve Your Skiing.* Helena, MT: Falcon Publishing, 1998. (800-582-2665 or www.falconguide.com)
This neo-classic is not only informative but also is illustrated with uproariously funny cartoons.

Parker, Paul. *Freeheel Skiing: The Secrets of Telemark and Parallel Skiing in All Conditions,* 2nd ed. Seattle: The Mountaineers, 1995. (206-223-6303, www.mountaineersbooks.org)
The instructional and equipment design guru of our generation has produced the undisputed classic free-heel overview covering parallel and telemark techniques, gear selection, maintenance, and fitness training.

APPENDIX G: Bibliography and Recommended Reading List (continued)

Randall, Glenn. *The Outward Bound Staying Warm in the Outdoors Handbook.* New York: Lyons Press, 2000. (800-836-0510, www.lyonspress.com)
This is a good overview on layering and other strategies for maximizing comfort when living and exercising in colder climates.

Vives, Jean. *Backcountry Skier: Your Complete Guide to Ski Touring.* Champaign, IL: Human Kinetics, 1998. (800-747-4457, e-mail: humank@hkusa.com)
Written by a veteran skier who completed his doctoral research work on backcountry skiing, this book is a well-rounded resource for all types of modern off-piste skiing.

Weiss, Hal. *Secrets of Warmth: For Comfort or Survival.* Seattle: The Mountaineers, 1988. (206-223-6303, www.mountaineersbooks.org)
Although somewhat text-heavy, this book contains well-researched, detailed information on staying warm, comfortable, and safe in cold climates.

Yule, Leigh Girvin, and Scott Toepfer. *The Hut Handbook: Planning and Enjoying a Backcountry Trip.* Englewood, CO: Westcliffe Publishers, 1996. (303-935-0900, www.westcliffepublishers.com)
Going out-of-print soon, this is a great primer for novice hut skiers.

Weather, Geology, and Ecology
Chronic, Halka. *Roadside Geology of Colorado.* Missoula, MT: Mountain Press Publishing, 1988. (406-728-1900, www.mountainpresspublish.com)
This is a best-selling guide to Colorado's "living geology museum" found along her highways and interstates.

Chronic, John, and Halka Chronic. *Prairie, Peak & Plateau: A Guide to the Geology of Colorado* (Bulletin 32). Denver: Colorado Geological Survey, 1972. (303-866-2611, www.dnr.state.co.us/geosurvey)
An excellent summary of Colorado's geologic history, this book is scheduled for revision and a new title by winter 2000–2001.

Halfpenny, James, and Todd Telander. *Scats and Tracks.* Helena, MT: Falcon Publishing, 1998. (800-582-2665, www.falconguide.com)
For those who are curious about the other animals living out in the hut systems, this is an exhaustive study of the tracks they leave behind.

Mutel, Cornelia Fleischer, and John Emerick. *Grassland to Glacier.* Boulder, CO: Johnson Books, 1984. (303-443-9766, e-mail: books@jppublishing.com)
This is the best-selling guide to the ecology of Colorado.

Nelson, Mike. *The Colorado Weather Book.* Englewood, CO: Westcliffe Publishers, 1999. (303-935-0900, www.westcliffepublishers.com)
This best-selling book provides a basic overview of the science and history of Colorado's weather phenomena.

Woodmencey, Jim. *Reading Weather: Where Will You Be When the Storm Hits?* Helena, MT: Falcon Publishing, 1998. (800-582-2665, www.falconguide.com)
This is a small, packable book full of expert advice on what is going on in the atmosphere, written by a leading mountain avalanche and weather forecaster.

Videos

Avalanche Awareness: A Question of Balance. Spokane, WA: Alliance Communications, Spokane, WA: (distributed exclusively by Pyramid Film & Video), 1989. (800-421-2304, www.pyramidmedia.com) *This video offers an easy-to-understand introduction to avalanche safety awareness.*

Avalanche Rescue: Not a Second to Waste. Lakewood, CO: Colorado Avalanche Information Center and National Ski Patrol, 1992. (303-988-1111, www.nsp.org) *This is an in-depth, 30-minute avalanche rescue how-to video.*

Beyond the Groomed: Freeheel Skiing Off-Piste. Curlew, WA: Freeheels, 1995. (800-227-2054, www.freeheels.com) *In this superb video, inspirational ski footage is interspersed with instructional segments that focus on the body mechanics of skiing, as well as skiing in different snow conditions.*

Big Mountain, Little Skiers. Curlew, WA: Freeheels, 2000. (800-227-2054, www.freeheels.com) *The awesome skiing footage shot throughout Canada, the West Coast, and Alaska will get you pumped.*

Freedom of the Heels. Curlew, WA: Freeheels, 1997. (800-227-2054, www.freeheels.com) *A nice introduction to backcountry skiing, this video covers topics such as skins, transceivers, route-finding, uphill travel, avalanche awareness, downhill skiing, and general backcountry awareness.*

Winning the Avalanche Game. Salt Lake City: Friends of the Utah Avalanche Center, 1993. (801-488-1003, or for Backcountry Access: 800-670-8735,www.bcaccess.com) *This overview features spectacular avalanche footage and interviews with people who were caught in slides.*

APPENDIX H: Map Sources

Colorado Atlas & Gazetteer
DeLorme Mapping
P.O. Box 298
Freeport, ME 04032
207-865-4171

United States Geological Survey
Denver Federal Center
P.O. Box 25286
Lakewood, CO 80225
303-236-7477

Trails Illustrated
P.O. Box 3610
Evergreen, CO 80439
303-670-3457
800-962-1643

USGS Topographical Maps
National Cartographic Center
507 National Center
Reston, VA 22092
703-648-6045

Most USGS topographic maps and Trails Illustrated maps can be purchased through outdoor, ski, and mountaineering shops. U.S. Forest Service maps can also be purchased through retail sporting goods stores as well as from their respective offices (see Appendix C for phone numbers).

APPENDIX I: GPS Coordinates

This third edition of *Colorado Hut to Hut* does not include the current crop of GPS coordinates. Within a year of press time, most hut systems that provide GPS coordinates are going to be in the process of re-gathering these data. Recent changes in U.S. Defense Department policy will allow for vastly more accurate readings to be taken. Though this process will take some time, these new, more reliable readings will be phased in.

In the meantime, please contact each hut system for the latest readings, and for further information refer to "On the Trail" in the introductory section of this book (page 23). Also, please consult Appendix G for suggested reading on navigation.

APPENDIX J: Difficulty Ratings for Tours

CRESTED BUTTE AREA	Difficulty Rating	Page
1 Friends Hut		
1a. East River Trailhead to Friends Hut	Advanced	41
2 Cement Creek Yurt		
2a. Cement Creek Trailhead to Cement Creek Yurt	Intermediate	44
3 Gothic Cabin		
3a. Gothic Road Trailhead to Gothic Cabin	Novice	49
4 Elkton Cabins: Elkton Hut, Silver Jewel, Miner's Delight		
4a. Meridian Lake Trailhead to Elkton Cabins	Novice/Intermediate	52
SAN JUAN MOUNTAINS		
SOUTHWEST NORDIC CENTER		
5 Grouse Creek Yurt		
5a. Grouse Creek Trailhead to Grouse Creek Yurt	Novice	60
6 Neff Mountain Yurt		
6a. Neff Mountain Trailhead to Neff Mountain Yurt	Novice/Intermediate	64
6b. Neff Mountain Yurt to Trujillo Meadows Yurt	Novice/Intermediate	65
6c. Neff Mountain Yurt to Flat Mountain Yurt	Intermediate	65
7 Trujillo Meadows Yurt		
7a. Cumbres Pass Trailhead to Trujillo Meadows Yurt	Novice	68
8 Flat Mountain Yurt		
8a. Cumbres Pass Trailhead to Flat Mountain Yurt	Intermediate	70
8b. Flat Mountain Yurt to Trujillo Meadows Yurt	Novice	71
9 Bull of the Woods Yurt (Sangre de Cristo Mtns./Taos)		
9a. Taos Ski Valley Trailhead to Bull of the Woods Yurt	Intermediate/Advanced	76
SAN JUAN SNOWTREKS		
10 Fisher Mountain Hut		
10a. Forest Road 526/527 TH to Fisher Mtn. Hut	Novice	84
10b. Fisher Mountain Hut to Lime Creek Yurt	Intermediate/Advanced	85
11 Lime Creek Yurt		
11a. Forest Road 528 Trailhead to Lime Creek Yurt	Novice	88

APPENDIX J: Difficulty Ratings for Tours (continued)

APPENDIX K: Hut Rental Rates

The hut fees listed here are for the 2000–2001 season. Although prices could increase in the future, this appendix enables a rough price comparison. These are base fees and do not reflect applicable taxes or hut association memberships if they apply. *Note:* Designations for days of the week are Su, M, T, W, Th, F, S and PPPN = Per Person Per Night.

CRESTED BUTTE AREA
Alfred A. Braun Memorial Hut System
Friends Hut: $15 PPPN, or $100 flat fee for entire hut

Adventures to the Edge
Cement Creek Yurt: $25 PPPN (F, S, Su, holidays), or $85 for entire yurt
Avalanche course, 2 days/2 nights, $250 PPPN (5-person minimum)

Crested Butte Nordic System
Gothic Cabin: $12 PPPN (F, S, Su, holidays)

APPENDIX K: Hut Rental Rates (continued)

Elkton Cabins
Elkton Hut: $18 PPPN, or $108 for entire cabin
Silver Jewel: $65 PPPN
Miner's Delight: $20 PPPN, or $200 for entire cabin

SAN JUAN MOUNTAINS

Southwest Nordic Center
Grouse Creek Yurt, Neff Mountain Yurt, Trujillo Meadows Yurt, Flat Mountain Yurt:
$80 F-Su, $65 M-Th, $90 S

Bull of the Woods Yurt (Taos):
Flat fees: $125, S; $100, F, Su; $85 M-Th

San Juan Snowtreks
Fisher Mountain Hut and Lime Creek Yurt: $25 PPPN or $85 for entire yurt F, S, Su,
and holidays; $15 PPPN or $55 for entire yurt M-Th

Hinsdale Haute Route
Jon Wilson Memorial Yurt, Rambouillet Yurt, Colorado Trail Friends Memorial
Yurt, Fawn Lakes Yurt: $100 for entire cabin for nights 1 and 2; $75/night for each
additional night

San Juan Independent Huts
Continental Divide Hut System
Lost Wonder Hut: $20 PPPN, or $200 flat fee

Cumbres Nordic Adventures
Spruce Hole Yurt: $99 for entire yurt F, S, and holidays; $89 for entire yurt Su-Th

Wolf Creek Backcountry
Pass Creek Yurt: $25 PPPN, with $100 minimum on F, S
($25 for each guest over 4 people)

Vertical Reality
Phoenix Ridge Yurts:
Phoenix Ridge Yurt: $100/yurt (1-4 people), $25 each additional guest
Meadow Yurt: $75/yurt (1-4 people), $25 each additional guest

Saint Paul Lodge:
Packages starting at $90/night

San Juan Hut System—Winter/Ski
Last Dollar Hut, North Pole Hut, Blue Lakes Hut, Ridgway Hut, Burn Hut: $22 PPPN

San Juan Hut System—Summer/Bike
Last Dollar Hut, Spring Creek Hut, Columbine Pass Hut, Big Creek Cabin,
Gateway Hut, La Sal Hut:
6 nights, 7 days (Telluride to Moab): $395
5 nights/6 days to Gateway Hut including last night at Gateway: $330
4 nights/5 days (last night at Big Creek Cabin or Gateway Hut): $264

Preserving

a quiet

The Backcountry Skiers
Alliance represents winter
backcountry recreationists by
advocating for the creation,
preservation, and manage-
ment of non-motorized areas
on Colorado's public lands.

Please join us.

Increased

membership

strengthens

our voice.

For more information:
Backcountry Skiers Alliance
PO Box 3067
Eldorado Springs, CO 80025

303.494.5266
303.499.5045 (fax)
bsa@backcountryalliance.org
www.backcountryalliance.org

backcountry

for you

Index

NOTE: Citations followed by the letter "p" denote photos; citations followed by the letter "m" denote maps.

Notes

Notes

Since his first hut trip to the Tagert and Markley Huts with the Denver Junior Group of the Colorado Mountain Club in 1977, **Brian Litz** has been a confirmed hut addict. His mountain travels began at an early age with family ski trips and climbing ventures with friends.

Litz is an avid downhill and cross-country skier, mountaineer, rock climber, and bicyclist whose insatiable appetite for exploration, adventure, and photography has led him through the western United States and Alaska, as well as Mexico, Canada, New Zealand, Australia, and western Europe.

A graduate of the University of Colorado, Litz is managing editor and founding partner of *Back Country Magazine*. He is also a member of the North American Snowsport Journalists Association and is coauthor of the book, *Skiing Colorado's Backcountry: Northern Mountain Trails & Tours,* with Kurt Lankford. His photos and articles have appeared in books, newspapers, and periodicals such as *Skiing, Ski, Powder, Outside Magazine, Outdoor Explorer, Outdoor Photographer, Summit,* and *Mercedes-Benz Momentum Magazine.* Litz's *Colorado Hut to Hut* calendar is also available through Westcliffe Publishers.

Litz serves as president of the Backcountry Skier's Alliance and as trainer/instructor for the Colorado Outward Bound School, where he has worked with mountaineering programs and the Professional Development Program. A Colorado resident for 35 of his 39 years, Litz lives in Boulder.

Brian Litz photo by Ruedi Beglinger